READING INTERVENTION
IN THE PRIMARY GRADES

The Essential Library of PreK–2 Literacy

Sharon Walpole and Michael C. McKenna, *Series Editors*
www.guilford.com/PK2

Supporting the literacy development of our youngest students plays a crucial role in predicting later academic achievement. Grounded in research and theory, this series provides a core collection of practical, accessible resources for every teacher, administrator, and staff developer in the early grades. Books in the series contain a wealth of lesson plans, case examples, assessment guidelines, and links to the Common Core State Standards. Issues specific to each grade—and the essential teaching and learning connections between grades—are discussed. Reproducible materials in each volume are available online for purchasers to download and print in a convenient 8½″ × 11″ size.

**Reading Intervention in the Primary Grades:
A Common-Sense Guide to RTI**
Heidi Anne E. Mesmer, Eric Mesmer, and Jennifer Jones

Developing Word Recognition
Latisha Hayes and Kevin Flanigan

Reading Intervention in the Primary Grades

A COMMON-SENSE GUIDE TO RTI

Heidi Anne E. Mesmer
Eric Mesmer
Jennifer Jones

Series Editors' Note by
Sharon Walpole and Michael C. McKenna

THE GUILFORD PRESS
New York   London

© 2014 The Guilford Press
A Division of Guilford Publications, Inc.
72 Spring Street, New York, NY 10012
www.guilford.com

Printed in the United States of America

This book is printed on acid-free paper.

Last digit is print number: 9   8   7   6   5   4   3   2   1

Library of Congress Cataloging-in-Publication Data is available from the Publisher.

ISBN 978-1-4625-1336-9 (Paperback)
ISBN 978-1-4625-1359-8 (Hardcover)

*To the spirit of collaboration and dedication
that makes a process such as RTI possible
for fostering reading success for all children*

About the Authors

Heidi Anne E. Mesmer, PhD, is Associate Professor of Literacy in the School of Education at Virginia Tech in Blacksburg. A former third-grade teacher, she has held tenure-track positions at Virginia Commonwealth University and Oklahoma State University. Since 1999, Dr. Mesmer has studied beginning reading materials and text difficulty. She has worked extensively with schools and teachers in Virginia and Oklahoma, serving as co-principal investigator on a number of funded projects, and has published articles in a range of journals.

Eric Mesmer, PhD, NCSP, is Associate Professor of Psychology and the coordinator of the school psychology program at Radford University in Radford, Virginia. He has served as an RTI consultant to local school districts and worked as a practicing school psychologist for several years. His research interests include the application of behavioral generalization principles to the academic responding of students with behavioral and learning difficulties, school psychologists' involvement in RTI, and teacher interpretation and use of progress monitoring data. Dr. Mesmer served as co-principal investigator of a teacher training grant providing professional development in data-driven reading assessment and intervention practices.

Jennifer Jones, EdD, is Associate Professor of Literacy Education in the School of Teacher Education and Leadership at Radford University. She is an award-winning teacher educator and scholar whose research foci include RTI and core comprehension instruction in the elementary grades, and who works with teachers through ongoing, research-based professional development. A former classroom teacher, Dr. Jones has served in leadership roles in state and national literacy organizations, and her research has been published in research and practitioner journals.

Series Editors' Note

"Everybody talks about the weather," Mark Twain is said to have observed, "but nobody does anything about it." We might say something similar about response to intervention (RTI). There is presently almost universal agreement that RTI is a splendid idea, but no one seems to know quite how to implement it. Our visits to schools have revealed an enormous variety of approaches, some well thought out but many more plagued with difficulties. If only there were a "how-to manual," one literacy coach told us, a book that outlines a step-by-step approach to sizing up the needs of a school and that offers explicit guidance about how to make RTI truly work. Now there is.

The authors of *Reading Intervention in the Primary Grades: A Common-Sense Guide to RTI* clearly recognize its potential to address the needs of children early on and to reduce the number who eventually enter special education. But the devil is in the details, and the details are what these authors take great care to explain. They view RTI as assessment-driven instruction and intervention raised to a schoolwide level. It is a goal that requires a complex system, to be sure, and they do not shy away from this reality. But as they carefully work through the details, it soon becomes evident that RTI can be accomplished with surprisingly few assessments and a modest range of instructional approaches and materials.

This is not to say, however, that such a goal is easy to achieve. The key to implementing and sustaining an RTI program is leadership. Principals, coaches, and grade-level leaders must coordinate the efforts of teachers if RTI is to succeed. This theme recurs throughout the book, not in the form of platitudes but in the specific guidance provided to school leaders. Because RTI requires decision-making for *every* student in an elementary school, leaders must not only convey their support for the program but ensure that teachers possess a shared understanding of how it works. They require the know-how to use assessment results to form flexible groups, to provide instruction targeted to identified needs, and to gauge the impact of their efforts.

Such know-how will come at a cost. It will challenge entrenched notions about instruction as teachers move beyond the status quo. Professional learning is clearly key to successful implementation, and this book can become a solid foundation of that learning. Its authors are careful to explain how a limited number of informal assessments can drive the system forward, how evidence-based instruction can actually be easy to plan and provide, and how progress monitoring can become a mainstay of reflective practice.

On the other hand, it is not necessary that all teachers know every aspect of RTI, and the book's organization makes relevant, differentiated learning easy. Beginning with the basics (an RTI primer, so to speak), the book follows the developmental trajectory of reading acquisition, from letter recognition and phonological awareness to word recognition and fluency. Teachers can view the entire book through a wide-angle lens and focus squarely on the sections most germane to their teaching assignments and the major challenges they face.

We need hardly mention that these challenges now include the expectations of the Common Core State Standards, particularly in the realm of foundational skills. If schools are to respond to the new challenges, they can ill afford a business-as-usual approach to beginning reading instruction and intervention. Fortunately, an effective alternative is possible in this straightforward model of screening, planning, monitoring, and reevaluating children. And children are what RTI is really about. This book, in tandem with those written by the other expert contributors to this series, is precisely the kind of "how-to manual" literacy leaders have been looking for.

In short, we are confident that elementary educators can rely on this wonderful book as the only blueprint they will need to put an excellent RTI program in place and keep it there. Unlike the weather, RTI can cease to be one of those things that everyone talks about but no one knows how to change.

SHARON WALPOLE, PhD
MICHAEL C. MCKENNA, PhD

Introduction

Response to intervention (RTI) is a framework that offers a process designed to meet the needs of *all* students. By providing supplemental support for readers, the RTI process addresses students' needs using various forms of data to inform instruction. Instruction is grounded in high-quality, research-based best practices in both classroom and intervention settings. The intensity of instruction depends on students' needs, which are identified by systematic, consistent use of assessment data. As educators, we can all embrace such a framework to support students' growth in thoughtful, informed ways.

Our experiences have proven that in many places and cases, RTI carries negative connotations in the schooling arena. Often, teachers have negative feelings as the result of the way RTI is "rolled out" by well-meaning officials at the state or district levels. Schools are sometimes faced with unrealistic timelines for implementing a thoughtful, strategically planned RTI framework. Attempting to meet the demands of state agencies and unstable federal regulation, schools rush to implement RTI and frequently make costly purchases of unnecessary boxed programs that claim to meet all RTI needs of schools, students, and teachers alike. In an effort to "get it right" quickly and respond to pressure, teachers are often burdened with excessive paperwork that only impedes the process of giving kids the instruction they need to flourish as readers. In our experience, teachers do want to "get it right," but they also want opportunities for professional learning through thoughtful study, collaboration, and professional development that require time. They want to implement RTI with careful planning and participation from various stakeholders to develop site-based, culturally relevant procedures. They want to resist the flurry of panicked RTI planning, ambiguity, and confusion that result from rushed collaboration and a lack of site-specific efforts. Mandates that lead to a rushing of the process, whether for RTI or other initiatives, foster a culture of resistance within school systems. This is true for *any* new program or process implemented in schools.

In this light, we offer one cautionary tale of how the messaging that precedes RTI implementation can "make or break" such efforts.

Washington Park School (pseudonym), a combined elementary–middle school, began to experience resistance from both teachers and parents to the RTI framework early in its implementation. The teachers were uncomfortable with RTI as a form of special education identification. Why should they have to use instructional interventions for students not identified with special needs? Parents resisted the RTI interventions as well. Mothers, fathers, and caregivers didn't want their children labeled as "special ed" as a result of being in intervention groups. They decided that their children would not participate in such groups.

In this case, the school's RTI intervention framework had been introduced to the teachers by the district Director of Special Education, who had emphasized the use of RTI with special-needs students. In the process, she unintentionally failed to relay the message that the RTI intervention framework was for all students. *RTI is a general education initiative, not solely a vehicle for special education identification.* Nonetheless, RTI began to be seen in the school and surrounding community as a vehicle for identifying students for special education. It was not seen as a system of support for everyone, regardless of their literacy-based needs.

As the school year progressed, administrators noted the underutilization of the RTI interventions and sought to rectify the problem. Although the teachers eventually did understand what RTI was intended to accomplish, the damage was done and a culture of resistance endured. Parents continued to refuse to let their children participate in small-group Tier 2 interventions for fear of "special-needs" labeling. Thus, many students missed out on intervention instruction that could have closed the gap for them. Finally, the administrators launched a campaign to rebrand RTI at the school, but change came slowly. Six years passed before RTI was fully implemented as a successful intervention for students.

In an effort to avoid situations such as the one described above, we like to remind administrators and teachers that they often have some components of RTI already in place. For example, many schools already have assessment systems to determine students' literacy needs. Likewise, schools already have frameworks for small-group interventions in many cases. We recommend that schools take time to reflect upon what components are *already in place*, and consider how these components might be slightly revised according to the guidelines provided in this book. There is no need to reinvent the wheel if you have pieces in place that are already working! Successful RTI implementation does not require that schools rush to purchase boxed programs for instructional interventions. Although some of these programs can be helpful in filling gaps in an intervention framework, they are not always necessary. We encourage schools to first examine components of the RTI process that are already up and working, and then consider what needs to be tweaked.

Successful RTI implementation efforts do not always look the same logistically, but all successful implementation efforts do encompass important key components: systematic screening and progress monitoring efforts, solid instructional intervention, diagnostic assessment, and dedicated teachers. For example, RTI frameworks may be different in rural and urban schools, taking into account the needs of the students, the diverse populations, and the support systems that are in place. Schools in rural settings may have fewer support personnel. There may be only one teacher per classroom level, whereas in larger urban settings, support systems and volunteers may be more readily available. In some schools, intervention is delivered during a dedicated, gradewide time period. In rural schools with smaller staffs, intervention may be delivered throughout the day by available personnel. Some schools ask reading specialists to administer screening and progress monitoring assessments, whereas other schools ask classroom teachers to handle these components. The culture of the school, the community, and the teachers must be taken into consideration. Each unique culture creates a different RTI picture with common elements threaded throughout.

Our focus in this book is not the specific logistical arrangements that schools make to enable instructional intervention to take place, but instead the "meat and potatoes" of RTI—the assessment, instruction, and analysis—that make it work. In working with many different schools, we have found that when administrators are dedicated to RTI and willing to work with their teachers, the logistics can be figured out. When schools get mired in the details of "why the scheduling won't work" and "why it's just not possible," the issue is rarely the logistics themselves but more likely the resolve, focus, and readiness of the school to implement RTI.

RTI should not be a monster that everyone fears and avoids. Neither should RTI be an elephant in the room—something everyone knows is there, but no one talks about. RTI should not be a new label for something already in place, although it may utilize resources and processes that are up and working. RTI *should* involve high-quality instruction at every level, offering every child equal access to instruction that leads to student achievement. RTI should be thoughtful, respectful, and collaborative on all levels.

While writing this book, we noticed that many states and local school districts are now using the term *multi-tiered instruction* to describe their RTI efforts. In some regions, this term is being used synonymously and interchangeably with RTI, as if they are the same thing. We have not used *multi-tiered instruction* as a label for RTI for several reasons. It is true that instruction and intervention lie at the heart of RTI; effective instruction transforms outcomes for struggling readers. However, RTI is more than simply offering various tiers of differentiated instruction. We use the terms *response to intervention* and *RTI* throughout this book because we believe this terminology more accurately reflects the comprehensive nature of the movement and the important factors that extend beyond differentiated instruction.

We believe *multi-tiered instruction* is restrictive in that it fails to capture key aspects of the RTI process. Beyond intervention instruction, the RTI process includes screening, data-based decision making, problem solving, progress monitoring, and reevaluation of students' needs. At a more fundamental level, the evolution of terminology often indicates a shift in our thinking and behavior. In this case, *multi-tiered instruction* may well reflect a myopic shift toward sole focus on instructional procedures. Lost in this shift is the concept of *responsiveness*, which ultimately speaks to the individual and dynamic nature of change. The term one uses to describe a movement or a school-reform effort does matter once the term becomes associated with certain assumptions and procedures. For these reasons, we refer to RTI rather than multi-tiered instruction throughout the book.

Administrators and teachers have many responsibilities, and we recognize this heavy workload as the contextual reality of RTI implementation. In this book, we approach RTI in a no-nonsense, practical way. We offer suggestions for each phase of the RTI process that are considerate of time, money, and meeting students' needs in the most effective, researched ways. We offer "before" and "during" suggestions for RTI procedures, and routines, timelines, and interventions specific to the primary grades. Fidelity checklists are provided throughout the book to keep the process focused and on track over time.

In Chapters 1 and 2, we set the stage for the book as we explain essential "must-know" concepts and procedures surrounding effective RTI. The process and framework for effective RTI are explained. Examples and tips for putting components of RTI into action successfully are provided. Chapter 1 lays the foundation by defining the basic components of the process and explaining the "why" behind RTI. Chapter 2 breaks the process down into more detailed components, which include (1) *screening assessments*, (2) *analysis of assessment data*, (3) *intervention and progress monitoring*, and (4) *problem solving through modifications in intervention instruction*. These steps in the RTI process are vital to its success in meeting the needs of all students. As these key steps are discussed, we offer practical suggestions along the way about how to start the process within your school, including the inclusion of an RTI leadership team, an assessment and materials audit, and the procedures to have in place *before* full RTI implementation.

Chapter 3 showcases the instructional intervention plan for the primary grades. Intervention is intended to interrupt a pattern of failure for students. Hence, this key step of intervening within the RTI framework is crucial to its success. The focus of this book is on Tier 2 intervention, which means strategic instruction that typically takes place in small groups. Tier 2 intervention instruction is most often delivered by the classroom teacher. In this chapter, you will learn how to plan effective intervention instruction that is research based, data driven, and engaging for students. Our approach to Tier 2 intervention is practical and teacher friendly, while remaining student centered. A structure for an intervention lesson plan is provided, along with guidelines for successful intervention planning.

In Chapters 4, 5, and 6, we offer content-specific guidelines for addressing primary students' literacy needs in three areas: letter naming and letter sounds, blending letters/sounds together to form words (decoding), and fluency. In each of these chapters, we share what research has to say about each construct, complete with practical ways to use data to diagnose students' issues in each specific area. We showcase focused, engaging intervention instruction strategies, along with samples of lesson plans. Suggestions for monitoring students' progress to make instructional intervention decisions are provided, as are fidelity checklists to keep interventions focused on meeting the specific needs of students. These chapters also offer intervention specifics and progress monitoring guidance.

Chapter 7 addresses problem solving, the final step within the RTI process. Some students continue to struggle even when they have received excellent Tier 2 instruction. This chapter provides direction for what to do with these struggling students and serves as a guide for designing more intense, individualized interventions. The problem-solving process is discussed in detail, and guidelines are offered for addressing struggling students in the context of a problem-solving team. Recommendations for monitoring student progress are also highlighted.

In the end, an RTI framework should be culturally relevant for the school population in which it is administered. It should capitalize on already-present procedures and routines. Here is the bottom line: Intervention is instruction thoughtfully designed to interrupt a pattern of *failure*. If intervention is successful, students do indeed respond to it. Interventions do not need to be complicated. Interventions *do* need to be focused, engaging, and informed by data.

We conclude with an RTI success story:

Westlake Elementary (pseudonym) is a school with a diverse population with various needs. Four years ago, Westlake was placed on a School Improvement Plan, as it was not meeting expectations of annual yearly progress. Scores were low. Morale was low. Expectations were low. Everyone on the "outside" had quick-fix solutions—sometimes boxed, sometimes not. RTI was just starting to become a priority at the district level.

School leadership, both at the district and building levels, chose to implement RTI to address the many instructional needs in the building. The school administrator eliminated competing initiatives and embraced RTI in a positive, proactive way. We worked with the district and school administrators, teacher leaders, and specialists to develop a thoughtful process that would work best in the Westlake Elementary setting. We collaborated to develop an RTI process that the school leadership and teachers could embrace. Data were studied and professional learning opportunities were provided not just once, but throughout a 2-year period. Teams were formed, processes and procedures developed, and professional development commenced with support provided for a 2-year period, phasing in various components of the process as goals were met. At the end of 2 years, the school's RTI process flowed smoothly at the Tier 1 and Tier 2 levels. Confusion among teachers was eliminated. In Year 3, the school focused its efforts on Tier 3; now in Year 4 it continues to refine and perfect the RTI system in place. Morale is up, students are learning (and proud of it), and scores prove that the process works. Westlake Elementary is a picture of one school that was struggling and is now moving forward successfully every day!

At Westlake Elementary, the following concepts guided the RTI process as outlined in our book:

1. *Having data and using data are not the same thing.* Data were used to inform every process connected with RTI at Westlake Elementary. Data collection and selection did not encompass hours and hours of effort. Westlake conducted an assessment audit to determine which data would be most useful in RTI implementation and developed helpful processes for using data in *smarter* ways, keeping in mind that achievement that is measurable is meaningful, and achievement that is meaningful can be measured.

2. *Teachers are not pencil pushers.* Forms and paperwork developed for the RTI process should be minimal and meaningful. Superficial practices and procedures that are not improving students' learning need not be documented. Westlake Elementary determined that paperwork should not comprise unduly onerous tasks for the classroom teacher.

3. *Engagement matters.* The best RTI processes in the world are no good if students are not meaningfully and actively engaged in targeted instruction. This engagement begins at the classroom level and continues for students who need additional intervention.

4. *Assumptions and beliefs have influence.* The Westlake Elementary RTI process had to be something the teachers could believe in; otherwise it would not translate into student achievement results. It was important to involve teachers in every step of the process to maintain a common-sense perspective. Teachers who believe in the process have high expectations and teach accordingly.

5. *High-quality professional development pays off.* Professional development (PD) is high in quality when it is ongoing, consistent, and supportive over time. One-shot workshops are not enough for something like RTI. PD should be guided by student achievement data as well as teacher input. The fruit of high-quality PD is teacher knowledge that translates into increased student achievement.

6. *Goal setting keeps RTI focused.* It is important for teachers to work together to define goals based on data, know them intimately, revisit them at least two to three times each year, and track goals to note progress. Westlake Elementary developed procedures for addressing goals during grade-level and school-level meetings throughout the year.

7. *Celebrating success is essential.* Too often, we forget to celebrate our success when we see students progressing or we succeed with new instructional strategies. Westlake Elementary made a commitment to take time to celebrate their successes. Doing so kept the initiative moving forward toward established goals.

Establishing an RTI framework takes careful planning and collaboration, all focused on one goal: improving opportunities and achievement for all students. It is a process that is surely worth the effort!

Acknowledgments

To keep three dedicated but very busy coauthors focused, organized, and unified requires someone with exceptional organization and management skills and a keen attention to detail. Anita Deck, doctoral student at Virginia Tech, has served as just this person for us, and we are so very appreciative. Thank you, Anita, for coordinating our schedules, organizing our planning and writing meetings, assisting with sidebars and references for the book, and your adroit use of technology to manage it all. We are grateful for the time, expertise, and attention you devoted to the project and the joyful spirit in which you operate. It was a pleasure to work with you.

Authoring a book on a process such as response to intervention (RTI) requires a significant amount of time in classrooms with teachers and students, as well as time with school leaders. Literacy leaders serve in various roles—as central office personnel, building principals, reading specialists, school psychologists, classroom teachers, special educators—so engaging in conversation and sharing valuable time with these literacy leaders are paramount. Without the shared expertise of such leaders, we couldn't have written a practical, "real-world" book on RTI.

It has been our privilege to work among leaders, teachers, and students in many schools who have greatly influenced and informed the contents of this book. They have welcomed us with warmth and hospitality, exhibited a willingness to learn and grow, embraced new ideas, and showcased the effort to implement new initiatives—all for a common goal: their students. Likewise, these many individuals have taught us so very much about the spirit of collaboration, expert teaching, core classroom, intervention, and how to make the most of each day—all for the children.

Contents

CHAPTER 1

Response to Intervention
BASIC CONCEPTS AND DEFINITIONS

GUIDING QUESTIONS

- What is RTI?
- Why did RTI emerge?
- What do the following terms mean: *screening, diagnostic assessment, instructional intervention,* and *progress monitoring*?
- Why do we place an emphasis on the mastery monitoring form of progress monitoring for primary grade students?
- How does RTI relate to the Common Core State Standards?

RTI, AYP, IEP, ELL . . . it seems as though our education system has perfected the art of creating an alphabet soup of abbreviations, and every few years the acronyms change. Most teachers and reading specialists are familiar with the abbreviation RTI—*response to intervention.* In our experience working with schools, RTI is like many other abbreviations: Everyone uses it and everyone thinks they're "doing it." Likewise, everyone thinks that they are sharing the same meaning. Most of the time, this is not the case, which can create misunderstandings.

"Cheryl, a veteran first-grade teacher of 10 years, first encountered RTI about 4 years ago during an inservice training and then when she initiated a special education referral for a student in her classroom. "The entire thing was the most complicated, convoluted process I had ever seen. They were throwing around all kinds of graphs and charts and using all this medical terminology. It seemed to me to be overcomplicating teaching. I mean, I just figure out what a kid needs to know and then I teach him or her and I don't need a bunch of fancy charts or handheld devices."

1

The following year when Cheryl had some concerns about a student in her classroom, she was asked to meet with a prereferral team. The team asked her to bring her progress monitoring results for the student to the meeting and to discuss his response to intervention. "I had no idea what they were talking about. I had gone to the RTI training, but I didn't remember what it stood for and I didn't know what they wanted me to bring. I quickly assessed the student on his letter-sounds and decoding and went to the meeting. Turns out they wanted me to have assessments for every 2 weeks, and they wanted graphs. They kept asking me what I was doing, what my instruction was, and if he was responding to my instruction. I remember thinking, 'I work with this kid every day. I know if he is responding or not. I don't need to prove it to you. I know what I am doing.' It was exasperating, and I felt really inadequate."

We have interacted with many teachers just like Cheryl, solid instructors who are baffled by RTI terms and requirements. One purpose of this book is to cut through the RTI jargon. Like many teachers, Cheryl also sees RTI as some sort of hoop to jump through in order to get her student tested for special education. It is not. RTI literally means *response to intervention*, specifically, a student's response to an instructional intervention. It is the focused intervention instruction given to a student with a particular need that can make a difference, and it is intervention instruction that teachers like Cheryl usually love. Identifying the skill or need that is holding a student back, teaching that specific skill, monitoring progress, and then seeing the results is gratifying. Good teachers love to see concrete evidence of the impact of their teaching. It is this *intervention instruction* upon which RTI success depends.

In this chapter we begin with a "just-the-facts" overview of RTI, an RTI primer, of sorts, to facilitate a basic understanding of key RTI terms, which is essential to understanding the RTI process. We begin with a section that provides a definition of RTI and an explanation of why RTI was offered as an option in the most recent reauthorization of Individuals with Disabilities Education Improvement Act (IDEIA) in 2004 (United States Congress, 2004). As it turns out, there have been many problems with inappropriate special education referrals, and RTI seeks to address these problems. In the second section we discuss several RTI terms, many of which are being used widely in schools.

What RTI Is and Why It Emerged

Since 2004 the number of books, articles, and implementation resources that have been developed on RTI is mind-blowing. These products have been written for various professions within education, including reading specialist, special education, general education, school psychology, and administration. Although the emphases within these resources varies somewhat, there is general consensus regarding what RTI is, why RTI emerged, and what it promises to do.

Defining RTI

We define RTI as *a process of collecting and using assessment data to inform and modify intervention instruction with the goal of preventing, intervening with, and possibly identifying learning or behavioral difficulties.* Depending on the source reviewed, RTI is frequently defined in one of two complementary ways. First, RTI has been described as an overall school improvement initiative with a particular focus on preventing and intervening early with academic and behavioral concerns. Second, other descriptions of RTI include prevention and early intervention activities but include an additional focus on the special education referral process. In this second approach, data documenting students' responses to interventions are ultimately used to determine which students are eligible for special education services due to learning disabilities. Again, these two approaches are complementary because both focus on improving learning and ensuring the delivery of appropriate instruction. The prevention arm of RTI focuses on identifying struggling readers as soon as possible and providing them with instruction that will prevent them from failing. If a student does not make progress at a pace that is commensurate with his/her peers, then the RTI process focuses on increasing the intensity and appropriateness of instruction, which may ultimately include special education services.

Both the prevention–intervention and special education referral parts of an RTI process incorporate multiple layers or "tiers" of intervention—levels of increasingly intense instruction for learners at increasing levels of need. The text box *Characteristics of Tiered Instruction* and Figure 1.1 illustrate the widely used concept of tiered instruction. Often within an RTI model you will hear people refer to *Tier 1, Tier 2*, and *Tier 3.* Typically, assessment data are used to make decisions about whether students should receive increased tiers of instruction.

Why Did RTI Emerge?

At the broadest level RTI emerged due to the increasing challenges schools have faced in successfully educating all students. As demands have been placed on classroom teachers for increased accountability, the "achievement bar" has gradually risen, and more and more students have had difficulty meeting mandated goals. Although schools have been required to have both general and special education supports in place since the 1970s, these supports have not always resulted in increased success for struggling students. Basically, more and more students have continued to struggle, while standards for learning and accountability have

CHARACTERISTICS OF TIERED INSTRUCTION

Tier 1

- General classroom instruction provided to all students in various arrangements (e.g., whole group, small group).
- Instruction reflects emphases within the core curriculum.
- The developmental, core reading curriculum is balanced with the many parts of high-quality reading instruction (i.e., decoding, alphabet, comprehension, fluency, vocabulary, phonemic awareness).
- Instruction progresses at a rate to meet curriculum objectives.
- Instruction is provided at grade level.

Tier 2

- Should not exceed more than 20% of student population.
- Small-group format.
- Strategic—focuses upon an identified area of instructional need that is preventing student from being successful in Tier 1 reading instruction.
- Standard protocol—students with the same identified instructional need receive the same/similar intervention.
- Multifaceted—may utilize multiple instructional techniques to teach the skill.
- Instruction is provided three to five times per week for at least 30 minutes per day.
- Intervention minimally lasts 8–10 weeks.

Tier 3

- Should not exceed more that 5% of student population.
- Individually focused.
- Targeted—focuses upon a singular skill that has not responded to previous intervention.
- Unifaceted—often focuses on using one strategy with a high number of repetitions to teach the skill.
- Instruction is explicit as skills are broken into small steps and directly taught.
- Interventions are expected to be implemented as long as necessary to demonstrate student growth.

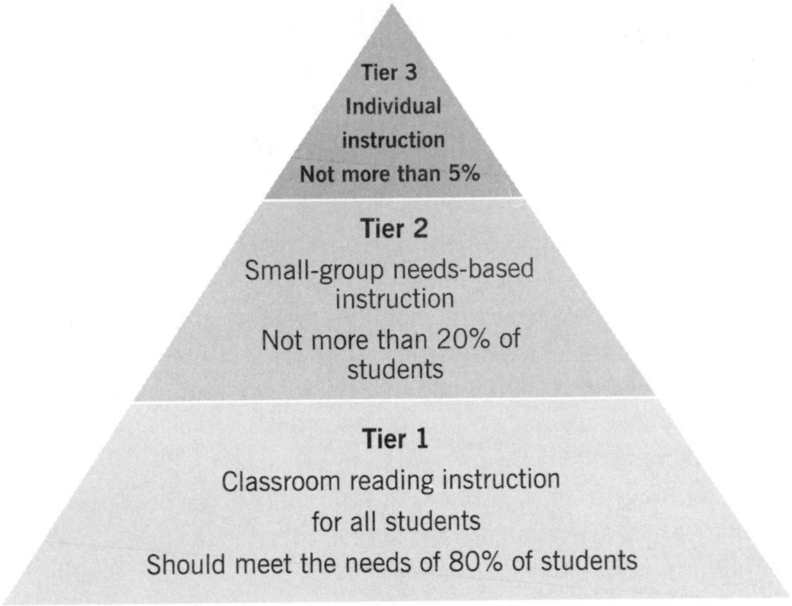

FIGURE 1.1. Tiered-instruction triangle.

increased. Thus RTI has emerged with the hope of strengthening both general and special education.

In 1974, the Education for All Handicapped Children Act was passed (Public Law 94-142) and later became the Individuals with Disabilities Education Act (IDEA). This was landmark legislation in that it ensured, for the first time, that all children with disabilities were guaranteed a free and appropriate education (FAPE). Educational needs would be documented in an individualized education program (IEP) and instruction delivered in the least restrictive environment (LRE) deemed appropriate.

We've all seen it. In the spring of each year, special education referrals often skyrocket in schools as a result of high-stakes testing or the rush to get kids "into the system" before the school year ends. Usually we see a flurry of child study meetings, and many students are identified as being in need of services (including low-achieving students) due to learning disabilities (Horn & Tynan, 2001). However, a greater number of kids is identified for special education services than really should be (Ysseldyke, Algozzine, Richey, & Graden, 1982). Hence, special educators often have overwhelming caseloads, making it nearly impossible to meet the testing and instructional demands placed upon them. Large numbers of kids needing special education services are a function of a referral system that just doesn't work. Special education is necessary for a portion of the population, but research tells us that too many students are typically referred for, and receive, services.

Using an RTI process offers a solution for meeting the needs of *all* children and a way to more appropriately and correctly identify the small proportion of students that is genuinely reading disabled.

Research dating back to the 1980s demonstrated the negative impact of special classroom placement for certain groups of students, with only small improvements documented for students with learning disabilities (Forness, 2001). Moreover, a more recent study demonstrated that reading instruction that was delivered in resource rooms had no impact on reading scores, whereas spelling scores and verbal IQ scores showed declines (Bentum & Aaron, 2003). Although the goal of special education is to remediate students and place them back in the regular classroom, many of these students never "exit" special education services (Horn & Tynan, 2001). Think about it: Do you ever recall someone coming to you and saying something like, "Well, Bruce has received special education services for a year now, and we have found that the progress he has made puts him at grade level and so we believe he will no longer need services." In fact, instruction often slows down significantly and changes qualitatively. In most cases, students' reading problems are never truly remediated. This was never the goal of special education and is surely not the goal of teachers when they refer a child for special education assistance.

A second unintended result of special education is that a disproportionate percentage of minority students has consistently been identified as disabled (Albrecht, Skiba, Losen, Chung, & Middelberg, 2012). For example, if you are a student, particularly a boy who is African American, you are far more likely to be referred for special education than if you are a white student. If special education identification were proportional to the minority populations in schools and districts, then we should see far fewer minority students in special education. This issue is particularly problematic in schools that enroll predominantly white students. In these schools the percentage of minority students placed in special education exceeds that of white students (Ladner & Hammons, 2001). Minority students are more likely to be identified as disabled when attending predominantly white schools when compared to minority students attending predominantly minority composition schools (Ladner & Hammons, 2001).

Third, strong dissatisfaction has also been expressed regarding traditional procedures that have been used to identify students with learning disabilities. At the heart of these procedures is a method known as the "discrepancy formula." This method attempts to measure the child's ability or potential and compare it to his/her actual academic achievement. Usually this is accomplished by administering an IQ test and an achievement test to the child, and then determining if the IQ score (ability) far exceeds the achievement test score. When a discrepancy between these two scores exists, then the student is often found to have a learning disability. Unfortunately, most experts now believe that the discrepancy formula is flawed because it (1) results in identifying many children as being learning disabled when in fact they are not and (2) often fails to identify students who truly do have a learning disability. Related to the first point, it is important to understand that a discrepancy between an ability score and an achievement score is frequently found in individuals who do not have any learning difficulties. Put another way, if every student in your class had his/her IQ and achievement tested, there would certainly be some students with a "discrepancy" who were, in fact, straight "A" students—overachievers. Conversely, there might be some students not doing too well in class, and they too might be found to have an achievement–ability discrepancy because they are underachieving. The discrepancy is actually something these two groups have in common, so something else must explain why one group struggles whereas the other does not. However, the fact that both groups have a discrepancy means that the discrepancy itself is not really meaningful in helping to identify a learning disability.

As noted above, there are times when a student has a real learning disability but the discrepancy approach fails to identify it. Many teachers have likely had the experience in which a student is referred and tested but the discrepancy between achievement and ability is "not large enough." This most commonly occurs in the early grades. When this happens, students who may truly need an intense level of help, which can only be provided through special education, will be denied the very help that is most needed. Unfortunately, the opportunity to intervene early with these students may be lost.

Finally, researchers and educators have pressed for RTI because many students who are labeled as learning disabled may actually be "curriculum/instructional casualties," and not disabled at all. They are, in a sense, *instructionally disabled* by a lack of appropriate instruction. This regrettable term implies that the difficulties of some referred students' can be traced to poor or inadequate instruction, rather than to a true learning disability (Spear-Swerling & Sternberg, 1996). This is not a reality new to RTI. Educational professionals, including school psychologists, have always been required to rule out environmental factors (including instruction) as the primary reason for a student's learning struggles. We believe that RTI forces educational professionals to more seriously consider the impact of instruction and other school environment factors that may be impacting a student's reading.

The following case scenario helps to illustrate this point. We have found that this situation is very real and very common.

> Carson is a second-grade student referred for assistance due to difficulties in reading. Specifically, Carson's teacher, Ms. Paul, indicates that he is unable to keep up with his classmates as they are reading grade-level materials. Ms. Paul believes that Carson's reading skills are at an early first-grade level, and she noted that she is not sure that Carson has fully mastered recognizing all the letter-sounds of the alphabet. Assessment data taken at the beginning of second grade revealed that Carson struggled in applying short-vowel sounds

in word reading. Carson has been receiving instruction in the "lowest" group since the beginning of the school year, in which he is placed with five other students who also struggle. At this point in the year, Ms. Paul believes that the average student within the group is reading at the mid-first-grade level. In describing the instruction that is provided within Carson's group, Ms. Paul reported: "We work on a number of different skills. Generally I allow the students to take turns reading in the leveled reader, and I provide assistance when they struggle. Carson often struggles with unknown words, and I prompt him to sound these words out. He is able to do this some of the time, but mostly he cannot." When asked about phonics instruction that might be provided in the small group, Ms. Paul replied, "I do some of that. Again, I try to embed that instruction within the story that the students are reading so that it is more authentic. I can anticipate that there are some words that they will struggle with, so I will sometimes pull those words out and review those words with the students. This really seems to work for most of the students, but Carson just does not seem to be making much progress. I think there are other ways he may learn better. Frankly, some students don't benefit from phonics instruction. I suspect that he may have a reading disability, and we need to get him help."

As is evident in the case scenario, the team is clearly interested in Carson's current skills and the type of instruction he receives. Through the brief information provided by Ms. Paul, it appears that there may be a mismatch between the instruction provided and Carson's current skills but that Ms. Paul has actually concluded that the problem is *with Carson*, as opposed to the instruction that he is receiving. Carson appears to need more explicit instruction in applying basic letter-sounds, and in particular short vowels, but this instruction is largely absent. Indeed, we have often found that students such as Carson often continue to fall further and further behind. The "differentiated classroom instruction" that struggling students receive in small groups may not be linked to their instructional needs.

This case study also illustrates that educators may struggle with pinpointing why a student struggles to read. Often educators will suggest that knowing exactly "why" a student struggles is not important and that instead we should focus on getting a student help if he/she needs it. We do not wholly disagree with this perspective. However, we do disagree with mislabeling a student as disabled in order to provide him/her with help. Misidentification can result in unnecessary social stigma and emotional scars. Thus, assuming that the student in the above scenario was referred for an evaluation, the school team would have to face the question as to whether instructional factors played a significant role in the student's reading difficulties. Certainly this is not an easy question to answer, and unfortunately some educators have interpreted the requirement to answer it as an attack on teachers and instruction. However, at the heart of RTI are teachers and instruction. RTI recognizes the power that instruction has in preventing learning difficulties from occurring. It should come as no surprise that instruction is one of the most important factors in determining whether a student will be successful. Moreover, we believe that identification of the instructional factors that may be contributing to a student's difficulties is often the first step in helping the student, because intervention will often address these factors.

Overview of Basic RTI Terms

In order to have a basic understanding of RTI, educators must thoroughly understand important terminology. Here we introduce basic RTI concepts, including screening assessments, diagnostic assessments, intervention instruction, and progress monitoring in two forms. In this chapter our goal is to simply define and illustrate these terms. In Chapter 2 we expand upon them, integrating them into an RTI process, illustrating how you could create a working and feasible RTI process in your school. Following each of these terms is a set of questions that will guide schools in evaluating their current RTI practices. We suggest that these questions be used to ground schoolwide discussions in RTI development.

Screening Assessments and Benchmark Scores

The RTI process begins with a method to identify those students within a school who are in trouble and may need additional targeted instruction (i.e., intervention instruction). A *literacy screener* is a type of assessment that has a very specific purpose—to sort students into two categories: those needing help (intervention) and those not needing it. The meaning of the verb *to screen* is to separate, divide, or partition, and that is exactly what screening measures do.

Literacy screeners are like the many other screening tests that already exist in our world (e.g., health screenings, security screenings). Just as a health screening seeks to determine if there are any body functions below the "normal" range at various times throughout a year, in a school some type of initial literacy screening assessment is given to every student at the beginning of the year as well as at the middle and end of the year. A screening test usually assesses students on a simple literacy skill that is correlated with success on a broader outcome measure such as a state test or a standardized survey reading assessment. Screening assessments are unlike survey reading texts, which might be designed to provide an overall picture of a student's reading level (e.g., the Gates–MacGinitie), or diagnostic assessments (e.g., a qualitative spelling assessment). Instead, they are designed to identify specific instructional content (e.g., high-frequency words, long-vowel patterns, oral reading fluency). In the primary grades literacy screenings may measure the following skills: letter-sounds, decoding pseudowords, spelling, phonemic segmentation, and/or oral reading rate.

Literacy screening tools have four important features. They are:

1. Quickly administered
2. Predictive
3. Universal
4. Objective

Screening assessments should be quick because they need to be provided to every student in the school and are primarily designed to identify students who need help. Screening assessments are not comprehensive, thorough, or very diagnostic because such onerous assessments may not be necessary for everyone. Although they are not designed to provide specific information about the exact nature of a student's reading needs, we have found that the information provided by some of the more popular screening measures, such as the Dynamic Indicators of Basic Early Literacy Skills (DIBELS) and the Phonemic Awareness Literacy Screener (PALS), do provide sufficient information to identify broad instructional needs. However, as we describe, many times teachers and schools will need to administer more specific diagnostic assessments to direct the content of interventions. This point is discussed in the section about diagnostic assessments. As we discuss in Chapter 2, having this information will allow grade-level teams to minimally identify more targeted instructional groups. However, it is also important to understand that schools may need to conduct additional diagnostic assessment with some students to determine specific literacy needs.

Literacy screening assessments are predictive. They should accurately identify students who are actually at risk. If a measure does not hold students to a high standard, then it will miss students who really need help (false negatives)—students who are not identified as at risk but who really are. These students will not be given help and might struggle in the future. If a screening sets a standard that is too high, it will inaccurately identify students who are not really at risk (false positives). This outcome will case some students as being at risk when, in fact, they are not, and the school will assign personnel and resources to help students who don't really need help. Clearly the former error is worse. We do not want false negatives. We do not want to miss students who need help, and so screening measures are more likely to err on the side of false positives rather than false negatives.

Third, literacy screening assessments should be universal; that is, they should be given to every student in the school at least three times per year. This point seems obvious, but we have frequently worked with schools and heard teachers say, "Oh, well, I don't really need to give her a screening, she's been reading since kindergarten and her mom's a teacher; I just use my own judgment and screen who I think needs it." This is a big mistake. All children should be screened because many times well-behaved, bright children, who do not otherwise indicate that they are having trouble, need help. We suggest that schools set a screening benchmark window—a period of time during which screenings take place. If using an online data repository, we also suggest setting a deadline for data entry, so that intervention planning can take place. We suggest that this deadline be not later than 3 weeks after the start of school or after the midyear point. In our experience, when a literacy screening window is not set, assessments do not get completed, data are inaccessible, and sometimes it can be up to 6 weeks after the start of school that intervention instruction begins.

This leads us to the final point about literacy screening: It should be objective. The use of the literacy screener should not vary from person to person. There should be an identified screener that all students receive, and the screener should be guided by a clear benchmark score (see below). In other words, the benchmark score and interpretation of that score should be so easy to interpret that everyone in the school would draw the same conclusion about whether or not the student met the benchmark score. Again, this sounds obvious, but many schools have a fuzzy screening system and teachers can (and do) come to different conclusions. This should not occur. Literacy screening should be simple and clear-cut, and it should challenge preconceived notions about students. We like to remind teachers that all assessments, and especially literacy screeners, *should* produce surprises. These screeners should tell us something that we would not otherwise know—students whom the screener indicates are in need of help but we would not have guessed it. We like to say, *"Don't dump your data!"* In other words, don't spend a bunch of time administering assessments, only to ignore those assessments or divert to personal opinions and hunches. Sometimes we might hear a teacher say, "Well, I know that this screener tells us that Susie needs intervention, but I think that she just had a bad day. I'm not going to put her in an intervention group." Although teacher judgments and opinions *should* always be one piece of data used in any assessment process, they should not be the *only* piece of data. If a screener shows that a student is in trouble, then that indicator should be taken seriously. If there is a belief that the screening data are invalid, then the screener can be readministered to a student.

What is often forgotten with screening assessments is the one important piece of information necessary to make the screener work: a *benchmark score*. The benchmark score is a level of performance (a target score) that is set as a cutoff point to separate students who are at risk from those who are not. Students who do not meet the minimal benchmark score are considered for additional help. For instance, a benchmark score for letter-sounds in first grade might be 24/26, with students who earn a score of 23 or lower being considered at risk. In order to use a literacy screener appropriately, users must know what the benchmark scores are. Many schools use established measures that were designed for literacy screening purposes and have clear benchmark scores, but many schools are also using other measures, such as the STAR, an informal reading inventory, or word lists. If a school is going to appropriately use a literacy assessment for screening purposes, then it must carefully set benchmark scores for each grade at each administration (e.g., beginning, middle, and end of the year). Importantly, the benchmark scores should be tested for their accuracy in predicting students who are at risk. We generally recommend that schools use well-established, researched benchmarks, instead of setting their own. We cannot tell you how many teachers and schools forget the purpose of the benchmark score. For instance, we might ask a teacher, "Okay, so you use the STAR as your screener, what are your benchmark scores for first grade?" only to be met with silence and a blank stare. Without a benchmark score, a screening measure is useless.

In sum, a literacy screening measure should provide the foundation for an efficient and objective identification of students who might be at risk of reading failure. The following questions are useful for evaluating your school's literacy screening process:

- What is your literacy screening tool?
- Does every student receive the screener three times per year?
- What are the benchmark scores?
  - Fall?
  - Midyear?
  - Spring?
- What is the screening testing window?
- Are the processes for identifying students for intervention and using the literacy screener objective? Or do identification and use differ from person to person?
- How long does is take between the time when students are screened and when intervention is received? (It should be no longer than 3 weeks.)
- Do we dump data? (In other words, do we administer assessments but fail to use the data for decision making?)
- Do we expect data to surprise us?

Diagnostic Assessments

As explained, screening assessments are usually surface-level measures that are quickly administered to indicate *if* a student has a reading problem and is in need of intervention instruction. Often, however, these screeners do not indicate *what* deficit or skill gap is causing the problem or how to help the student. A diagnostic assessment is a detailed measure that diagnoses or identifies the exact nature of the problem and, in so doing, the solution. A diagnostic assessment specifies what the student is missing and pinpoints the content that a student should be taught during an intervention. For instance, an oral reading fluency screener might indicate that a student is not reading at the accuracy and reading rate levels that are typical of his/her peers, but the screener does not identify why. The student may be able to accurately read the words, but is doing so too slowly and needs an intervention that focuses on developing fluency. The student may not be able to accurately read the words and may in fact need more instruction in long-vowel patterns. A follow-up diagnostic measure would indicate exactly *what* kind of instruction is needed.

Diagnostic measures tend to focus on one skill and tend to represent all the elements of that skill that a student should learn. For instance, a thorough diagnostic decoding measure would contain multiple items to represent the full range of letter-sound patterns (e.g., consonants, consonant blends, short vowels, consonant digraphs). Diagnostic measures should be thorough and comprehensive so that teachers and interventionists have a complete handle on how to fill in the literacy gaps. These measures are usually more informal as well because their purpose is not to compare a student's score to a normative group but instead to simply identify gaps. High-frequency word lists, letter inventories, phonics inventories, spelling assessments, and phonemic awareness batteries are all examples of diagnostic assessments that are used to detect the precise information and skills that students need to be taught in order to progress in their reading development.

Intervention Instruction

The RTI process is built around intervention instruction. An *intervention* is a series of steps or procedures used to address a problem. It is the intervention instruction that actually makes the difference for students, and all other parts of the RTI process wrap around the intervention (see Figure 1.2). The RTI process prepares for the intervention, assesses it, and/or modifies it. Intervention instruction is one type of differentiated, small-group instruction, the purpose of which is to fill in a knowledge gap so that a student can progress. Instructional interventions have many different foci, but usually prekindergarten (PreK) and primary grade students receive intervention instruction in areas that are developmentally related to emergent and beginning reading. These interventions might focus on recognizing letters, learning letter-sounds, developing phonemic awareness, decoding words, and/or developing fluency and high-frequency word knowledge. Intervention instruction often occurs in small groups with students who have similar needs. However, as intervention instruction becomes more intense, it may occur one on one. Although the major focus of this book is on intervention instruction, it should also be noted that sometimes intervention incorporates noninstructional methods that involve the classroom environment and classroom management (see the text box *Characteristics of Tiered Instruction* on p. 4).

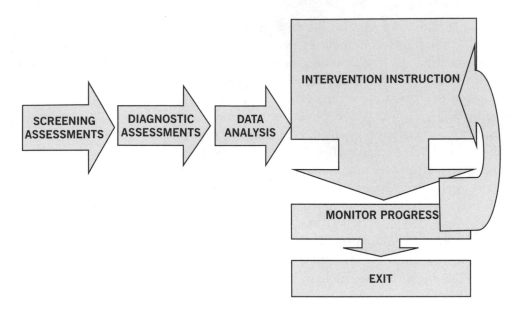

FIGURE 1.2. RTI processes.

Targeted Instruction

Intervention instruction has four essential characteristics. It is:

1. Targeted and specific
2. Intense
3. Delivered with fidelity.
4. Part of an integrated program

The specificity of intervention is a characteristic that significantly contributes to its effectiveness. This characteristic exists on a continuum, and the specificity of instruction increases as students' needs are addressed in tiered instruction. Tier 2 interventions are often more specific than the high-quality instruction offered at the classroom level (Tier 1), and Tier 3 interventions are more specific than Tier 2 interventions. Whether delivered at Tier 2 or 3, intervention instruction is *not* comprehensive and does not replace the classroom reading instruction, which will include comprehension, vocabulary, phonemic awareness, decoding, and fluency instruction, as well as a great deal of supported and independent text reading.

For instance, take into consideration the following scenario involving Sheila. A first grader, Sheila was receiving small-group decoding instruction and word study in her classroom, but at the middle of the year she did not pass the benchmark for the literacy screener. Diagnostic follow-up indicated that she, along with another group of students, was unable to blend together a simple short-vowel word and required a small-group intervention at Tier 2. Although she was receiving decoding instruction in her classroom, that instruction was not having the desired effect, and so she needed intervention instruction. Importantly, the intervention instruction had to be different qualitatively from that which she received in the regular classroom. Intervention that simply repeated the same instruction at the same level of intensity was not what Sheila and the other students needed. Even high-quality classroom instruction may not be sufficient for some students to learn some essential skills.

For this small group, the interventionist used two new strategies. In the classroom, the teacher was using a phonograms, or word families, approach to teach decoding, and that instruction was working well for the majority of the class. Using this approach, the teacher would ask students to interchange initial sounds at the beginning of a phonogram (e.g., -*ap*) to create new words (e.g., *tap, nap, cap*). Although Sheila could do the phonogram activities during small-group reading instruction, she was not generalizing her decoding skills. When she encountered simple short-vowel words in other contexts (i.e., word lists, text reading), she could not decode them. The interventionist had to do something different. Instead of a phonogram approach, she modeled for students how to cover the final consonant in a word, blend the first two sounds together, and add the final sound. Then she gave them word cards with which to practice. She also asked students to spell the target short-vowel words so that they would be required to pay attention to each letter-sound in the word. The focus of the intervention (70% or more of the time) was decoding short-vowel words, but some skill review was necessary to support this intervention. The interventionist did spend time reviewing letter-sounds and practicing phonemic segmentation to support students' abilities to decode. Thus, the goal of the intervention was decoding words with short vowels (i.e., *a, e, i, o, u*) in a consonant–vowel–consonant pattern, but there were some ancillary support skills reviewed during the intervention. Intervention instruction usually takes place in 20- to 30-minute segments, and it must be focused, brisk, and lively instruction.

Let's say that after 4 weeks, this intervention had worked for the majority of the intervention group, but, despite its specificity, was not having the desired effect for Sheila. In this case, the interventionist could make the instruction even more specific, in what might be called a Tier 3 intervention. Perhaps instead of working on all short vowels, the instruction might just focus on Sheila's learning the techniques for decoding one sound, such as a short *a*.

Sheila's intervention instruction illustrates the nature of targeted interventions that are qualitatively different from regular classroom instruction. Intervention instruction is not the only type of differentiated instruction that can occur for a student. A high-quality, comprehensive classroom reading program will have differentiated small-group instruction based on reading level, decoding knowledge, fluency, and/or other needs. For instance, a student in first grade might need additional intervention instruction in phonemic awareness in order to be able to decode, but this will not replace all the text reading, comprehension, and other instruction he/she will receive in the regular classroom. Intervention instruction should *never* replace the classroom program.

Interventions should be well defined, meaning that the instructional activities are very clear. Not all interventions are created equal. Not all support approaches can be defined as an intervention. Sometimes students receive what the school is calling an intervention, but it is actually what we call *ad hoc instruction*. To us, ad hoc instruction is extra, improvised instruction usually offered "on the fly" by whoever is available. This may occur at a different time each day without a clear purpose or goal. Ad hoc instruction is *not* intervention.

An intervention also is not a service. For example, within RTI approaches, "seeing the reading specialist" or "receiving Title services" are not interventions. What the reading specialist or Title teacher actually does to address a specific reading deficit is an intervention. Although this may seem to be a matter of semantics, the distinction is critically important. Interventions should be specific, well articulated, and understandable. Professionals delivering interventions should be able to articulate for others (1) what actions they are taking in working with a struggling reader, (2) what those actions are addressing, and (3) the goal for their intervention instruction (see the text box *Goal Setting for Interventions*).

Intensive Instruction

At times an intervention does not necessarily need to be qualitatively different, but it needs to be quantitatively different or more intense. Like specificity, intensity also exists on a continuum, and strategies for intensifying instruction can be applied during small-group interventions and during more focused and individual interventions. There are four techniques for increasing the intensity of the instruction that a student receives. The first is the group size, which can be reduced to allow for more teacher contact and feedback. Hall (2006) recommends that students at the highest levels of risk work in groups containing no more than three students and those at a lower level of risk should be served in groups of five.

The next technique for increasing intensity is breaking down a task more than it would be broken down in the regular classroom. For example, Jennifer, a kindergarten teacher, was working with a group of children at the end of year who needed help in phonemic segmentation, or breaking words down into their parts. In the regular classroom she was using Elkonin boxes, a strategy in which students push counters into boxes as they say the sounds of a word. After using the technique, she found that a small group of students was still unable to do it independently and had not passed the midyear literacy benchmark. So Jennifer formed an intervention small group.

GOAL SETTING FOR INTERVENTIONS

As we discuss in greater detail in Chapter 2, the intervention is preceded by a diagnostic assessment and a grade-level planning meeting in which the details of the intervention are specified. An important part of this process is identifying a progress monitoring measure with which to evaluate the intervention and setting a goal for the intervention based on the progress monitoring measure. The goal is the concrete criteria for "success." It is the way that a team of teachers will know in the future if the intervention has been a successful or not. For example, a goal might be that a student increases his/her reading rate by 1.5 words per minute per week. Another goal might be that a student would be able to accurately decode 10 new words for each of the short vowels. Teachers tell us that setting goals at the *beginning of an intervention* makes the entire process so much more focused and clear. When they come back together to review the progress monitoring data to see if the interventions are working, they know what they want, and the discussions can be grounded by the goals, instead of feeling directionless.

Jennifer thought very carefully about what she was asking the students to do by analyzing the tasks in the activity. In order to push the counters accurately, students had to be able to orally break up the word (e.g., *c-a-t*), then coordinate their voices with their fingers while pushing counters, making sure not to say two sounds together when they were pushing counters into boxes (e.g., saying "*ca—*" while pushing only one counter into a box). When Jennifer thought about the activity, she realized that the students were not able to orally segment the words, a prerequisite for handling the counters and coordinating the movement of the counters with their speaking of a segmented word.

So she took a step back and simply asked her students to work on orally segmenting words. When Jennifer analyzed the task that she was asking students to do, she realized that she was asking them to perform several different tasks in one step and that the number of phonemes in the word was complicating the activity. It is possible that despite these changes, one or two students might still have difficulty. In a more individualized intervention, perhaps at Tier 3, Jennifer might break down the task even more. For example, she may discover that orally segmenting phonemes could be simplified, starting with words that contained only two phonemes as opposed to three (e.g., *he, she, be, to, do*). Attention to this detail was not needed for the students who responded to the small-group intervention, but it may be needed for a select student or students. Good intervention instruction often requires teachers to break down tasks further than they would in the regular classroom.

A third strategy for increasing intensity is simply providing students with more practice and repetition. This strategy is so simple, it is frequently overlooked. Often students just need more opportunities to respond. For example, Janice, a PreK teacher, was working with her class on naming the first five letters of the alphabet. In a whole-class exercise, she held up cards and asked the class to name letters, thinking that students were getting daily practice with naming these five letters. However, when Janice assessed them at the midyear literacy screening, one-third of her class did not meet the benchmark and did not know the letters. After some observation, Janice realized that many of the students were not paying attention during the whole-group instruction and that frequently students were simply parroting their neighbor's responses. Clearly, they needed intervention instruction in small groups but they also needed more individual practice opportunities. Janice began working with a group around a table, presenting the children with individual letter cards and asking them to name the letters. She thought carefully about making sure that each child had the opportunity to practice naming each of the five letters three times during the small group. She used a fun game format in which the children could "earn" teddy bear counters and watched as they each became more skilled in naming their letters. She had simply increased the number of practice opportunities available to the students. A very simple way to increase intensity of instruction involves attention to the number of practice opportunities that students are getting. When teachers do not know how many opportunities students are receiving to practice target reading skills, we frequently find that students are not receiving enough practice.

Lastly, intervention instruction can be made more intense by increasing the amount of corrective feedback that students are given. *Corrective feedback* involves the careful use of language following the observation of a target skill that specifies for the student *if* he/she gave the right answer; *why* the answer is/is not right; and if the answer is wrong, *how* to make it right. One of the unfortunate experiences common to struggling readers is a lack of feedback about how to improve. Sometimes teachers do not even tell them if their answer is correct, and they remain confused. For example, let's say that Pedro is trying to decode the word *peg*, but instead says "pug." Some teachers might say, "Almost. Let's try that again," in which case Pedro doesn't know *why* his answer is wrong, or *how* to fix the problem. Instead a teacher can be more explicit and corrective and say:

> "No, that is not *pug*. Let's look at it. The word has the letters *p, e, g*. Watch me put them together, /p/. You got that right. The first sound is /p/. Now look at the second sound. That's where you were not right. You said '/p/' and then you said '/u/,' but look, that's an *e*. The sound should be /e/. So it should be /p/ then /e/, *peeee* and then /g/. You got the /g/ at the end right. Now you do it. Put that word together; remember the sound in the middle is /e/."

Corrective feedback often needs to be more explicit in an intervention because students have not been able to infer what they need to do from regular classroom instruction where the feedback may be vague (see the text box *What to Do about Intervention Programs*).

WHAT TO DO ABOUT INTERVENTION PROGRAMS

In our work with schools we have often encountered RTI programs that use computer-aided design and responsive structures to deliver instructional intervention. These programs claim to be all schools need to deliver intervention. In our experience these programs rarely provide a targeted instructional intervention that is tailored specifically to the needs of the students. Most of the time, they focus on too many different skills in one session. For instance, a first-grade program might provide letter-sound practice, high-frequency word practice, decoding practice, and fluency in one 20-minute session regardless of whether the student needs it. In addition, we find that if these programs are used daily, students get bored with them and become what we call "autoclickers," randomly clicking answers without thought. If you must use such a program, we suggest that you do not use it daily and that you intersperse it with live, teacher-directed intervention. We believe that these programs are best used for review and maintenance.

Fidelity

Interventions must be well implemented. Intervention *fidelity* or *integrity* is the consistency with which the intervention instruction is delivered. If the intervention is well specified and clear, the activities will be very consistent from session to session or according to directions. In other words, if the goal of an intervention is to support a student's skills in phonemic segmentation (i.e., breaking words into sounds), we would not expect to find unrelated activities taking place during the intervention. Although this seems obvious, our experience indicates that it is not. For example, we once encountered a teacher who was charged with a phonemic segmentation intervention, but we observed that about two-thirds of the intervention was focused on high-frequency words and phrases. During classroom instruction the teacher had determined that the students needed work with Dolch words and had decided to do this work during the intervention time. This explained why the progress monitoring data, which measured phonemic segmentation, was not showing progress. The intervention had been derailed, and it was not being implemented with integrity or fidelity. Although the students needed high-frequency word practice, they also needed segmentation support, and this skill was determined by a team to be the most pressing need of the students receiving intervention instruction. Intervention "drift" like this can happen more easily than expected. We recommend that when developing an intervention, a grade-level team develop a simple checklist with three to five key intervention ingredients.

Interventions are most likely to be successful if implemented with integrity (Duhon, Mesmer, Gregerson, & Witt, 2009). We like to remind people of the common quote found on many household products, "For best results follow instructions as directed." For example, most tubes of toothpaste indicate that the user should "squeeze from the bottom." Certainly, one could squeeze from the top, but eventually no toothpaste will come out of the tube. The same holds true for research-based instructional interventions. Although these interventions may be partially effective even if they are not implemented the way that they are supposed to be, it is just as likely that they will not be effective at all. When it comes to interventions, it appears that following directions is, indeed, important.

Integrated Intervention

One of the important elements of instructional interventions within an RTI model is that the interventions do not stand alone. Simply implementing intervention instruction does not mean that an RTI model is in place. Reading interventions have been in use for some time. However, reading interventions in the past were not part of a systematic RTI process. Interventions within RTI are integrated into a process of screening and identification, continued progress monitoring, review of data, and modifications to instruction if the intervention is not working. In previous approaches to intervention, teachers often did not assess in an ongoing way but instead used more static assessments that took place one or two times at the beginning or end of the intervention. For instance, in previous approaches to intervention, a teacher might give a pretest at the beginning of the intervention and then 5 months later given a posttest. Often, teachers did not even assess interventions using equivalent tests at the beginning and the end of the intervention, making it impossible to know if the intervention was effective or not because the tests changed. The RTI process is about systematically delivering and assessing instruction and making changes to that instruction in order to understand if, with focused instruction, a student can *respond to intervention instruction.*

In sum, instructional intervention is at the heart of RTI. As we describe in Chapter 2, there are specific processes that schools can incorporate to plan for intervention instruction, communicate about it, and support it. In this chapter we simply defined *intervention*—a targeted type of instruction that is both qualitatively and quantitatively distinguishable from other types of differentiated instruction. Importantly, intervention within an RTI model does not stand alone but is part of an integrated system with multiples parts. The following questions may guide you as you examine your school's approach to intervention:

- Are we delivering "ad hoc instruction" (extra, improvised instruction offered by random people in an inconsistent manner) and calling it *intervention*?
- Does intervention instruction replace any part of the comprehensive classroom program? (It should not.)
- Does intervention instruction look qualitatively different from small-group classroom instruction?

- Do we have *clearly targeted* interventions, focused on *one* prioritized skill, with a small portion of time used to review supporting skills?
- Is it easy to identify the skill being targeted when observing an intervention lesson?
- Do we alter the intensity of instruction by changing group size, analyzing and breaking down tasks, providing more practice, and/or giving specific and corrective feedback?
- Does our intervention instruction exist within an integrated system that includes screening and progress monitoring?
- Does every student who needs intervention (e.g., does not meet the benchmark on the literacy screening test) receive intervention?
- Do we design interventions based on the *students' needs* rather than what *a program offers*?

Progress Monitoring

Instructional interventions are the most effective when students' responses to them are monitored on a regular basis. *Progress monitoring* is an ongoing assessment procedure designed to evaluate the effectiveness of a targeted intervention. When we think of progress monitoring, we often ask two questions. First, "Is the student learning the skill I have been teaching?" To answer this question, we assess the child on the exact skill that has been taught during small-group intervention. This form of progress monitoring, called *mastery monitoring/measurement* (MM), gives us a "micro-level" look at students' responses to intervention in a specific way (Deno, 2008; Fuchs & Deno, 1991). Next we ask, "Are the student's skills improving to a level beyond the current skill being taught?" Naturally, we want to know if the student's progress is generalizing to a level beyond the current skill that is being targeted during intervention instruction. In other words, we want to know that the intervention instruction is translating to a greater proficiency in reading. This type of progress monitoring is referred to as a *general outcome monitoring/ measurement* (GOM; Deno, 1997; Fuchs & Deno, 1991). GOM gives us more of a "macro-lens" on students' progress. Both forms of progress monitoring can prove useful as we check to see if students are responding to our intervention efforts in both specific and more general ways.

As intervention instruction is going on, teachers are assessing and evaluating that instruction weekly or biweekly. Although research-based interventions are effective for most, they may not be effective for all. Therefore, it is never safe to assume that any one intervention or instructional approach will be the ultimate answer for any single struggling student. For any intervention that is implemented, teachers must routinely determine whether it is working by using progress monitoring data. Again, an analogy to the medical field is useful. Physicians often check and recheck and check again the vital signs of their patients. These checks, of course, are conducted to see if the patient's condition is improving. If the patient is not responding to the medical intervention, then this lack of response will be reflected in their vital signs and the physician will prescribe a change in treatment. Such is the case with instructional intervention. If the student does not improve, then changes in intervention instruction will be necessary. If RTI data are being used in a special education referral process, progress monitoring data and charts are necessary to evaluate if the student has *responded to the instructional intervention*. Progress monitoring and the instructional regrouping that is informed by it are vital to ensuring that intervention groups continue to be flexible and appropriately matched to students' needs.

Teachers often ask us about the burden of weekly assessments with intervention groups that might be larger than average (i.e., greater than five students). First, we always say that you would want to do progress monitoring no less than every other week. Without progress monitoring, you cannot say that the intervention is working for everyone. Remember, assessment data will *produce surprises*, and progress monitoring is no different. Teachers will sometimes believe that a student is responding perfectly to an intervention based on small-group responses, but when the progress monitoring data are collected, he/she may not be. Then we always try to remind teachers that progress monitoring is not so different from other forms of weekly assessment, such as a spelling or vocabulary test. The issue is usually that the progress monitoring measures need to be given individually, and teachers are not sure what to do with the other students while they are assessing. Teachers have legitimate concerns about losing an entire intervention day to progress monitoring assessments.

To address these issues teachers have created a number of solutions. Some design a schedule that allows them to assess each student on a different day, during the last 5 minutes of intervention time, with other students engaging in independent practice. Other teachers dedicate an entire intervention period per week to assessment with students doing independent work during the entire invention session, but only if the week is a *full* week. (You would actually be surprised how frequently the school week is not a full 5 days.) So, if there is a Monday holiday or snow day, then assessment is done the next week. This approach prioritizes intervention.

Finally, we don't believe that teachers should have to spend a significant amount of time designing their own progress monitoring measures. The good news is that MM measures are easily developed or may already be available to teachers as part of the instructional materials that they are using. Because MM directly assesses the skill being taught, these materials will be easy to find or develop. Regarding GOM, most schools choose to adopt an assessment system that includes these measures. Two commonly used assessment systems for monitoring early literacy skills includes DIBELS Next and AIMSweb. Both of these systems include specific tests that can be easily matched to the focus of intervention instruction.

RTI and the Common Core State Standards

We are often asked how RTI relates to the Common Core State Standards (CCSS) for the English language arts. The CCSS have been adopted by over 45 states and are clearly impacting literacy instruction across the country. All teachers know that the CCSS are front and center in the minds of American educators. It seems that everything—webinars, conference sessions, books, and professional development efforts—has been geared toward equipping schools for the new standards. When new initiatives such as the CCSS come to the forefront, it feels like the latest "hot topics," such as RTI, begin to wane and fade. We know many teachers and schools may be asking, "Where does RTI fit in with the CCSS? Is there any point in devoting efforts toward RTI when it seems that assessments and instruction now lean toward the CCSS?" Unfortunately, education in the United States, like so many other things, can be prone to fads, but RTI is not a fleeting fad. In the reading field, it developed out of a decades-long line of research on early reading intervention. Further, there are some important connections between the CCSS and RTI. So, we encourage schools to not "throw the baby out with the bath water." High-quality reading intervention, the focus of RTI, is what will enable students to reach the high standards articulated in the CCSS. The two initiatives actually complement one another: RTI ensures student capacity for the high-level skills articulated in the CCSS.

The CCSS are designed to reflect the knowledge and skills that are necessary for students to succeed in college and careers (Common Core State Standards Initiative, 2010). The CCSS set grade-level expectations that are specifically designed to develop proficient readers. Proficient readers have the capacity to comprehend texts of various types and disciplines. Both CCSS and RTI are focused on facilitating success for *all* students. As McLaughlin and Overturf put it, "the Common Core has provided the Standards. Teaching students how to meet the Standards is in our hands" (2012, p. 35). RTI places emphasis on helping students achieve success through research-based, data-informed instruction, both in the core classroom and via instructional interventions. Through the CCSS, we know what students need to be able to do, grade by grade, in order to leave our school system deemed *proficient*. Through RTI's focus on research-based intervention, we can teach students how to meet the CCSS in effective ways. Let's take a closer look at CCSS and RTI as we highlight some important considerations for ensuring success for all students in the primary grades.

Foundational Skills

Foundational skills, according to CCSS and most reading experts, include print concepts, phonological awareness, phonics and word recognition, and fluency. As the CCSS states, foundation skills should not serve as end points for reading development. In grades PreK–2 there is a great deal of focus on students' acquisition of foundational skills. We agree that foundational skills are *necessary*, but they alone are *not sufficient* for reading success. In other words, we know that it would be fairly difficult for kids to be good readers if they lacked these skill sets. In order to comprehend complex texts, readers need to have phonological awareness, the ability to decode words based on letter-sound knowledge, and recognition of high-frequency words. Kids need to be able to read with accuracy, appropriate rate, and prosody in order to make meaning when reading. It is unlikely that any proficient reader is without these foundational skills. Likewise, foundational skills are easily measured and have a "ceiling" for mastery (i.e., a maximum level of achievement that can be obtained). For example, students can only learn 26 letters of the alphabet.

Foundational skills are paramount to RTI, because they do what they suggest: They provide a foundation, a "ground-level" base, upon which readers build to become proficient readers who make meaning as they read. It would be incredibly difficult to comprehend a complex text successfully without adequate word knowledge or fluency. Foundational skills are the necessary building blocks to prepare proficient readers. RTI provides a system for ensuring that students develop these foundational skills. Through RTI, we can address students' needs early so that they move onto more complex texts efficiently and smoothly.

Teaching What Students Need

The CCSS state that teachers should teach what students *need*, not what they already know. Further, the CCSS state that teachers must discern when students, or activities, warrant more or less attention. These determinations cannot be made by hunches, general wisdom, judgment, or even experience. We believe that the ability to determine when students or activities need more or less attention resides in *data*. This is where RTI enters. RTI provides a systematic way to determine *who* needs more or less help and *what* needs more attention. Universal screenings help us determine *who* needs intervention. Diagnostic assessments help us determine *which* activities (instruction) are specifically needed. Further, progress monitoring helps us determine *when* struggling readers no longer need attention or when they need more.

Through strategic and systematic use of data in an RTI framework, we can design RTI instructional intervention groups. Intervention groups in the primary grades should focus on specific foundational skills and build upon them with targeted, data-informed instruction. Because we rely on data to inform our instruction for RTI, it is possible that first graders may be working on foundational skills from the kindergarten CCSS. For example, Mr. Lopresto's first-grade phonological awareness intervention group may need to target the kindergarten phonological awareness CCSS. RTI makes sure that kids don't get pushed forward when they need more attention in particular skills. For primary grade students, these are usually the foundational skills outlined in the CCSS.

The Case for Instructional Urgency with Foundational Skills

The CCSS were designed to develop more proficient readers who can succeed in an ever-changing world that places high demands upon readers. Comprehension is vital for such success. As a result, a clear emphasis is placed in the CCSS on critical thinking skills, including the comprehension of complex texts in a variety of genres. This emphasis on high-demand reading and thinking begins in kindergarten, not after students have learned to read, and continues to build throughout the grade levels. So, students must master the foundational skills as early and as quickly as possible in order to have the capacity to fulfill the CCSS for literature, informational texts, and writing.

Likewise, the CCSS are organized and structured so that skills progress from year to year. From grade to grade, standards build upon one another, and students are expected to adhere to each grade-level standard while *retaining and/or further developing* skills mastered in preceding grades. For example, the CCSS Foundational Skills for phonics and word recognition require that kindergarten students should associate the long- and short-vowel sounds with common spellings. As students move to first grade, they should learn consonant–vowel–consonant–final *e* (CVCe) and common vowel team conventions for representing long-vowel sounds. On into second grade, students should know the spelling–sound correspondences for additional common vowel teams. Each grade level builds upon the other with gradients of learning. Pacing and gradients of learning are swift and high. Swift and accurate attention to the foundational skills for struggling students is key.

Struggling readers can easily get lost or left behind in the CCSS system, leaving foundational "cracks" and frustrations along the way that lead to greater difficulties and struggles as instruction builds and paces ahead from grade to grade. RTI provides a system that is designed to identify struggling readers as quickly as possible and to fill in cracks in foundational skills with research-based intervention instruction that is informed by data. Through RTI, we can identify "cracks" in learning to read as quickly and efficiently as possible, maximizing students' instructional time and time in text. With RTI, we can give kids what they need to construct their own strong foundation so that their focus can then move to comprehending more diverse and complex texts from grade to grade.

CCSS, RTI, and Connections in This Book

Because this book focuses on RTI in the primary grades, the CCSS foundational skills for reading serve as the focal points for our intervention instruction. Table 1.1 highlights how we address CCSS within the context of Tier 2 interventions.

TABLE 1.1. How Common Core Standards Relate to Tier 2 Interventions

CCSS foundational skill	CCSS	RTI in the primary grades connection	Points to ponder
Print concepts	Kindergarteners should be able to name all upper- and lowercase letters of the alphabet.	Chapter 4 addresses alphabet recognition, to which we refer as *letter naming*.	There are additional CCSS print concept standards, such as the concept of *word* that may require intervention beyond letter naming. However, letter naming will contribute to students' development of word concept.
Phonological awareness	Various elements of phonological awareness are addressed for kindergarten and first-grade students. Emphasis is placed on blending and segmenting various aspects of the speech sound system.	In Chapter 5, we specifically address the important role of phonemic segmentation in intervention instruction that is focused on decoding.	The ability to segment and blend individual sounds is put into play in the process of decoding written words. Hence, we believe it is important to teach phonemic segmentation, which is a phonological awareness component, while also teaching decoding skills—for students who need it. The two go hand in hand.
Phonics and word recognition	Kindergarten, first-grade, and second-grade students are required to "know and apply" phonics and word analysis skills at each grade level. These skills build upon one another from grade to grade.	In Chapter 5, we provide intervention strategies for improving students' decoding skills, equipping them with tools to analyze, or break down, unknown words.	Because the CCSS tell us *what* kids need to know and not *how* to teach it, much autonomy is placed in the hands of the teacher. Teachers must be knowledgeable about the developmental phases students go through as they apply knowledge of letters-sounds to read unknown words. Teachers must be equipped to use this knowledge base for offering intentional interventions that target specific decoding/phonics needs.
Fluency	In kindergarten, first grade, and second grade, students must read with sufficient accuracy and fluency to support comprehension. This includes reading with purpose and understanding, accuracy, appropriate rate and expression, as well as using of self-monitoring strategies.	In Chapter 6, we discuss research-based intervention strategies for addressing students' reading accuracy, rate, and expression (or reading prosody), with particular emphasis on rate and prosody. Whereas the CCSS include high-frequency words in the phonics and word recognition category for foundational skills, we include high-frequency words in Chapter 6 on fluency, because without efficient and accurate reading of high-frequency words on sight, students will lack the ability to read with appropriate rate and expression.	Fluency has such a very important connection to comprehension. Whereas fluent readers have the brain capacity to focus on making meaning, struggling readers are often fixated at the word level, leaving little "brain power" left to make meaning of what they read. Note that the CCSS address this very notion within the foundational skills for fluency. We wholeheartedly agree that readers should not be considered "fluent" by accuracy, rate, and prosody alone. Comprehension, or reading with purpose and understanding, is paramount in the definition of fluent reading.

We provide additional points to ponder regarding RTI and CCSS for each foundational skill.

In sum, RTI has an important role to play in helping schools meet the CCSS. Because of its reliance on data, RTI ensures that students are being taught what they need to learn and not what they already know. RTI provides more attention to students who need help through tiered intervention instruction. The CCSS demands instructional urgency. In the primary grades, RTI intervention instruction works to build foundational skills that are necessary for success as proficient readers in effective and efficient ways. This book shares the research behind the foundational skills found in the CCSS and provides practical ways to assess and monitor students' progress, as well as teacher-friendly ways to deliver intervention instruction in the foundational skills. In closing, there is no need to wave goodbye to RTI with the dawning of the CCSS. Together, RTI and CCSS will improve literacy instruction, resulting in success for our children across the country.

Conclusion

This chapter has provided the reader with a basic understanding of the RTI process. We have focused on defining RTI and explaining why it is being used at this time. We have also provided extended definitions and examples related to three important RTI concepts: screening, intervention, and progress monitoring (MM and GOM). Certainly these are not the only terms used in RTI, but they are basic, and understanding them will provide teachers and schools with basic grounding in building a successful RTI model.

In Chapter 2 we take these basic ingredients and embed them into a system for implementing the RTI process. In our experience, schools have the most difficulty in *applying* these concepts and principles, and in Chapter 2 we describe how to put RTI into action. Although the focus of this book is reading, the information in this chapter would be broadly applicable to any RTI process, including interventions that focus on behavior or math.

CHAPTER 2
• • • • • • • • • • •

Putting the RTI Steps into Action

GUIDING QUESTIONS

• What characteristics of active leadership are necessary for successful implementation of RTI?

• What are the five major processes associated with RTI Tier 2 intervention instruction?

• What types of preplanning efforts are key to creating a firm foundation for RTI success?

• How is universal screening interconnected with both Tier 1 and Tier 2 intervention instruction decision making?

• On what should Tier 2 place the most time and emphasis?

• How does progress monitoring serve as a "thermometer" for making instructional decisions for students' interventions?

The purpose of this chapter is to provide guidelines regarding the actions that might be taken to implement the basic steps in the RTI process. This guidance is based upon experience that we have had in working with several school districts. In particular, we examine the major processes associated with the Tier 2 level of RTI. These processes are illustrated in Figure 1.2 (p. 14) and include screening, analysis of data (and sometimes additional diagnostic assessment), instructional intervention with progress monitoring, and either modification of the intervention or exiting the student from the intervention due to success. We have used this graphic with schools for several years and find that it provides a simple "big picture" framework for teachers to understand the process. With an overarching organizational structure, people can grasp the steps of RTI and understand how the particulars fit into a larger structure. Universal screening, which is associated with Tier 1, is intertwined with decision making for Tier 2 level instruction.

Following screening, identified students are placed into instructional groupings that best match their instructional needs. As instructional interventions are implemented over several weeks, assessment data (progress monitoring) are collected to determine whether the instructional interventions are working. Finally, decisions are made regarding the level of success of interventions and appropriate changes are made to these interventions. Notice that the largest square in Figure 1.2 is devoted to intervention. This proportion reflects the importance of the intervention itself and that the majority of time should therefore be devoted to it. It is the *instructional* intervention that actually makes the difference, and all other parts of the process are simply preparing for the intervention or assessing its effects.

RTI is a sequential process in which early steps inform subsequent steps. So, it is important to have an understanding of *all* parts of the process. The process then repeats, possibly multiple times, in an effort to help students who struggle the most.

As a starting point we believe that the foundation of any RTI effort is embedded in a building's leadership. Thus we begin with an exploration of issues, and ultimately decisions, that must be addressed by a leadership team before the RTI process can begin. Having an understanding of these issues is also important in fully appreciating the major components of RTI.

The Importance of Leadership

In every school that we have worked with, we have learned that change is never easy. You may know from your own personal experiences that even small changes in behavior can be challenging. For example, one us made a vigorous attempt to increase teeth flossing over the course of a year. Although this is a small behavior which only takes a few minutes each day, making this change required conscious effort, self-reminders, and fighting the urge to simply stop. Over time, however, this change in behavior became a habit, simply part of the routine and was no longer experienced as a burden. The same can be true for changes in the school setting. It is true that new behaviors or practices will likely be retained once they have been done many times. The daunting question is, however, what factors get us to initially sustain our change efforts?

In the districts that we have worked with, one factor has largely influenced whether the school was successful in their initial efforts: the degree to which *active leadership* was present. We mention this factor here because there is no way to carry out the procedural logistics of RTI without it. Each school has unique characteristics, and the solutions necessary to carry out plans for change will inevitably vary.

Active leaders demonstrate three characteristics (Murphy, 2004). First, they are *committed*. Commitment means:

- Making RTI a priority in the face of other pressures and initiatives.
- Believing in the basic assumptions and premises of RTI.
- Engaging in RTI practices firsthand and thereby demonstrating for others the willingness to practice change.

In one school we worked with, commitment was exemplified by a principal who reviewed progress monitoring data with the grade-level team, obtained input from his teachers, and made clear statements about possible ways of furthering assistance for students in need.

Second, active leaders are *flexible*. Flexibility in this context involves the willingness to think about and utilize resources in new ways. Flexible leaders are able to come up with and/or endorse solutions that provide school personnel with opportunities to do things differently. School leaders who are flexible are often heard saying, "We can figure that out." These leaders endorse flexibility by making changes in the school schedule and finding paths of action to make change happen. One leader we worked with, when asked if the school could find an additional 30 minutes of reading time each day, was famous for saying, "We will make that happen because these students need more time reading."

Finally, active leaders *enable* change by actively supporting teachers and by not accepting excuses. We have seen active support expressed in numerous ways, such as reassigning and dropping duties, eliminating competing or duplicative assessments or initiatives, and actual engagement in assessment or interventions activities, to name a few. Moreover, these leaders do not drown in negativity or "cave in" to the resistant efforts of a vocal few. When these leaders truly believe in the outcomes and the process, we have generally found that they are willing to make RTI efforts a priority. Teachers working with active leaders feel safe to try new things, and they feel supported in all ways, including time and resources. We sum up these characteristics in the old adage, "Where there is a will, there is a way." We truly believe that RTI requires committed and active leadership as a necessary condition for success.

Putting the Steps into Action

What we have found is that *logistics do matter* when implementing RTI. A sound plan is helpful in navigating the twists and turns that inevitably occur during RTI implementation. In the sections below we discuss two action steps that will assist in implementing RTI. Each action step includes a number of activities that should be accomplished. Action Step 1 includes important leadership planning activities that are relevant to Tiers 1 and 2 of RTI. We have included this action step because we believe teachers should have some understanding of the "background" that is intended to facilitate their active involvement. We have found that this background information eliminates misunderstandings and helps to ensure greater buy-in to the process. Action Step 2 reflects the active RTI processes that occur during Tier 1 (screening) and Tier 2 (group instruction and decision making), as seen in Figure 1.2. The figure representing the RTI process is a reminder that RTI is not simply "doing" a reading intervention or administering a reading test, but is instead an integrated system of interdependent assessment–intervention steps.

Reading interventions have been used for years and years, but not until RTI have we seen systematic assessment of these interventions, continued progress monitoring, review of data, and modifications to instruction if the intervention is not working. The RTI process is about *systematically* delivering and assessing instruction and making changes to that instruction in order to understand if, with focused instruction, a student can *respond to intervention*.

Action Step 1: Developing Your Leadership Team

At the school level we recommend that the leadership team generally consist of four or five representatives who are respected members of the school staff. Minimally the team should include the school principal and the lead reading instructor. These two individuals set the tone for the reading program in the building and both formally and informally endorse the credibility of the RTI efforts. We also suggest that at least one member of the team have in-depth knowledge of the screening and progress monitoring measures and a background in assessment (e.g., the school psychologist). This individual will play an important role in selecting assessments and organizing and interpreting data. We also recommend the involvement of a special education teacher because he/she will have knowledge about explicit intervention strategies. Finally, because classroom teachers will be most impacted by changes that accompany the RTI process, it is important that one or two teachers take a leadership role in the initiative. In one school with which we are familiar, there is a teacher representative for each grade level on the RTI leadership team. This makes the team a bit larger than we typically recommend, but teachers at all grade levels feel they have a contact and a voice in the process through their grade-level representatives. Once the leadership team is established, several important tasks should be addressed in moving efforts forward.

Select the Screening Measure

In Chapter 1, we outlined the central questions to ask when considering the use of a universal reading screener. In sum, screeners should be brief, predictive, objective, and universally administered. In addition, screening assessments must be psychometrically sound and might also have some diagnostic value. *Psychometric soundness* means that the measure should be accurate and that it was, in fact, developed for purposes of screening literacy needs. This requirement underscores an important point: Not all screening measures are equal. In fact, some are likely better than others with regard to the accuracy of the results provided. *Accuracy* means that the screener is able to identify those students who are truly struggling or "at risk" while not identifying students who may appear to be struggling but are really not "at risk." We have found a disturbing trend in many of the schools in which we have worked, in that an assessment tool is used for screening primarily because the district has already adopted that assessment for other purposes. Although we certainly recommend using existing assessments whenever possible, we remind schools that assessments still must be used *appropriately* for a given purpose, in this case screening. Some districts/schools have chosen to use a state outcome test as a screening assessment to determine which students in their schools are struggling. Keep in mind that state outcome tests were not developed to identify struggling readers. They were designed to evaluate the progress of a school and to inform stakeholders (e.g., parents, business, community) of this progress. Moreover, these outcome tests were intended to be just that, a measure of end-of-year mastery of concepts and skills (i.e., outcomes). Screening assessments are intended to be administered prior to outcome assessments and should predict or identify those students who will not do well on the outcome test—thus allowing schools to intervene with these students and improve the possibility that more students will pass the outcome assessments.

A second situation that we often encounter is that schools sometimes choose computer-based screeners due to their significant convenience. We have no problems with computer-based screeners in general; however, they should be selected based upon the criteria already outlined. Fortunately, most non-computer-based screening assessments that must be individually administered by a teacher are brief and can be accomplished rather quickly. That said, the use of a computer delivery format may be very appealing to many school administrators. Unfortunately, the independent research base evaluating these screening tools is scarce. For schools that are considering the adoption of a computer-based screening assessment, we would minimally recommend that you visit the National Center on Response to Intervention website (*www.rti4success.org*). That center provides a resource that allows users to review the available data on several computer-based screeners, as well as non-computer-based screeners, in addition to cost and feasibility information.

The last issue for teams to consider when selecting a screener has to do with their diagnostic value. As previously discussed, many universal screeners provide little information as to why a student is not performing well. In the event that your school has chosen such a screener, it will be imperative that the team collect additional information on those students who fail to meet the benchmark score so that these students' reading needs can be better understood. Minimally, for grades K–2 the screening process should provide you with information about students' phonemic awareness skills, alphabet knowledge, and early decoding skills. This information can then be used to identify broad reading needs for purposes of instructional grouping (Tier 2).

Establish the Screening Window

A *screening window* is the time frame within which the screening should be completed. Teachers are given a period of several days or weeks to complete screening. In determining the screening window it is first important to remember that the screening process should occur three times per year (fall, winter, and spring). The purpose of conducting screenings multiple times each year is to increase the chance of "catching" struggling students who may not have been identified from an earlier screening. For example, it may be that some new students move into a school after the fall screening has been completed. Or, a student who performs above the benchmark in the fall may not maintain adequate progress during the year and as a result may fail to meet the benchmark in either the winter or the spring. In both of these cases, the provision of interventions may be delayed if additional screenings were not performed and the students' reading needs not identified. Waiting until the following fall, close to an academic year, to identify these students and provide needed supports could prove disastrous to their reading development. Screening three times per year increases instructional urgency to meet students' needs as quickly and efficiently as possible.

We recommend that the timings of screenings occur so that students have had some opportunity to "knock the rust off" their skills upon returning from extended school breaks. Conversely, schools should not wait too long to conduct screenings, as this may prolong the time that students with reading needs do not receive help. As a general rule we recommend that schools conduct the screenings during the second to third week of the school year each fall. This time frame allows students sufficient time to become reacquainted with school and testing situations. Keep in mind that students returning from summer break may not have had the opportunity to practice their reading skills over the summer. Thus, it is not surprising to see many students' scores decrease from spring of the previous year to fall of the current year. However, for most students, this decrease in scores will quickly rebound after several weeks of instruction. During the winter we recommend that screenings be conducted approximately 2 weeks after returning from winter break (mid-to-late January). Finally, we recommend that the spring screening occur approximately 4 weeks prior to the end of the school year (mid-April to early May). Waiting until the very end of the school year increases the likelihood that the results will not be used because there is no further instructional time remaining in the year. Moreover, given the pressure of other end-of-the-year activities and the desire to begin the summer break, it is possible that the results would not be given ample attention.

Consider Intervention Materials

As we have already discussed, intervention is the heart of RTI. In the end, the progress of struggling readers will largely be determined by the quality of the instruction/intervention that is provided. Early in the RTI process it is important that schools begin accumulating instruction/intervention resources that specifically address the essential reading skills that students need to acquire in the early grades. The materials used for intervention include teacher professional resource books with strategies, manipulatives, existing curriculum guides, and sometimes programs. For example, to address phonological awareness a school might use the teacher professional resource book *Road to the Code* (Blachman, Ball, Black, & Tangel, 2000). Similarly, to address development of phonics skills a school might use the Sound Partners program available through Sopris Learning. Although schools have access to many materials, we have found that the quality of these materials varies from school to school (and within schools).

Quality refers to the extent to which the materials are both empirically validated (i.e., research shows them to be effective) and socially valid (i.e., they fit the pedagogical perspectives embraced within a school). In addition, often the materials may not be used or may not be used effectively. In selecting intervention materials, we recommend that the characteristics of effective interventions (discussed in Chapter 1) be addressed as part of your selection process. As part of those deliberations it may be helpful to ask the following questions:

- Are the materials specific in that they provide detailed information regarding how to use them?
- Do the materials allow for differentiation in intensity of delivery?
- Are the interventions relatively straightforward, or will they be too complex to implement with fidelity?
- Will this intervention match or fit my instructional objectives?

In order to answer these questions, schools must often obtain the materials and spend sufficient time examining them. Commercially available information about these products usually does not provide enough detail to make an informed decision. In addition, we have found that discussions with sales representatives can also lead to insufficient information. Finally, it does seem important to determine whether there is any evidence of the effectiveness of the intervention materials that you are considering. We have found two websites that we feel provide sufficient information about the evidence supporting various reading intervention programs and products. One of these sites is hosted by the Center on Teaching and Learning at the University of Oregon. This website has a page entitled, "Review of supplemental and intervention programs," which can be found at *http://oregonreadingfirst.uoregon.edu/inst_curr_review_si.html*. Information provided at this site focuses on criteria for selecting and evaluating core reading curriculum as well as supplemental intervention programs. The second site is the What Works Clearing-house, which is supported by the Institute of Education Sciences (*http://ies.ed.gov/ncee/wwc*). This site is described in the text box *Using the What Works Clear-inghouse to Evaluate the Effectiveness of Intervention Programs*. As described in the text box, teachers can search for reading programs and read reviews of published studies evaluating the effectiveness of each program. A third website, which is hosted by the International Reading Association, can be used to evaluate core reading programs that are being used with all students (not just those receiv-ing Tier 2 supports) and can be found at *www.reading.org/General/Publications/Books/SupplementalContent/bk707_supplement.aspx*.

Determine the Need for Professional Development

Another critical step for the leadership team is to determine the extent to which teachers will require professional development training. In our work we have found that training as many teachers and staff as possible is a crucial compo-nent in communicating the central importance of this work and to ensure a truly "schoolwide" effort. Many consultants often conduct a needs assessment to deter-mine the strengths and weaknesses of a school building, which subsequently helps with planning professional development. Schools may find, however, that experts working in their buildings can themselves identify professional development needs.

In Table 2.1 we provide a list of the skill areas that are critical to success-fully initiate RTI efforts. As school personnel examine this list they will see that there are many skill areas that need to be considered. Many of the profession-als in a building or district are already well trained in these skills. However, we have often found that staff training will need to occur. Training sessions should occur throughout the year. We usually remind schools to make their professional development timely by focusing on the skills that are to be used first. Moreover, follow-up sessions, in which consultants can observe staff and provide feedback as well as facilitate grade-level and RTI team meetings, are important. In this role, consultants serve as *teacher support*, not as evaluators (see the text box *Finding the Right Consultant*). Finally, provision of "booster" sessions is also important as RTI efforts continue across multiple years.

Prepare to Conduct "State-of-the-School" Meetings

One of the great benefits of RTI is that the assessments used to evaluate students' reading performance can also be used to provide insight into the instructional strengths and weaknesses of a school building. We believe that it is important for administrators and teachers to take responsibility for the quality of instruc-tion provided to students. Within RTI there is an accepted belief that if schools

USING THE WHAT WORKS CLEARINGHOUSE TO EVALUATE THE EFFECTIVENESS OF INTERVENTION PROGRAMS

Research-based practices are essential to instructional intervention, but, as one principal asked us, "How can we tell if something's research-based without spending a day in library?" He was right on with his question; teachers and schools do not have the luxury of time. They need answers right now. What Works Clearinghouse (WWC), a website sponsored by the Institute of Education Sciences, is a resource for evaluating the degree to which various products and practices are research-based. WWC evaluates the effectiveness of practices, products, and strategies in a *simple* report format (and you can read it in about 10 minutes).

There are two ways to use the information in WWC. First, schools can evaluate a program or strategy that is being promoted for intervention. Second, schools can identify the area of reading in which they are intervening and peruse high-quality programs and strategies that would impact this area. This tool is indeed helpful, especially for commercially produced programs. In fact, we like to ask sales representatives, "Do you have a What Works report?" Such a report shows serious commitment to quality and efficacy. That said, there are many products and practices that are not listed on WWC and have not been evaluated but are nonetheless research-based.

To access reports, go to the WWC website (*http://ies.ed.gov/ncee/wwc*) and begin by clicking on "Topics" on the homepage. A drop-down menu will appear that lists "Literacy." From the Literacy page the user can either search a key word for a specific program (e.g., Wilson Reading Program) or click on area of reading instruction (e.g., alphabetics, reading fluency, print knowledge). Over 300 different strategies and programs have been evaluated.

Each WWC report contains a brief description of the program or strategy and highlights four easy-to-read pieces of information about the program:

1. Effectiveness rating—positive effects, no discernible effects, potentially positive effects, potentially negative effects, mixed effects, and negative effects.
2. Extent of evidence—how much evidence supports the effectiveness.
3. Improvement index—the average amount improvement in a student who was taught with the strategy.
4. Student outcome—the specific area of reading measured or impacted by the intervention (e.g., fluency, alphabetics).

A sample table found in the nine-page report for a program called Sound Partners is shown below:

Sample WWC program evaluation.

Effectiveness *Sound Partners* was found to have positive effects on alphabetics, fluency, and comprehension and no discernible effects on general reading achievement on beginning readers.

(continued)

	Alphabetics	Fluency	Comprehension	General reading achievement
Rating of effectiveness	Positive effects	Positive effects	Positive effects	No discernible effects
Improvement index	Average: +21 percentile points Range: −6 to +39 percentile points	Average: +19 Range: +6 to +33 percentile points	Average: +21 percentile points Range: +11 to +27 percentile points	+9 percentile points

The Sound Partners program was tested on four student outcomes: (1) fluency, (2) alphabetics, (3) comprehension, and (4) general reading achievement (e.g., a survey test). The *effectiveness rating* was *positive* in all areas but general reading achievement, where there were no differences between a treatment group and a control group. The average improvement index was 19–20 percentile points, which is high. One area that can be a little confusing about these reports is that the effectiveness rating supersedes the improvement index. In other words, if the effectiveness rating is not *positive* or *potentially positive*, then the improvement index means nothing. So, although we see that there was a 9-point improvement index for general reading achievement, we note that there were no discernible effects, meaning that the 9-point increase was not statistically significant. What this means is that the 9-point difference was not shown to be different than chance. On one day the group receiving Sound Partners might score 9 points better than a comparison group on general reading achievement, but on another day the comparison group might score better in this area. After reading this report, we would come away with an understanding that this program would show high levels of improvement in the areas of fluency, comprehension, and alphabetics.

are providing quality instruction, then only a small percentage of students will truly struggle. In other words, the provision of high-quality reading instruction throughout grade levels should serve to eliminate or prevent the majority of students from developing reading problems. The state-of-the-school meeting is a way to provide feedback to school staff regarding the quality of instruction (Walpole & McKenna, 2012). More specifically, during this meeting assessment data from the reading screening are presented to each grade-level team. The data are presented in such a way that teachers can see the percentage of students who are meeting benchmark versus those students that are not. When classroom (Tier 1) instruction is functioning as it should be, 80% of students should meet the benchmark scores, about 15% might require Tier 2 type interventions, and only 5% of students would require the most intensive instruction at Tier 3. We tell schools that these are the numbers to shoot for when evaluating their screening data. If the percentages are significantly different, with the majority of students needing Tier 2 instruction, significant steps to strengthen Tier 1 classroom instruction must be taken.

TABLE 2.1. Needed RTI Skill Sets and Possible School Staff Conducting These Activities

Skills	Staff				
	School psychologist	Reading specialist	Special education teacher	School administrator	Classroom teacher
Access and critically evaluate empirical evidence of group- and individual-level intervention	×	×		×	
Group-level test administration (reading screenings)	×	×	×		×
Individual assessment of student needs/skills	×	×	×		
Assessment of instructional environment	×			×	
Data analysis and decision making	×	×	×	×	×
Development of intervention strategies	×	×	×		
Progress monitoring and determining intervention effectiveness	×	×	×	×	×

FINDING THE RIGHT CONSULTANT

Finding the right expert consultants to deliver training to school staff is critical and can be overwhelming. How the leadership team goes about finding an expert(s) to conduct training may depend upon your location. In general, we recommend that your search include consideration of recognized experts (i.e., those with numerous publications and presentations in the area of RTI and reading), discussions with colleagues in other districts, obtaining recommendations from your state's Department of Education, and utilizing resources such as regional training and technical assistance centers. We recommend the use of consultants who have skills and experience in the various areas of knowledge represented in RTI, including reading instruction, assessment, intervention, data analysis, and consultation. Keep in mind that using too many consultants can sometimes cause confusion and can even seem "choppy" in regard to the support provided to teachers. When possible, using one or two consultants consistently throughout a school year will avoid conflicting messages across consultants, build rapport and "street credibility" with staff, and allow for growth across time.

Importantly, the reading data are presented in aggregate for the entire grade level as opposed to being broken down and presented by classroom. We see this last point as critically important because we don't believe teachers should be shamed or publicly embarrassed by this process. Instead the message and tone of these meetings should speak to how *we* as a team are performing and that *we* could be doing better. Explaining the purpose of the meeting and why examination and discussion of the data are important should occur prior to the meeting. Simply presenting the data and asking the question, "What do you think?", is often enough to stimulate productive conversation.

Communicate Roles to Staff

We believe that teachers play the central role in RTI efforts. It is critical, however, that the leadership team clearly delineate the responsibilities of the staff in a building. Planning efforts should include discussions regarding who will do what. Experience tells us that RTI will not adequately move to the stage of implementation without clear communication and commitment from all involved parties. In the sections that follow regarding implementation of Tiers 2 and 3 procedures, we give special consideration to the role of teachers. We believe that teachers must shoulder some responsibilities in RTI efforts, and we indicate these. However, we also believe that RTI is truly a schoolwide effort that must be shared by other staff with important expertise.

Action Step 2: Tier 2 Grade-Level Team Efforts

Once a school's leadership team has addressed the issues previously discussed, a foundation is set that will enable classroom teachers to begin the process of implementing RTI. We cannot overstate the importance of engaging in RTI efforts as a team. RTI is not a process that can be tackled alone. Thus in the sections that follow in the remainder of this chapter, we emphasize that these procedures be implemented in relation to decisions made by your grade-level team. Refer back to Figure 1.2 (p. 14) for the processes or steps of an RTI framework, beginning with conducting universal screening assessments, analyzing assessment data, intervening, monitoring progress, and modifying the intervention or exiting the student.

Screening Assessments

The first step in the universal screening, following selection of assessments and the training process, is determining *who will administer the assessments*. We have worked with schools that have ordinarily taken one of three approaches in ensuring that the screenings are conducted within the established testing window. Each approach has advantages and disadvantages.

One approach is to have each teacher assess each student in his/her classroom. Logistically, this approach requires little planning and is easily accomplished with group-administered universal screening assessments. However, this approach is more challenging when universal screenings require additional one-on-one assessment. Schools using this approach will frequently designate specific days and times in which students rotate from their home classroom to other teachers' classrooms until their home teacher has assessed every student in his/her class. Although conducting the screening assessment in this manner takes away some time from instruction, we believe that teachers benefit from the firsthand knowledge they gain of their students' weaknesses or strengths by seeing their students perform on the assessment. We recommend that grade-level specialists or paraprofessionals be available during these assessment times to assist the nontesting teachers, who may be receiving an additional 15–20 students into their classrooms.

A second approach often employed is using non-classroom professionals to administer the screening assessments. This approach avoids burdening teachers with additional responsibility and largely solves the problem of having to rotate students to different classrooms. In this approach the non-classroom teachers can both administer the group assessments and then pull individual students, as needed, into a quiet space for additional assessment. Unfortunately, although this approach is logistically appealing, the classroom teacher is not able to see students perform on the reading assessment.

The third approach represents a hybrid of the first two. In this approach the classroom teacher administers and scores the group-administered portion of the screener. Any follow-up assessment with individual students is then conducted by other non-classroom professionals such as the reading specialist or special educators. Based upon our experiences, we believe that the classroom teacher should be involved in conducting part or all of screening assessment. There are at least two critical reasons why we recommend this. First, we have found that teachers have a more accurate understanding of their students' reading skills when they observe them performing on a standardized assessment. It is likely that witnessing all the students do the exact same task assists in providing the teacher with an objective anchor that allows for comparison with classroom peers. By administering the assessments themselves and seeing their students' performances, teachers observe that the data collected are not just numbers; there are faces behind those numbers. Second, we have found that teacher involvement increases the chances that teachers will believe or trust the data that are generated from the assessment.

Determine What Time of the Day the Assessments Should Be Administered

Although the screening window should already be established, there is the question of when, during the day, the screener should be administered. We pose one simple question when determining the time of day for testing: When are the students most likely to put forth their best effort? Generally speaking, this usually is in the morning, possibly during the block of language arts/reading. Although other times of day may be equally effective, we like to ensure that students are well rested and approach the screening as they would any other schoolwide assessment practices.

Prepare the Assessment Materials

Because taking on an RTI initiative requires significant effort, one consideration in adopting a universal screener is whether the materials are largely prepared and ready for use. As noted earlier, computer-based screening instruments are popular most likely due to the fact that they are convenient to use and require little preparation time. Unfortunately, computer-based assessments do not lend themselves to tasks that require more complex responses on the student's part, such as reading aloud or providing a detailed oral response, or in cases when the teacher is required to model an answer or provide the student with specific feedback. Fortunately, paper-based assessments have become more convenient to use because materials can be easily downloaded and student responses can often be recorded by the teacher, using a handheld computer device. With such a device student responses can be recorded individually by the teacher, and the data are directly downloaded into a database associated with the handheld assessment application, thus saving the time needed to create databases and enter data. As suggested earlier, computer-based screening tools can present some difficulties with regard to test content and administration. However, we do suggest using computer-based resources to store, organize, and generate schoolwide screening reports.

We have typically found that the paper-based assessments are most economical and provide the type of assessment information most beneficial for screening purposes. These assessment materials can be purchased in a prepackaged format in which all the materials are prepared and ready for assessment. On the other hand, some of these assessments are available online and thus must be downloaded, printed, collated, and stapled. In general, we recommend that materials be prepared by a central school-based coordinator and not by individual teachers. This method will cut down on frustrations and time spent trying to find the correct materials and will ensure uniformity of materials within a particular grade level. When testing day arrives teachers should be prepared with (1) all student response booklets, (2) the teacher test instruction booklet, and (3) several pencils to record student responses.

Conduct the Assessment

Compared to the other steps, this one is straightforward in that teachers should already be trained to administer the screener. However, we have found that questions arise during administration, and someone should be there to answer those questions. Three frequently asked questions include:

1. *Should the administration directions be followed exactly?* It is paramount that teachers follow the directions exactly as provided. If there is room to deviate from these directions, this will be indicated. We like to tell teachers, "Take off your teaching hat and put on your assessment hat." Without realizing it, teachers sometimes want to support, coach, or help students, because that is their nature. However, in an assessment situation, this cannot happen because an assessment must indicate what students can do on their own. Remember, the purpose of the assessment is to determine if the students might have, or be at risk for, reading difficulties. This determination is based upon whether the student performs above or below a particular benchmark score. Most often these scores are determined by how many students of a particular age or grade perform on the same assessment. Changing the directions may provide your student with an unfair advantage or in some way may inadvertently penalize him/her. Either way, providing the directions in a way other than indicated makes it difficult to compare the student's performance to other students who were given accurate directions.

2. *Can we help students if we feel they don't understand?* In general, students should not be provided with extra or improvised instructions just to make sure they understand the test directions. However, you may often find that directions are included by the test publisher to provide students with additional instructions or practice items when they demonstrate that they do not understand. Most commonly there are sufficient teaching and practice items for all students to understand. In those cases where a student is unable to successfully perform the task (even one item), it will be up to you and your team to determine whether the student simply does not have the skills to perform the task or failed to understand the task due to other reasons (e.g., difficulties following oral directions, attention difficulties). The reasons that explain the student's difficulty will be important to confirm in order to accurately interpret the results and provide the student with meaningful supports.

3. *What if the student's dialect makes it difficult to understand his/her pronunciation of letter sounds or words?* Pronunciation issues may be due to regional dialect, expressive language difficulties, or speaking English as a second language. Again, most screeners will provide you with information about how such instances should be handled. As a general rule, however, students' reading performance should not be penalized due to factors that impede their expression. If children can accurately read (decode) the word but have difficulty orally pronouncing that word, they should not be penalized if you can determine that they are reading the word correctly. For example, a student who consistently says "wocket" when reading the word *rocket* would not be penalized. The fact that the student consistently

pronounces /r/ as /w/ would be evidence that he is correctly identifying the letter sound but that the difficulties lie with accurate pronunciation.

Collecting and Preparing the Data for Further Use

We feel strongly that there is no purpose in collecting assessment data if that information is not used in an effort to assist students. Thus, data collected from the universal screening represents the first step, not the last step, in truly helping students. The question is, *How can information about students' performances be efficiently and meaningfully used once the assessment data are collected?* The pieces involved in answering this question require consideration of several substeps. First, the screening assessment must be scored. We strongly encourage classroom teachers to complete the scoring so that they have a confirmed understanding of students' performances. Sometimes a student's actual performance can be misleading when compared to the obtained score. Importantly, if a computer-based system is being used, then scoring will be completed automatically.

Once scoring is completed, all of the data must be collected and entered into the data system. In our experience we have found it useful to designate one individual (not a classroom teacher) per grade level or for the entire school (depending on school size) to collect all screening data and enter the data into the designated database/website. All of the major universal screening assessments available will subsequently generate reports documenting student performance and determining whether students met or failed to meet the benchmark score. In addition, reports should be available to aggregate the results of students within each grade level, thus indicating the percentage of students meeting benchmark versus those who did not. Having this information is critical to conducting the *state of the school* meetings discussed previously.

Analyze Assessment Data to Form Tier 2 Instructional Groups

The universal screening will provide schools with an understanding of which students are in need of intervention. The next step is to understand which skills students need in order to move forward in the process. Thus, at this stage, grade-level teams should meet to determine students' specific needs and to assign students to specific instructional intervention groups. Remember, however, if the universal screening chosen by your school does not provide any information that would assist in identifying instructional needs, the team will likely require additional diagnostic information before proceeding with this step. In order to assign students to Tier 2 instructional groups, schools will need diagnostic information about phonemic awareness, alphabet knowledge, and phonics skills for students who did not meet the benchmark score on the universal screening. Specific diagnostic assessments required for each type of instructional intervention (i.e., letters, decoding and phonemic awareness, and fluency) are specified in Chapters 3–6. Data on word recognition may also be helpful, particularly for students in late first or second grade. In our work, we have found that the use of flowcharts with easy-to-follow decision-making rules are important in facilitating the task of assigning students to instructional groups. These flowcharts are particularly useful when the screening data include scores from multiple subtests.

From a pragmatic perspective, we have found that teachers rarely have enough time to sort through and discuss every student who did not meet the benchmark on the literacy screening. It is therefore important that teams prioritize the students whom they feel should be discussed. In our work we have suggested a multistep process. Before the meeting, we ask teachers to write each student's name and data on a notecard. Then we ask them to identify all of the students who have met the screening and to put those cards aside, coding them with a green dot. The remaining students will need intervention instruction, but the trick is to find out exactly what kind. Teachers then organize the students into two groups: one composed of students who have a very clear-cut intervention need and one of students about whom they are not sure.

We established a coding system for the types of interventions that we regularly see (i.e., Mostly Letter-Names, Mostly Letter-Sounds, Mostly Decoding, and Mostly Fluency). The adjective *mostly* is used in front of each description because within an intervention, there will always be additional support or "capacity-building" skills. For example, in a mostly letter-sounds intervention, some phoneme awareness is included. When teachers come to their grade-level meeting, they briefly identify the students in the easily matched intervention groups and say why. Then the bulk of the meeting is dedicated to discussing the students who are more difficult to place. We have found that teachers do a great job of selecting students for group discussion who have particularly perplexing data. To facilitate this discussion we often ask that student data be presented to the team on an overhead projector and that one team member take a lead in attempting to make sense of the student's scores. Other team members can then step in and provide input, with the ultimate goal of determining which instructional group will best meet the student's needs. At the end of the meeting, a sheet is completed that lists the intervention that each student will receive and who will deliver that intervention. We have seen that teachers are often not immediately comfortable in leading these data-driven discussions. However, after modeling the process for teachers and providing feedback, we have seen teachers quickly gain confidence.

Intervene for Tier 2 Instruction

We view the instructional task with a sense of urgency because "waiting to start" only deepens the gap between struggling students and their peers. Thus, once your instructional groups are formed, it is important that instruction begin as quickly as possible thereafter. As a general rule we believe that Tier 2 instruction should be delivered by the classroom teacher. This will serve to ensure that the teacher is highly aware of the student's needs, will remain invested in seeing student progress, and will readily link intervention instruction to broader instructional goals. In instances where a great number of students is identified for Tier 2 help, it may be necessary to employ other trained reading instructors or well-supervised and skilled paraprofessionals to deliver this instruction with the goal of ensuring relatively small instructional intervention groups. Our experience suggests that small-group instruction is most beneficial when the number of students in a group does not exceed five or six. Thus, if additional staff must work with students to ensure a smaller teacher-to-student ratio, then this goal should be prioritized. Smaller instructional groups will help to optimize the amount of active engagement that each student will experience within the group. *Active engagement* refers to the frequency and quality of student responses to instructional prompts and the frequency with which students receive and respond to teacher feedback.

As a general rule we have recommended that Tier 2 instruction occur 5 days per week for 30 minutes each day. Keep in mind that these 30 minutes are *in addition to* the regular daily classroom reading instruction. Given full and busy schedules in schools, it can be a struggle to ensure an extra 30 minutes of intervention instruction each day, but finding the time is a must-do. Fortunately, in the successful schools that we have worked with, the building principal views the decision to increase reading instruction time as a critical priority and works with teachers to make this time a priority in scheduling. Implementing this intervention requires balancing schedules so that each instructional group can meet while retaining the optimal student-to-teacher ratio. We recommend that Tier 2 instruction be delivered using the collective resources of an entire grade level, such that students can be sent to another grade-level teacher to receive instruction. By utilizing this approach multiple groups with different instructional foci can be offered at the same time. Generally, we have found that this approach works best for schools that have three or four teachers at each grade level. In smaller schools it becomes imperative to utilize additional teachers such as reading specialists or Title I teachers. It should also be apparent here that if a school identifies too many students as being in need of Tier 2 supports, the instructional groups could exceed five or six students. As we pointed out earlier, if more than 20% of your students (within a grade level) are failing the screening measure, then some critical deficits may be present in the general core reading instruction program. In these cases steps should be taken to strengthen the reading instruction that is provided to all students.

The content of Tier 2 instruction should center on the common identified need of the students within the group. Thus, students with fluency needs should receive instruction that *mostly* focuses upon fluency. We use the term *mostly* because it is important to recognize the simultaneous development of multiple reading skills. Thus, there will be times when it makes sense to emphasize a reading skill that will enhance or complement reading fluency development. The actual content of instruction should closely follow adopted materials that your RTI team has selected (see previous section on selection of materials). In our experience teachers appreciate the structure provided by well-developed and detailed strategies and products. Although we do not feel that "scripted" lessons at this level are necessary, we have found that products and lessons that are not specific or detailed often result in too much ambiguity and confusion. In Chapters 3–6, we recommend that teachers implement 6-week intervention plans, using their resources to guide their instruction. Teachers who do not engage in long-term planning or who do not have materials that provide sufficient detail may be confused subsequently and have difficulty providing quality instruction. The key here is to find quality products that provide details regarding instructional format and that match the instructional objectives of the group. Although teachers should have some flexibility in choosing the types of activities that are emphasized on a particular day, it is important that instructional interventions are delivered in a manner that maintains the integrity of the approach.

Progress Monitoring

Once instructional interventions are under way, the next step in the process is progress monitoring. As discussed in Chapter 1, progress monitoring is the process of collecting ongoing assessment data. These data are collected in order to determine whether instructional interventions are having an impact on students' reading skills. Ultimately, the purpose of collecting progress monitoring data is to determine whether a student is responding to instructional intervention efforts, and if not, to make timely decisions about the need to change those efforts.

After Tier 2 interventions commence, progress monitoring should begin almost immediately. There are two types of progress monitoring: *mastery monitoring* (MM) and *general outcome monitoring* (GOM) (Deno, 1997; Fuchs & Deno, 1991). Mastery monitoring is the progress monitoring that we heavily emphasize and demonstrate in Chapters 3–6. This is progress monitoring that is closely aligned with the specific skill being taught during the intervention. MM measures the degree to which a student is acquiring exactly what is being taught in the intervention. A GOM measure evaluates the degree to which what is being taught in the intervention is generalizing to another area. For example, if teachers were conducting a decoding intervention, then the MM measure might be a list of words with the target sounds and the student would be asked to decode these words. A GOM for this decoding intervention might be an oral reading fluency passage because ultimately the goal is that the decoding skill that the student is learning should transfer to fluent automatic reading. In terms of the student's long-term reading development, decoding is not the end. Reading efficiently in connected text is the end, as measured by fluency.

At Tier 2, we recommend that progress monitoring data be collected once per week. We also suggest that classroom teachers conduct these assessments in order to witness, firsthand, student progress. The good news is that progress monitoring assessments should be brief, taking only a few minutes. With both MM measures and GOM measures in hand, teachers will be equipped with very important information about reading progress. Progress monitoring assessments have been compared to the use of a thermometer with a patient who has begun treatment. The purpose of taking the patient's temperature at relatively regular intervals is to determine whether the treatment is effective in addressing the infection. Seeing changes in the patient's temperature tells us something very important about the patient's progress toward wellness, but it certainly does not tell us everything about his/her health. Likewise, seeing changes in progress monitoring scores tells us something very important about reading progress. Progress monitoring assessment serves as the "thermometer" for our intervention effort and whether or not it is moving students ahead in their reading skills.

Given the purpose of progress monitoring, it is critical that schools select brief assessments that accurately capture student progress. In Chapters 4–6 we provide much detail about the skills on which teachers should focus when conducting MM.

Modifying Instruction or Exiting Students: Grade-Level Review of Data

Once progress monitoring data have been collected, those data should be prepared for grade-level review. First, data should be entered into a database as soon as scores are generated from the progress monitoring assessment. MM data should be recorded after each assessment is conducted, either in a spreadsheet, such as an Excel database, or within an intervention notebook, where the teacher might keep all of his/her intervention materials. Regarding GOM, we have found that most schools choose to purchase a commercially available system such as the DIBELS Next or the early literacy assessment from AIMSweb. Fortunately, most progress monitoring systems that are commercially available offer an online method for entering scores that subsequently allows for the generation of various reports. We recommend that a report be selected that visually demonstrates the students' progress (i.e., their progress monitoring scores) plotted over the period of time in which the intervention has taken place. This method of reporting data is known as a *line graph* and is represented in Figure 2.1. As can be seen in the figure, data points are plotted from left to right across the page. The bottom (horizontal) axis represents the time the intervention has been in place, and the side (vertical) axis represents

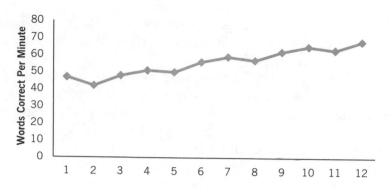

FIGURE 2.1. Basic progress monitoring graph.

the possible scores on the progress monitoring measure. In this case the progress monitoring data indicate that the student made positive gains over a 12-week period. In particular, whereas the student read 47 words correct per minute when the intervention started, he read 68 words correct per minute 12 weeks later. When visually examining this chart, it is possible to see the trend in the student's progress over a period of time.

In examining progress monitoring data for any particular student, the critical goal of the grade-level team is to determine whether the progress the student has made is satisfactory. In order to make this determination, two critical questions must be answered:

1. What is the goal for the student?
2. How many points of progress monitoring data are needed in order to make an accurate decision?

In answering the first question, we generally recommend that schools pay attention to their MM assessment to see if the student is improving on the taught skill. The goal of MM is to promote mastery. That is, the goal should reflect a very high level of accuracy, at least 90%. Once a student demonstrates that he/she can perform the skill at the designated level of mastery on several consecutive assessments (three or four), the teacher can feel confident that mastery has been reached.

If the student shows progress toward the mastery goal, then the team should also examine the GOM assessment data. These data can be examined in several ways. As a general rule, we recommend using the benchmark "cutoffs" that are provided by the progress monitoring assessment system that has been adopted (e.g., DIBELS Next, or AIMSweb). These benchmark goals are typically provided for the fall, winter, and spring for most of the measures that would be used for progress monitoring. The goals that are provided are based upon data that have been collected from thousands of students who have been given the measure at the various times of the school year (fall, winter, or spring). Another approach, which can be particularly useful when providing interventions to a small group of students, is to compare each individual student's performance to one another as a way of determining which students are responding and which are not. We illustrate this approach with an example in Chapter 4. Similarly, a third approach is to collect "local norms," which allow comparison of a student's progress to all other students within the student's school at his/her grade level.

Once the goal is set for a student, then the student's scores can be compared to the goal. As we indicated above, for MM data we would expect students to demonstrate gains in learning for some goals, such as letter naming, rather quickly. Thus, at a minimum we recommend that these data be examined rather frequently. In general, we recommend that grade-level teams meet every 4 weeks in order to make interim or *short-term* decisions about a student's progress. At this level of frequency, teams can determine whether instructional modifications should be made if the data indicate that the intervention is not working. Specifically, we recommend that teams meet after four and eight progress monitoring assessments have been completed (i.e., after 4 and 8 weeks of intervention) in order to make *short-term* decisions about a student's progress. Based upon consideration of the progress monitoring data, teams should determine whether the instructional intervention being provided should be (1) continued as is, (2) modified to focus on a different instructional intervention, or (3) discontinued because the student has met the goal.

Finally, we believe that before *long-term decisions* can be made (i.e., the decision to refer a student for more intensive supports or assessment), at least 12 weeks of GOM data should be collected. Given that we believe that Tier 2 interventions must be given time to have an impact on student performance, we recommend that at least 12 progress monitoring data points (approximately 3 months of intervention) be collected before decisions are made regarding the need for more intensive interventions (i.e., Tier 3). It should be noted that research continues to emerge regarding how much progress monitoring data are needed to make accurate decisions about student progress; however, available research indicates that as more progress monitoring data points are collected, the more likely it is that the data are reliable (Christ, 2006).

The last task facing the grade-level team is determining whether "nonresponders"—students who have failed to respond to Tier 2 intervention efforts—should be referred to the Tier 3 problem-solving team. This is the team responsible for developing more intensive individualized interventions for nonresponding students (see Chapter 7). It is likely that your school district will have specific policies and procedures in place for determining which students should be referred to this team. Minimally, we believe that 12 weeks of progress monitoring data should be collected indicating minimal progress before making this decision.

Conclusion

In sum, RTI is a process with important cyclical steps for which active leadership is integral to its success. Each step in the process is integral to it and cannot stand alone. Active leaders are an important key to RTI success because they are committed, flexible, and supportive. Prior to full implementation of RTI, it is wise to engage in important preplanning efforts aimed at selecting universal screenings and instructional interventions, as well as determining the need for professional development training in the RTI process. State-of-the-school reports to each grade level provide discussion and action steps to start the process. Tier 2 intervention instruction should be based on a universal literacy screening and additional diagnostic data. Clear plans for conducting, scoring, and using the results of screening assessments to form instructional intervention groups must be in place. Finally, progress monitoring of students in Tier 2 intervention should be conducted at least once weekly. Data should be examined every 4–8 weeks for short-term decisions about interventions and every 12 weeks for long-term decisions. When every component of the RTI process is carefully planned and clear processes and expectations established, RTI implementation can be done effectively and with less stress, ultimately working to improve students' reading.

CHAPTER 3

The Primary Grades Intervention Lesson Plan

GUIDING QUESTIONS

- What are helpful ways to evaluate programs, strategies, or content for a research base?
- How is the developmental continuum key in planning effective interventions?
- How should diagnostic assessments be used to inform intervention instruction?
- What is the framework for effectively and efficiently setting intervention goals and timelines and for monitoring students' progress?
- What lesson planning guidelines are important for successful interventions in the primary grades?
- How do instructional leaders (administrators and teachers alike) evaluate the effectiveness of instructional interventions?

Across many years of both clinical work and RTI work we have learned how to help teachers and schools structure RTI and deliver interventions successfully. In this chapter we provide a structure for planning Tier 2 reading interventions in the primary grades. As described in Chapter 1, reading interventions are qualitatively different from small-group instruction in the classroom. We like to say, "Do something different!" Remember, the student is in intervention because business-as-usual instruction did not work. Interventions should not be extra, improvised, "ad hoc" instruction offered by random people. They should be planned, but the planning should not overwhelm a school or teachers (see the text box *What Is an Intervention?*). Our approach supports effective instructional intervention with

WHAT IS AN INTERVENTION?

An intervention is:

- Based on universal screening and diagnostic data.
- A specific research-based strategy or technique targeted to improve a particular reading skill.
- A strategy or technique that requires planning and progress monitoring.
- Typically delivered in a small-group or one-on-one format.

Interventions are specific instructional strategies or techniques targeted to improve a particular aspect of reading. Intervention needs are determined by using universal screening and diagnostic data. Universal screening data identify students who are not performing as they should in reading, and diagnostic data can further pinpoint specific literacy needs. Intervention instruction should use strategies that are research-based and are used to meet the needs of specific students.

Interventions are offered to students *in addition to* core classroom reading instruction; they are most effective when delivered in small-group or one-on-one settings. Intervention requires intentional planning and the monitoring of students' progress in order to inform instruction. Examples of intervention programs might include the Wilson Reading for students with decoding needs or Read Naturally for students with fluency needs. Chapters 4–6 in this text provide intervention instructional guidelines and strategies for students with specific needs in the primary grades.

An intervention is *not*:

- A person.
- An accommodation.
- A modification.
- A program.
- A piece of computer software.

In many cases, schools mistakenly view interventions as people. For example, Ms. Rodriguez may be referred to as "the intervention" for a particular group of students because she is the classroom teacher who delivers small-group instruction to students who need mostly fluency work. In fact, Ms. Rodriguez is the *teacher* who delivers the intervention. She is not the intervention itself.

Accommodations are changes made in instruction or assessment. For example, a student's needs might be accommodated with additional time to complete reading assignments or by being allowed to respond to questions orally, rather than in written form. With accommodations, students are expected to perform at the same level of all their peers with these slight changes. As you can see, an accommodation is *not* a specific strategy, does *not* involve additional instruction, and is *not* focused on a specific reading skill. Students receiving interventions may also receive accommodations.

Modifications are also changes made to instruction or assessment, but modifications *lower* the performance expectation or standard. For example, students with modifications may receive shortened vocabulary lists or fewer choices on multiple-choice tests. Again, modifications are *not* instructional strategies or techniques matching data to students' reading needs in research-based ways.

reasonable investments of time and pragmatic routines and practices. Schools and teachers can undertake reading interventions without burying themselves in paperwork and planning. The process that we share in this chapter is supported by some simple forms for organizing notes, plans, and progress monitoring (see Figure 3.1). In Chapters 4–6 we illustrate how these forms are used within the context of different types of lessons (i.e., letter-sounds, decoding, fluency). Our approach unifies RTI procedures, provides schools with a common language for working together, and helps to avoid the instructional fragmentation that can happen when multiple educators are working with struggling students.

The lesson planning structure offered in this chapter is also repeated in the content-specific chapters (4–6) that follow. Our lesson plan scheme contains the following seven elements:

1. A research basis.
2. Attention to developmental reading.
3. Diagnostic assessments.
4. Determining the focus of the intervention.
5. Careful instructional planning and activities.
6. Goal setting and progress monitoring.
7. A plan for evaluation.

The goal of this chapter is to set the stage for the skill-specific chapters that follow. We have found that many books supply the theoretical tenets of RTI or offer intervention ideas. Few books put it all together and show the steps for planning RTI. Each of the skill-specific chapters in this book is structured around the seven essential ingredients in our lesson plan scheme.

Essential Elements of an Intervention Lesson

Research Basis

According to IDEIA (United States Congress, 2004, Sec. 614.b.6.B), an RTI model is grounded in research-based interventions—that is, interventions for which there is verifiable evidence of effectiveness. At a very basic level, when we say that an intervention is *research-based*, we mean that there is some reliable information indicating that the intervention will result in students' learning a specific content. In other words, the approach has been tried before and proven to be effective. Someone has used the approach, product, or strategy and collected pretest data to show that the students did not demonstrate the skill *before* the research-based approach but were able to demonstrate the skill *after* the research-based approach. In Chapter 2, the text box *Using the What Works Clearinghouse to Evaluate the*

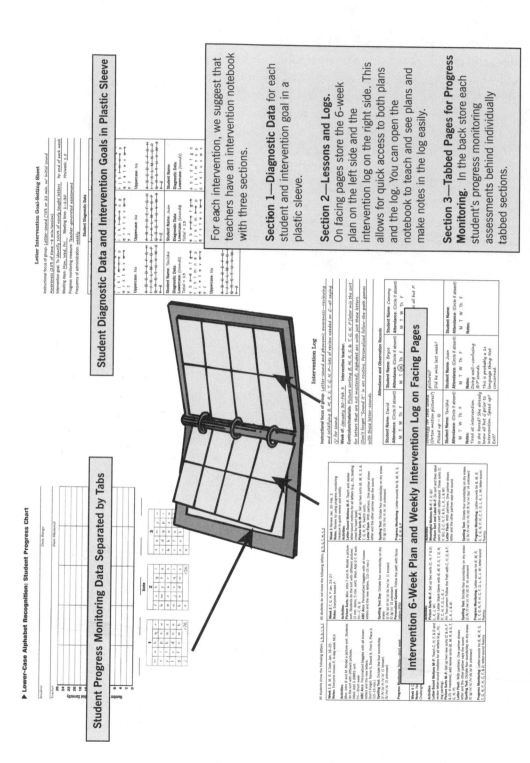

FIGURE 3.1. An interventionist's notebook.

Effectiveness of Intervention Programs (on pp. 36–37) describes one tool used to ensure a research base for programs and practices.

Instructional interventions must be research-based for two reasons. The first and most obvious reason is that research-based interventions help students. They make a difference, and by using them teachers and schools will not be wasting time with unproven strategies. The second reason that interventions should be research-based is that federal regulations require that a student's response to intervention using research-based instruction is the litmus test for determining a learning disability. If the approach, strategy, or program is not research-based, then a student might not respond to it because it is not effective and not because he/she has a learning disability.

Effective schools and teachers use high-quality practices and strategies to deliver instructional intervention. The strategies that we describe in this book are all research-based, and many are common strategies that teachers know and love. Fortunately, there are many new and exciting strategies that are also research-based that can help students. We use several resources to find strong, engaging strategies. First, we like to use articles from practitioner journals such as *The Reading Teacher* and *Teaching Exceptional Children*. These pieces tend to have a solid research backing and step-by-step instructions. We also like ReadWriteThink (*www.readwritethink.org*), a website sponsored by the International Reading Association and the National Council of Teachers of English, with links to hundreds of reading lessons, many based on *Reading Teacher* articles. This website is searchable by topic and each is linked to an in-depth article. We also like the Florida Center for Reading Research at Florida State University website, which also has links to solid, fun activities for students (*www.fcrr.org*). In addition, we have found many strong activities at the Center on Instruction (*www.centeroninstruction.org*).

Developmental Continuum

An understanding of reading development is absolutely essential to the delivery of high-quality reading interventions. Students go through the same general sequence of developmental steps but not at the same rate. The key to delivering intervention is identifying a student's position on the developmental continuum, at which there is trouble, and then matching instruction to need. A common problem in schools is that students come into classrooms at a point on the developmental continuum that is below their peers. These students are not at the same place as their peers, but they are developing nonetheless. Often these students are characterized as being disabled or having an innate problem when they simply have not been taught what they now need (Spear-Swerling & Sternberg, 1996). In fact, as mentioned earlier, students with reading difficulties, whether "learning disabled" or not, will need research-based reading instruction that is fundamentally similar in nature (Snow, Burns, & Griffin, 1998; Vellutino, Scanlon, & Lyon, 2000).

The developmental continuum that we present in Figure 3.2 shows a set of developmental milestones that research has established to be associated with reading success. There is nothing innovative about this continuum. It is supported by the DIBELS continuum, which is informed by a rich literature on literacy stages that is empirically supported by many studies (Chall, 1967; Ehri, 2005; National Early Literacy Panel Report, 2008; National Institute of Child Health and Human Development, 2000; Snow et al., 1998). Although there is not perfect agreement, generally the research has converged around a set of milestones or benchmarks that appear to be strongly associated with reading success. The milestones that we identify on our continuum represent only essential behaviors that signify progression in learning to read. Teachers will achieve much, much more with their students than the skills we have listed on this continuum. These benchmarks simply form a loose set of criteria that schools can use to gauge if a student is behind or not.

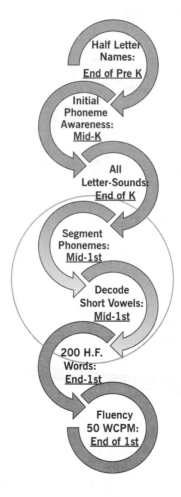

FIGURE 3.2. Developmental continuum.

We list seven milestones across PreK through first grade. (Students in second grade who are struggling usually have not met milestones in the first-grade year.) At the beginning of the continuum in PreK is *letter naming*. As described in depth in Chapter 4, the ability to rapidly name letters is strongly associated with later reading achievement (Adams, 1990; Bond & Dykstra, 1967; Chall, 1967; Vellutino & Scanlon, 1987).

At the middle of kindergarten students should demonstrate *awareness of initial phonemes* (e.g., the /b/ sound heard prior to the vowel in <u>b</u>at), because this level of phoneme awareness supports their attainment of the alphabetic principle and helps them apply letter-sounds. The *alphabetic principle* is the awareness that letters represent speech sounds. Students should be able to identify the beginning sounds in pictures or orally spoken words. Without this ability, letter-sound and decoding instruction will not move forward. By the end of kindergarten students should demonstrate letter-sound knowledge for all letters, both upper- and lowercase. In order to enter first grade ready to read, *accurate, automatic knowledge of letter-sounds* is required. In Figure 3.2 we shaded the shapes for initial phoneme awareness and letter-sound knowledge to reflect that initial sound awareness builds capacity for letter-sound knowledge. These two skills are linked.

By the middle of first grade students should be able to easily *decode an unknown short-vowel CVC (consonant–vowel–consonant) word*. This skill is often measured with pseudoword instruments. Pseudoword assessments present nonsense words containing common letter patterns to students, such as *zat*, in order to assess their ability to read unknown words. Pseudoword assessments ensure that students have not holistically memorized a word (see the text box *Discussion about Advantages and Disadvantages of Pseudowords* in Chapter 5, p. 000). The ability to blend sounds together into a word shows that the student has integrated and applied letter-sound knowledge and can access the English alphabetic system. Some students struggle with this skill, typically because they do not have awareness of phonemes or speech sounds. The ability to *segment phonemes*—that is, to break an oral word into its sounds (*cat* = /c/ + /a/ + /t/)—is a prerequisite to decoding words. Therefore, this milestone is shown *before* decoding. We find that phonemic segmentation practice builds capacity for decoding, and if a student is struggling to blend sounds together, practicing this skill will help.

By the end of first grade, two additional milestones should be reached: (1) *fluent reading* at a rate of 50 words per minute and (2) *accurate recognition of about 200 high-frequency words*. As with phonemic segmentation and decoding, these two skills are linked with sight-word knowledge-building capacity for fluent reading. Once first graders can decode and have a requisite store of high-frequency words, they are ready to move toward faster and more fluent reading. We once worked with a school that did such a good job with code skills in the first grade that they wanted to keep going and going and going. At midyear we had to help them shift their instructional focus toward fluent reading. Throughout the first-grade year, students are usually learning lists of high-frequency words, such as the Dolch list, that support their emerging fluency.

This instructional continuum essentially forms the framework for reading interventions provided in this book. As indicated by the graphic, certain skills are linked and build capacity for others (e.g., initial phoneme awareness–letter-sound, phonemic segmentation–decoding, high-frequency words–fluency).

Table 3.1 translates the continuum into a set of measurable reading behaviors that schools and teachers can check at different grades and different times in the year. This table is used to follow up with students who have not passed the literacy screening. The best way to use the table is to identify the grade level of the student and the time of the year. If a student has not passed the literacy screener, then this table provides guidance for administering additional diagnostic assessments. In general, we think of the beginning of the year as the first 2 months of school, mid-year as January, and spring as early April, when teachers can still have an impact on students. The skills are listed from the easiest at the top to the most difficult at the bottom. When working with an older struggling reader, perhaps in second grade, it may be necessary to work up the table to find the appropriate focus for intervention instruction (see Stahl, Kuhn, & Pickle, 1999). For instance, Cal, a second grader with whom we worked, could not read 50 words correctly per minute at the beginning of second grade. In fact, he read less than 25, so we moved up the table to check his ability to decode CVC words and found that he was unable to do so. We started our intervention instruction with Cal at decoding, but had we not probed earlier skills listed on the chart, we might have inappropriately started with fluency instruction.

We believe that teachers who have internalized knowledge of a simple developmental continuum and receive guidance in how to evaluate where their students are located on that continuum can be more flexible in how they view students. Using the continuum, teachers can identify struggling students and appropriately differentiate reading instruction in the classroom, as well as design appropriate instructional interventions for them. Teachers who locate students on a developmental continuum can identify specific needs that will move their students to the next position on the continuum. When teachers do not have this fundamental understanding, they default to grade-level expectations or grade-level standards as their continuum. Their focus then falls to the ways that a student is *not* like the others in a grade, and this perspective does not point to the type of instruction that a student needs. When teachers use a developmental continuum, they act as problem solvers as opposed to simply problem identifiers.

Diagnostic Assessments

As described earlier, the literacy *screening assessment* may or may not provide specific diagnostic information that can inform instruction. *Diagnostic assessments,*

TABLE 3.1. Developmental Continuum with Specific Reading Behaviors

Grade	Skill	Standard indicating potential risk[a]
Middle of PreK	Letter naming	Fewer than 7 letter-names—upper- or lowercase (approx. one-quarter)
Spring of PreK	Letter-naming	Fewer than 10 letter-names—upper- or lowercase (half)
Beginning of K	Letter-names	Fewer than 10 letter names—upper- or lowercase (half)
Middle of K	Letter-sounds	Fewer than 13 *letter-sounds*—both upper- and lowercase
	Initial phoneme awareness[b]	If below letter-sound standards, check to see if the student can identify the initial sound of spoken word presented orally or in a picture.
Spring of K	Letter-sounds	Fewer than 20 *letter-sounds*—both upper- and lowercase
	Initial phoneme awareness	If below letter-sound standards, check to see if the student can identify the initial sound of spoken word presented orally or in a picture.
Beginning of grade 1	Letter-sounds	Fewer than 23 *letter-sounds*—both upper- and lowercase
	Initial phoneme awareness	If below letter-sound standards, check to see if the student can identify the initial sound of spoken word presented orally or in a picture.
Middle of grade 1	Decoding	Unable to consistently read *unknown* CVC words with short vowels (e.g., *vut, heg, dop* or *bag, hit, tell*).
	Phonemic segmenting[c]	Unable to consistently break *oral* words into each of their sounds.
	Fluency—reading rate	Reads less than 25 words per minute in a first-grade-level passage.
	High-frequency words[d]	Knows fewer than half of the 200 most frequently occurring words.
Spring of grade 1	Fluency—reading rate	Reads less than 50 words per minute.
Beginning of grade 2	Fluency—reading rate	Reads less than 50 words per minute.

[a]If the student is below this level, intervention may be needed.

[b]Initial phoneme awareness builds capacity for a student to learn letter-sounds. If a student doesn't know letter-sounds, initial phoneme awareness should be checked.

[c]Phonemic segmentation supports full alphabetic decoding. It builds capacity for a student to sound out a CVC word. If a student cannot consistently sound out CVC, then phonemic segmentation should be checked.

[d]Knowledge of high-frequency words supports fluent reading in grade 1. Students who are below reading rate standards may need additional support with high-frequency words.

in contrast, are thorough measures that guide instruction by providing detailed information about exactly what content a student needs to learn. Sometimes screening measures do provide diagnostic information and sometimes they do not. For instance, there are several measures of letter-naming fluency that present a series of randomly interspersed upper- and lowercase letters. The student is asked to name as many letters has he/she can in 1 minute. Then this number of letters is compared to established standards. If a student doesn't meet the standard, however, a teacher would not know exactly which letters the student does not know. For this reason, a diagnostic letter-name or letter-sound measure would need to be administered for at-risk students. Such a measure would contain a complete listing of the letters in both upper- and lowercase forms, informing teachers about specific letters the student does and does not know. However, a screener that includes all 26 letters would provide the kind of diagnostic information that indicates which letters require specific focus. In contrast, a fluency measure, which indicates that a student is reading inefficiently, may or may not indicate the precise content on which a student needs to work on.

States across the country use many different literacy screening assessments to identify at-risk children in PreK through second grade. Many of these assessments tap the very skills that we highlight on the developmental continuum (e.g., letter naming, letter-sound knowledge, initial phoneme awareness). In the primary grades, screening measures and diagnostic measures sometimes intersect. Many primary grade skills, such as decoding, letter-sound knowledge, and fluency, are very discrete and can be easily measured. For instance, the PALS measure in Virginia uses a complete letter-sound measure as part of the screening, so a teacher using this measure would have both screening and diagnostic information all in one measure (Invernizzi, Meier, Swank, & Juel, 1997).

In some states and schools districts the screening measures are not diagnostically transparent. For example, some school systems use computer programs such as STAR Early Reading to identify at-risk students—which, as discussed in Chapter 2, are criterion-referenced assessments. These programs typically identify the students' levels of skill, but not the specific needs that would inform the content of an intervention. The developmental continuum that we provide would help to inform teachers who are not sure how to follow up if a student is identified as at risk. In PreK, for instance, a teacher would want to follow up with a letter-naming measure. A kindergarten teacher at the beginning of the year would want to use a letter-naming or letter-sound measure. Table 3.2 lists a series of easily accessible assessments for the various skills listed (e.g., letter naming, fluency, decoding). In addition, in each of the chapters we provide a skill-specific diagnostic template for recording diagnostic information in a way that guides planning. These forms look different depending on the skill being assessed, and teachers will have to use their judgment and a careful analysis of their state's literacy screening measure to decide whether or not additional diagnostic measures should be administered.

TABLE 3.2. Diagnostic Assessments for Literacy Skills

Area	Assessment name	Website
Phonological awareness		
Initial phonemes	Dynamic Indicators of Basic Literacy Skills—Initial Sound Fluency	*https://dibels.uoregon.edu*
Initial phonemes	Abecedarian Reading Assessment	*www.balancedreading.com/ assessment/abecedarian.pdf*
Phonemic segmentation	Yopp–Singer Test of Phonemic Segmentation	*www.balancedreading.com/ assessment/freeassessments.html* (see Figure 5.3 for example)
Phonemic segmentation	Abecedarian Reading Assessment	*www.balancedreading.com/ assessment/abecedarian.pdf*
Phonemic segmentation	Easy CBM—Phoneme Segmenting	*https://easycbm.com*
Letters		
Letter naming and letter-sounds	Abecedarian Reading Assessment	*www.balancedreading.com/ assessment/abecedarian.pdf*
Letter naming and letter-sounds	Easy CBM—Letter Names and Letter Sounds	*https://easycbm.com*
Letter naming and letter-sounds	Really Great Reading—Predecoding Survey	*www.rgrco.com*
Decoding		
Decoding real words	Abecedarian Reading Assessment	*www.balancedreading.com/ assessment/abecedarian.pdf*
Decoding pseudowords	Dynamic Indicators of Basic Literacy Skills—Nonsense Word Subtest	*https://dibels.uoregon.edu*
Decoding real words and pseudowords	Really Great Reading—Diagnostic Decoding Survey	*www.rgrco.com* (see Chapter 5 for a sample and more details)
High-frequency sight words		
Automatic word recognition	Easy CBM—Word Reading Fluency	*https://easycbm.com*
Dolch words	Dolch Word Kit (by frequency)	*https://theschoolbell.com* (see Chapter 6 for more details)
Fluency		
Reading rate	Dynamic Indicators of Basic Literacy Skills—Oral Reading Fluency Passages	*https://dibels.uoregon.edu*
Reading rate	Easy CBM—Passage Reading Fluency	*https://easycbm.com*

In Chapters 4–6 we specify the type of information that is needed to conduct a literacy intervention in a given area and then leave it to teachers to obtain that information from the assessment sources available to them.

Determining the Instructional Focus of an Intervention

As described in Chapter 2, schools using RTI conduct regular grade-level meetings prior to instructional interventions to discuss the details involved in implementation. These conversations usually address the intervention focus and the goal. In addition, the progress monitoring measure to be used is also identified. Such professional conversations are important for intervention success.

The team begins by identifying the focus of the intervention. Table 3.3 lists the forms included in this book that can be used by the team. First is the Intervention

TABLE 3.3. Forms and Their Purposes

Form	When used?/frequency	Purpose
Intervention Goal-Setting Sheet (Form 3.1)	Preplanning Once per intervention	This form is used during a grade-level or team meeting in which teachers are preplanning interventions. Teachers record the following information about the intervention: • Focus • Goal • Progress monitoring measure • Days and times the intervention meets • Diagnostic data for each student (baseline)
Six-Week Intervention-Planning Sheet (Form 3.2)	Preplanning During intervention (once per intervention)	Teachers use this form to record their tentative plans for 6 weeks of instruction. The form provides support for establishing the scope (content of instruction) and sequence (order) of instruction. Activities, notes, and progress monitoring days are also planned. The form serves as a guide for intervention instruction that can be revised in response to students' progress.
Intervention Log (Form 3.3)	During intervention During evaluation Once per week	This form is a "log" or record of what *actually* happened during the intervention on a weekly basis. It provides space to record the attendance for each student. Teachers also record specific notes about each student as needed. These notes are useful in evaluating the intervention and revising it.
Fidelity Checklist (Forms 4.2, 5.3, 6.3)	During intervention During evaluation Occasionally as needed	The purpose of this form is to check the fidelity of the intervention or the degree to which the lesson activities will fulfill the goal or purpose of the intervention. Fidelity checklists often contain a list of "essential" activities that should be taking place during the intervention. This form is used to evaluate an intervention to make sure that it is "true" to its intended goal.

Goal-Setting Sheet (Form 3.1), which includes space for individual student data as well as for recording the intervention focus, goal, and timeline.[1] The intervention focus is the content of the intervention lesson—in other words, what will be taught (e.g., letter-sounds, decoding, and fluency). Sometimes there will be a little additional instruction during the intervention that *supports* focus. For instance, when teaching letter-sounds, many times readers will need some initial phoneme awareness practice with pictures to build their sensitivity to sounds. Although this is not directly teaching letter-sounds, it supports letter-sound learning. The intervention goal is the measurable objective of the intervention, the skill that will be captured by the progress monitoring measures.

In the Goal Setting and Progress Monitoring section of this chapter we discuss how to quantify progress monitoring goals in more detail. However, at the planning stage, when teachers are formulating an intervention, they also must specify their progress monitoring assessment. As described in Chapter 2, there are two types of progress monitoring: mastery monitoring (MM) and general outcome monitoring (GOM). The MM directly reflects the content of the intervention and sometimes helps to clarify exactly what should be taking placed during the intervention. Jamie, an experienced educator, explained:

> "When I go to a meeting, I want to know what I am supposed to do. I don't want to sit around having long discussions about the intervention. I just want to cut to the chase. I have a whole classroom program that I am trying to deliver, and I don't have time to waste. We have the diagnostic data that tell us where the gaps are and we know that we want to fill those gaps. So if a kid is not able to decode, we go straight to a progress monitoring measure. How are we going to assess that content? That clarifies everything else that we are going to do. Then all the other stuff is planned, like how long the intervention will be, and who will do it."

Also, teachers may need to identify a GOM that represents a skill to which they would eventually hope the intervention would transfer. In the primary grades GOMs differ based on the student's stage of development. A GOM for a decoding intervention would likely look different than a GOM for a fluency intervention. In Chapters 4–6 we specifically describe the GOMs that might accompany different types of interventions.

Once the progress monitoring measure has been established, the next question is timing and scheduling. Decisions about time and personnel are essential. Who is delivering the intervention? What amount of time will be dedicated to the intervention? The answers to these questions impact both the quality of the intervention and the quantity of time devoted to it. We suggest making a record of *who* the

---

[1] All reproducible forms are found at the ends of the respective chapters.

interventionist will be and which *days* and *times* he/she will meet with a student. In addition, we suggest that a decision be made about *how many hours* per week the intervention will take place and *how much time* will be spent in the intervention each meeting day.

As with any other skills, students will improve in direct proportion to the amount of time they spend doing or practicing something. We recommend that interventions occur five times per week for 30 minutes per meeting. When this is not feasible, we believe that interventions should last at least 1.5 hours, three times per week. The amount of time dedicated to intervention should ultimately match the intervention goal and the amount of time that it will take for students to learn a content. We have often found that letter naming is a very teachable content that does not usually require daily treatment. However, letter-sound instruction can be more difficult, especially for students who do not have an awareness of initial phonemes in words. When phoneme awareness is deficient, intervention lessons must include both phonemic awareness activities and letter-sound instruction. Usually this type of intervention requires daily intervention time. Similarly, deeply entrenched fluency issues require more practice and time. In the subsequent chapters we address the amount of improvement that one might expect over a particular period of time with different literacy skills. Ultimately, the amount of time dedicated to intervention should be sufficient for consistent instruction to take place and should match the difficulty of the focus (more difficult content will require more time). In the planning section, we provide more insight about time and its distribution within the lesson.

Personnel decisions about interventions relate to quality. We do not recommend that volunteers be responsible for intervention instruction. However, with Tier 2 interventions, we have found that well-trained and well-supervised paraprofessionals with good attendance records can often be very successful in delivering interventions. Paraprofessionals are most successful with a very well-specified intervention. In one elementary school, we remember Shirley, who was very successful in delivering interventions designed by the reading specialist. Kathy, the reading specialist, used a blend of professional resource materials and her own knowledge to preplan an intervention and then checked in with Shirley every 2 to 3 weeks. Shirley enjoyed delivering intervention because she felt that she was really contributing to the success of the children and was often bored and overwhelmed when assigned to do clerical work and copying. The planning provided by the reading specialist proved to be a "win–win" situation for everyone involved, most importantly the students.

Usually a reading specialist, Title I reading teacher, or classroom teacher is a better choice for delivering interventions. The person delivering the intervention must want to teach the intervention, be skilled in the content focus, and able to consistently deliver the intervention. In our opinion, teachers *do* need to feel some level of control over the interventions they teach. They should be able to give input about the interventions that best connect with their gifts, and they should feel motivated to do the intervention. Intervention should be a positive, energetic instructional time for both students and teachers. Ultimately, the person delivering the intervention should possess the skills and motivation to deliver it. We also recommend placing the students with the greatest needs with the professionals in the building who have the most extensive training and experience to meet those needs. For example, students with extreme phonological awareness weaknesses would likely be best placed with the reading specialist. Students with language difficulties might be best placed with the English language learner (ELL) teacher or speech pathologist.

Schools should consider the following questions as they establish a progress monitoring measure, the intervention goal, timeline, and personnel:

- Is the person delivering the intervention willing to do so? (motivated)
- Does the person delivering the intervention possess the skills necessary to effectively deliver the intervention? (competent)
- If a paraprofessional is to deliver the instructional intervention, will the person be supervised and supported?
  o Who will provide plans for the paraprofessional to execute with students?
- If a paraprofessional is to deliver the instructional intervention, does the person have a good attendance record?
- Is the amount of time devoted to the intervention reasonable for the content being taught?

Planning for an Intervention

We suggest that teachers who are providing interventions plan in larger chunks and then reevaluate their plans every 3 weeks. Form 3.2 provides a template for planning the content, activities, and progress monitoring measures for up to 6 weeks, or about one-half of the time of a typical intervention period. Because interventions are so focused and consistent, teachers find extended planning useful from time to time. Each box on the form represents one week of intervention planning. The Six-Week Intervention-Planning Sheet provides a scope and sequence for the intervention. The sections of the Six-Week Intervention-Planning Sheet are illustrated in each of the content chapters (e.g., Chapter 6, Letters, and Chapter 7, Decoding). The Six-Week Intervention-Planning Sheet has space to record the focus content, which is what will be taught (e.g., letter-sound knowledge, decoding short vowels, fluency reading rate, and expression). Each week's content is sequenced or put into a specific order over the 6 weeks of the intervention (e.g., B, M, R, S—first week). In addition, the instructional activities for each week are also recorded. Instructional activities are the planned actions that teachers choose to teach the content and accomplish the goals of the intervention (e.g., word or picture sorting, repeated oral reading, sound boxes).

Writing Plans

We do suggest that brief, written plans be used during instructional interventions. When we have introduced the planning approach using the Six-Week Intervention-Planning Sheet to teachers, they have been initially skeptical. Often it seems easier to simply sit down and plan for a week, but we find that this does not work for two reasons. First, teachers tell us that investing about an hour of time up front on planning actually *saves* time in the long run. We did a little experiment and asked teachers to do the planning their way and then to do it our way. Teachers reported that going back to the plan each week, in a sense, was like reinventing the wheel. Carol explained:

> "I actually ended up spending about 30 minutes per week on intervention planning when I did it my way and I started to dread it. It was like, 'What are we going to do this week?' But when I sat down and did it for 6 weeks, I would basically review my plans each week for about 10 minutes and make changes based on data that I had on the students. I found it much easier to refine established plans than to do new plans each week."

The second reason that we believe long-term planning is more effective is that it leads to more consistent and coherent instructional intervention. When teachers plan for 6 weeks, the content is delivered in a more sensible fashion. Carol explained:

> "So when I plan for 6 weeks, I know where I am going this week and then I know where I want to be in 3 weeks. It keeps me focused on the goal. Yeah, I do change the plans if the kids are not responding, but it keeps urgency in my teaching and direction."

With intervention, the unit of instruction is usually the period of time in which the intervention will take place. Planning for the end goal and pacing the content are very important.

Different contents will lead to different types of pacing. With code-level skills, such as letter-sound instruction, decoding, or phonemic awareness, there are many resources to guide the scope and the sequencing. Sequencing of letter-sounds, for instance, can be done using *Words Their Way* (Bear, Templeton, Invernizzi, & Johnston, 2012), or the Neuhaus Reading Readiness materials. Phonemic awareness activities can be structured based on the type of phonemes (e.g., vowels, continuant consonants, stop consonants) and the number of phonemes in a word (e.g., *at* vs. *trap*).

With instructional intervention, teachers must be systematic in their presentation because the approaches that worked in the classroom did not work with these students. Attention to introducing the content from the easiest to the hardest or from the least complex to the most complex is particularly important with Tier 2 interventions. In addition, we suggest specifying the number of minutes dedicated to each activity. This step helps teachers move the lesson along and ensures that the lesson focus is receiving the requisite amount of time. For example, if the focus of the lesson is increasing fluency and reading rate, then the majority of the lesson, or 70% of the time, should be geared toward fluency instruction. In one fluency lesson, we found that the teacher was spending about 15–17 minutes on high-frequency word practice (50–56% of a 30-minute lesson) and the rest of the time on repeated reading and oral reading. In actuality, to keep the focus of the lesson on the target skill—fluency—only about 7–10 minutes of time should have been dedicated to high-frequency word practice. The majority of the lesson time, about 20 minutes, should have focused on fluency practice. Although these distinctions seem nitpicky, the cumulative effects of time are compounded across 6 weeks. Students get better at what they practice the most, and so the intervention time should be dedicated to the focus of the intervention.

Selecting Instructional Activities

The selection of activities is also very important to the intervention. We like to tell teachers, "Establish your content, be research-based, and then HAVE FUN!" Keep activities simple and repetitive, but not boring. The content of the intervention should be kept very consistent from day to day, but the lessons should be brisk and engaging, with different student-friendly activities. Students should receive multiple opportunities to engage in active learning/participation within each intervention session. In a letter intervention, this means that the students might focus on the same five letters and/or letter-sounds but engage in three different activities with those letter-sounds. From the perspective of the child, a variety of activities makes the lesson interesting, and from the perspective of the teacher the variety provides different opportunities to reach the student. The litmus test for an instructional activity is the degree to which it *meets the goal of the intervention and improves the students' performance on the MM progress monitoring measure.* When in doubt about an activity, ask yourself, "Would I expect this activity to result in a student's performing better on my progress monitoring measure?"

There are several activities that we suggest interventionists steer clear of or minimize. One nonproductive activity involves cutting, pasting, and coloring. Such activities do not contribute to improvement on a progress monitoring measure, and they eat away at precious instructional time. Sometimes we have observed teachers doing picture or word sorts or letter matching activities with word cards or pictures in which students are asked to cut up cards, color pictures, or paste cards *during* the intervention. This is not a wise use of intervention time, especially with young learners. Cutting cards and pasting them could easily consume 20 minutes of a 30-minute intervention session and do not sufficiently improve performance in the target area. As much as possible, we suggest that teachers avoid paperwork during interventions. Students love manipulatives and even writing activities can incorporate dry erase boards and colorful markers. In addition, we suggest that teachers minimize choral responding or whole-group instruction.

The intervention activities should allow children to handle their own manipulatives and to have as many practice opportunities as possible. We suggest that teachers evaluate their activities by also thinking about the number of practice opportunities that each child is given. For instance, we love games, but some formats do not provide a lot of practice opportunities per child. A Follow-the-Path-type game might give each student only one opportunity for response every four turns. A bingo game, on the other hand, might offer an opportunity for response each time. Follow-the-path games can be altered so that individual children must respond during everyone else's turn. Last, avoid nonspecific feedback or vague language. The intervention time is a time to provide students as much individual, specific, corrective feedback as possible in a small group.

Following is a list of questions to use in guiding intervention planning:

- Do you create long-term plans for instructional interventions?
- Does the content during the instructional intervention reflect a logical, research-based sequence?
- Do the plans include days to monitor progress?
- Are the instructional activities well matched to the progress monitoring measure (e.g., no cutting and pasting)?
- Are the instructional activities lively and varied?
- Is the amount of time dedicated to each instructional activity specified?
- Is the time dedicated to instructional activities aligned with the content focus (e.g., not too much time on support skills or ancillary activities)?
- Do games and instructional activities optimize the amount of individual practice for each student?

Goal Setting and Progress Monitoring

On the Intervention Goal-Setting Sheet, there is room for the interventionist to write the intervention goal (see Form 3.1). As described in Chapter 2 the intervention goal is a very precise statement of exactly what kind of progress monitoring score will constitute success. The first goal that should be established is the MM goal. The intervention goal addresses questions such as these:

- How will we know when the student has been successful?
- How many items must a student answer correctly to be considered proficient?
- How many words correct per minute must be gained?

Often these goals are based on the benchmark scores in a given screener for the next screening period (e.g., winter or spring). For example, a teacher who is working with a student in fluency may use the fluency benchmark scores for the next screening to shape a goal. At other times, a more specific goal is set that specifies a target relative to the instructional intervention. As described in Chapter 2, at least 12 data points or 3 months of intervention should be conducted before moving into more intensive Tier 3 interventions. However, it is often the case that students at the primary levels will make sufficient progress and meet goals before 12 weeks' time. The earlier that intervention begins in a student's school career, the more likely that he/she can be "caught up," and the less likely that a full 12 weeks of intervention will be needed. Our goal statement can be found on the intervention planning form in Form 3.1. Following are a few examples of goals for intervention groups:

- To read pseudowords containing short vowels *a, e, i, o, u* with 90% accuracy by March 1st.
- To identify the sounds for 24/26 letters by May 16th.
- To read 50 words per minute correctly by May 1st.

Evaluating an Intervention: Intervention Logs, Progress Monitoring, and Fidelity Checklists

Teachers have planned and delivered instructional interventions long before RTI, but what distinguishes RTI from other approaches is a thorough approach to assessing the effectiveness of instructional interventions. We recommend three tools to evaluate instructional interventions: (1) intervention logs, (2) fidelity checklists, and (3) progress monitoring data.

Intervention Logs

An intervention log is a weekly record of what actually happened during the intervention. Like a ship's log, it is a dated journal, in this case documenting the conditions of the intervention and the responses of each student. Form 3.3 shows a blank intervention log with boxes for all participating students, their attendance, and notes about their progress. After the intervention has been running for several weeks, teachers use the intervention log to support their discussions of student progress. With the notes that they have on the intervention logs, teachers complement progress monitoring data with information about attendance, students' demeanor during interventions (e.g., cooperative, eager, discouraged, sleepy), and responses (e.g., "James read accurately and his time improved, but he sounded robotic" or "Kayla takes a longer time to blend words than other students"). Frequently, the intervention log will include teachers' hypotheses about why an intervention might not be working effectively.

Because the intervention log is simple and anecdotal, teachers usually find it helpful. In each of the following chapters we include a sample intervention log for the particular content focus, such as letter teaching, fluency, or decoding. These sample logs show the types of comments that teachers typically make about students. Many of these comments are hypotheses. Teachers reflect upon the progress (or lack thereof) that students are making. For example, in Chapter 4, which focuses on letter-sound learning, a teacher comments that a student, Juan, an English language learner, may be confusing the /b/ and /p/ sounds because of his first language, in which these sounds are very similar. When we see a high-quality intervention log, we can almost see the wheels turning in the brain of the interventionist.

Intervention logs are also important because they help teachers improve instruction when an intervention is not working. With an intervention log teachers can maintain brief notes about students' immediate responses to instruction. Danielle explained to us:

> "I like having data in front of me during a meeting because I can provide examples of how a student responded to instruction. For example, I was doing this fluency intervention group and everyone was doing so well except for Felicia. I just couldn't figure out was going on and why the intervention wasn't working with her. When I looked at my notes, I had occasionally made notes that she read the passages silently because she told me she was shy. I don't know why I let her do that, but I did. I realized that she should have been reading the passages orally and so I insisted and I saw her improve."

We particularly believe in the importance of tracking attendance on the intervention log. We worked in one school where we remember a third grader who had made marvelous progress in a decoding intervention and then started to drop off. When we consulted the intervention logs, we realized that she was only attending about 3 days per week of a 5-day intervention. Although she was attending school regularly, she was frequently being pulled out of class for appointments or going home sick or even in school suspension. If we had relied on the school's attendance records, we would have assumed that she attended intervention much more than she did.

Fidelity Checklists

A fidelity checklist is simply a listing of the essential elements of an intervention used to evaluate it. Most often someone will use the fidelity checklist to observe an intervention and look for the essential components. A fidelity checklist for a fluency intervention might include questions like the following:

- Did students read orally?
- Was the oral reading timed?
- Were the students reading expressively (e.g., not robot reading)?

The fidelity checklist is essentially a way of making sure that the intervention is on track.

In all of our work with teachers doing RTI, we have found that the fidelity checklist can be the most misunderstood element of RTI. Some teachers are resentful of someone "checking up on them." Our friend Cheryl from Chapter 1 had many questions about the fidelity checklist. "It bugged me," she told us. "I am a professional and I don't need someone 'checking on me.' I can do my job, and I have been doing it for several decades." This perspective is common and certainly understandable. However, fidelity checklists are not evaluation tools for people. They are evaluations of the *intervention*. They are not shared with parents, administrators, or even other teachers. People who use them are not curriculum police. We use these when students are struggling and not making progress. A fidelity checklist is usually a good way to clarify the active ingredients in the intervention. Susan explained:

> "It's funny. When you put everything into a simple checklist, it's like a set of priorities. I find it clarifying. After we did this, I had a reading specialist ask me about my intervention when we were doing lunch duty. I used to hate those kind of on-the-fly conversations because I always floundered, but since we started to use fidelity checklists like this, I can quickly tell someone what I am doing and why."

One way to alleviate the negative feelings that good teachers have about fidelity checklists is to ask them to draft a few bullet points that capture what *they* believe to be the most important components of the intervention. If something is missing, the committee can discuss that at the onset. After being part of developing the checklists, Cheryl softened a bit.

> "I still bristle a bit with the fidelity checklists, but that's because I usually stay on course pretty well with what I do. I have found that it's really helpful if I am coaching another teacher or if I am sitting on a team and an intervention is not working. I have been asked by my principal to go in and observe interventions, and I use the checklists to help me think clearly. Sometimes I don't even share them with the teachers I am observing but they help me be organized and specific in supporting a teacher, if I need to. Also, it helps me to stay grounded in what's important in the intervention. I like being creative and I think that interventions *can* be lively and fun, but they can't veer from the focus of the intervention. When I am coming up with intervention activities, I look at the fidelity checklist and ask myself, 'Is this going to contribute to helping the kids do what we set up as the goal? Is the activity matched to the target behavior that we want the kids to display?' You just have less time to play around in an intervention, and this keeps me focused."

Teachers should not feel as if the fidelity checklist is a secret "gotcha" tool. It should be clear to everyone which elements of the intervention are most important. We include sample fidelity checklists in each of the chapters on specific types of interventions.

Progress Monitoring Data

Perhaps the most important tool used in evaluating the quality of a reading intervention is progress monitoring data. Without this information we cannot really judge the student's *response* to the intervention. When evaluating data, we first suggest that teachers look at the MM data to see if the student has responded to the content of the intervention. Chapter 2 provides a detailed description of analyzing data. If the student has not shown progress in acquiring the content in the intervention, then looking at the GOM will not be helpful. We would not expect a student to generalize an unlearned skill. When teachers see a lack of progress in MM, they know that they must examine the intervention instruction for the student. If the student has shown progress at the MM level, then we suggest that the GOM data be examined to see if there is some impact on a broader goal and if the discrete content of the intervention is having a more extended effect. Keep in mind, however, that any impact on GOM data will usually take longer because it is not as closely aligned with the intervention.

Following are several questions that we suggest schools and teachers use in guiding the evaluation of interventions:

- Does the intervention log provide a weekly review of what happened during a reading intervention?
- Does the intervention log track student attendance during interventions?
- Are anecdotal comments included on intervention logs and do they complement the progress monitoring data?
- Does the intervention log show hypotheses about why an intervention might *not* be working?
- Are simple fidelity checklists created collaboratively when the intervention is set?
- Are fidelity checklists shared with teachers at the outset of the intervention time and used in a transparent, professional, and respectful fashion?
- Do the elements on the fidelity checklist reflect the *essential* ingredients of the intervention that will lead to results on the progress monitoring measure?
- Is a fidelity checklist used to guide observations when an intervention is not working?
- Is the fidelity checklist treated as a constructive tool to improve interventions rather than a teacher evaluation instrument?

Conclusion

As we discuss specific intervention content in the coming chapters, it is important to begin with an overarching plan for intervention instruction. Interventions should be research-based, considerate of the developmental continuum, and informed by diagnostic assessments. When schools take the time to thoughtfully investigate the research base of intervention programs and strategies, teachers can confidently embark on interventions knowing that their instructional approach is supported by research, thereby eliminating a "trial-and-error" saga. Knowledge of the developmental continuum, coupled with diagnostic data for struggling learners, further inform teachers on exactly what kids need and where they need to be.

Lesson planning for intervention instruction need not be tedious and time-consuming. By setting goals and timelines and determining progress monitoring measures ahead of time, interventions can be targeted and well-informed. Long-range, 6-week planning for interventions keeps instruction consistent and allows content to flow from session to session. The planning sheets provided within this chapter serve as helpful resources in the planning process.

Finally, it is helpful to determine ways in which to ascertain the effectiveness of interventions and to provide opportunities for self-reflection regarding intervention instruction. Intervention logs, fidelity checklists, and progress monitoring data can serve as key components in this process. Intervention logs provide important information from teachers regarding students' attendance and progress during intervention sessions. Fidelity checklists contain essential components that should be found in every intervention session. Such checklists are helpful when observing interventions as well as serving as "thought points" for teachers as they plan intervention instruction. Progress monitoring data help teachers identify who is progressing as a result of instruction and who is not. When logs, checklists, and progress monitoring data are considered in conjunction with one another, decisions about students' progress are well informed and supported.

Intervention Goal-Setting Sheet

Instructional focus of group: _____

Intervention goal: To _____

Meeting days:_____ Meeting time: _____ Hrs/week: _____

Progress monitoring measure: _____

Frequency of administration: _____

Student Diagnostic Data

Student Name: Diagnostic Data:	Student Name: Diagnostic Data:	Student Name: Diagnostic Data:
Student Name: Diagnostic Data:	Student Name: Diagnostic Data:	Student Name: Diagnostic Data:

FORM 3.2

Six-Week Intervention-Planning Sheet

Content focus: _____

Specific student needs: _____

Week of:	Week of:	Week of:
Content:	Content:	Content:
Notes:	Notes:	Notes:
Activities:	Activities:	Activities:
Progress Monitoring:	Progress Monitoring:	Progress Monitoring:
Week of:	Week of:	Week of:
Content:	Content:	Content:
Notes:	Notes:	Notes:
Activities:	Activities:	Activities:
Progress Monitoring:	Progress Monitoring:	Progress Monitoring:

Intervention Log

Instructional focus of group: _____

_____

_____

Week of: _____   Intervention teacher: _____

Curriculum/materials: _____

_____

_____

_____

Attendance and Observation Records

Student Name:	**Student Name:**	**Student Name:**
Attendance: (Circle if absent) M T W Th F Notes:	**Attendance:** (Circle if absent) M T W Th F Notes:	**Attendance:** (Circle if absent) M T W Th F Notes:
Student Name:	**Student Name:**	**Student Name:**
Attendance: (Circle if absent) M T W Th F Notes:	**Attendance:** (Circle if absent) M T W Th F Notes:	**Attendance:** (Circle if absent) M T W Th F Notes:

CHAPTER 4

Interventions for Letter Instruction

GUIDING QUESTIONS
• •

- How does letter knowledge develop in young children?
- What are the guidelines for determining if a student is behind?
- How should diagnostic information be used to set intervention goals for letter instruction?
- How do you set a progress monitoring measure for letter interventions?
- What are some research-based, engaging activities for letter interventions?
- In what ways might you evaluate student progress in a letter intervention?

We typically think of letter knowledge as a very simple and straightforward concept, a set of 52–54 visual symbols that students must recognize in order to acquire literacy in English. However, closer inspection of this content suggests that *learning letters* may not be simple after all.

Have you ever had a parent or even friend or relative brag to you that their 2-year-old "already knows the whole alphabet"? "Wow! That's great!" you might say. Proudly, the parent then says, "Go ahead, Isabella, sing it!" Clearly, what parents think of when they say *"knows the whole alphabet"* is not the way that you, a literacy educator, think about it. Of course, singing the alphabet song is a fun activity, and it builds children's confidence with names of the letters and can be used as a scaffold for more challenging activities. But as educators we know that, in fact, learning letters requires more than singing the alphabet song. Letter

knowledge is layered and complex, consisting of many different levels and components. The alphabet song familiarizes children with the spoken names of letters,
but children must learn to attach these names to visual figures, then learn the corresponding phonemes or speech sounds and then even write letters. For a young
child this can all be rather tricky. For example, sometimes the upper- and lowercase forms of a letter look dissimilar even though they actually share the same
name (e.g., *Rr, Gg*), and this can be confusing to a young child. Something else
that can be confusing is that the names of the letters themselves, although helpful
in some cases, are not as important as the sounds that the letters represent. Eventually children must learn to write letters and recall their visual shapes and sounds
without prompts, pictures, or clues, and they must analyze these forms when they
begin reading. The content, which seems quaint and simplistic to adults, is actually
formidable for children. For most children learning the letters takes some time,
and not all children acquire this information easily.

In order to make use of letter-sounds in their reading and writing, children
must understand the alphabetic principle—that letters represent speech sounds.
Without this key understanding, they may learn what they have been taught and
be able to parrot adults, but they will not be able to *apply the knowledge.* We
recall a little guy, Terry, who could easily tell anyone the sound that accompanies
each visual letter symbol. He would just crank through them as we presented letter
cards, "/vvvvv/, /t/, /mmmmmm/, /aaaa/." When he attempted to read, however, he
frequently glanced around the page to look for picture clues or appealed to us for
help. Terry did not know *why* he knew the letter-sounds. He did not know what
to do with that knowledge. Like any conscientious kindergartener, he had eagerly
learned what he had been taught to make his parents and teachers happy, but the
information was useless to him without an insight about how the alphabet worked.

We begin this chapter with the very important reminder that children need
rich, meaningful experiences that support their acquisition of the alphabetic principle. Although this chapter focuses on letters, they should not be taught without
shared reading experiences with big books, shared writing experiences in which
teachers demonstrate the use of the alphabetic principle, or journal writing with
invented spelling. A wonderful quote by Vygotsky reminds us that although we
can directly teach children the alphabet, we must develop their construction of
the alphabetic principle over time and with many experiences. "Direct teaching of
concepts is impossible and fruitless. A teacher who tries to do this usually accom-
plishes nothing but empty verbalism, a parrotlike repetition of words by the child,
simulating a knowledge of the corresponding concepts but actually covering up a
vacuum" (Vygotsky, 1986, as cited in Downing, 1969c, p. 185). Terry had been
giving us empty verbalism that appeared to reflect knowledge he didn't possess.
Instead, what he did know was empty because he had no understanding of what
the knowledge was for.

Letter Knowledge:
What Does the Research Say about Instruction?

The ability to name letters is important. In fact, it is the single best predictor of beginning reading achievement (Adams, 1990; Bond & Dykstra, 1967; Chall, 1967; Vellutino & Scanlon, 1987). Of course, we know that much more is required to learn how to read, but letter knowledge is a great start. As is turns out, research suggests that children learn letter names in predictable patterns, a fact that many PreK and kindergarten teachers know (see Figure 4.1). According to research by Evans, Bell, Shaw, Moretti, and Page (2006) and Treiman, Tincoff, Rodriguez, Mauzaki, and Francis (1998), students usually learn uppercase letters first and then lowercase letters, beginning with unique or salient forms (e.g., the letters in a student's name, the letters *x* and *o*). Among the lowercase forms, they learn those with similar uppercase parents first (e.g., *Vv, Ww, Ss*) and then those with dissimilar uppercase parents (e.g., *Bb, Qq, Rr*) (Evans et al., 2006; Treiman et al., 1998).

As children learn letter-sounds, research tells us that they often will use the letter-names to help them (Ehri & Wilce, 1980). For instance, they will first learn the letter-sounds that have the target sound at the beginning of the name (e.g., *b, d, j, k, p, t, v, z*) (Evans et al., 2006; Kim, Petscher, Foorman, & Zhou, 2010). Think about the name of the letter *B* "*Bee*." It has the target sound /b/ at the *beginning* of the name of the letter. This information in the letter-name will often cue students to the sound of the letter itself. We call letter-names such as *B transparent*. Next, students learn the letter-sounds for letters with names that have the target sound at the end of the name (e.g., *f, l, m, n, r, s*). For instance, the sound for *F*, "*Eff*," actually has the /f/ sound at the end of the name. These are letter-names that we call *opaque*. Lastly, students learn letter-sounds where the name offers either no sound information or even conflicting sound information (e.g., *h, y, w*). For example, the

• Uppercase letters   o Salient forms first (e.g., letters in name, *X, O*)

• Lowercase letters
  o With similar uppercase parents (e.g., *Cc, Oo, Ss*)
  o With dissimilar uppercase parents (e.g., *Aa, Bb, Gg*)

• Sounds for letters with names that have the target sound at the beginning of the name   o *b, d, j, k, p, t, v, z*
• Sounds for letters with names that have the target sounds at the end of the name   o *f, l, m, n, r, s*
• Sounds for letters with no information in the name   o *h, y, w, x*

FIGURE 4.1. Developmental learning patterns in letter-names and letter-sounds.

name for *H*, "*Aych*," does not contain the target sound /h/ that we usually associate with H. Letters such as this are called *ambiguous*.

Research tells us that children can use the names of letters to help them learn the sounds, especially for transparent and opaque names (Share, 2008). However, a child's ability to exploit the sound information in the name depends upon his/her phonemic awareness. *Phonemic awareness* is the ability to identify the speech sounds or phonemes in a spoken word. For example, a student who can tell you that *fish* and *fun* both start with the /f/ sound have an awareness of the initial phonemes in these words. A slightly more sophisticated level of phonemic awareness is the ability to break an *oral* word into its sounds (e.g., *bag* = /b/ + /a/ + /g/). When children have some awareness that words have sound parts, they can use this skill to isolate the relevant letter-sounds in letter names (Share, 2008). So, whether it is taught or children figure it out on their own, some level of phonemic awareness is acquired in the process of letter-sound learning. The reports of the National Reading Panel (National Institute of Child Health and Human Development, 2001) and the National Early Literacy Panel (2008) both advised teachers to pair phonemic awareness training with letter learning for optimal results. This means that teachers should combine letter-sound instruction with phonemic awareness activities. The letters themselves provide a concrete referent for sounds (phonemes), which are abstract to young children. We suggest augmenting letter interventions with 20–30% initial sound/phoneme instruction. In the classroom this might mean that a teacher focuses on listening for the initial phonemes in spoken words. A teacher might say two words and then emphasize the initial sound (e.g., /fffffish/ and /ffff-fun/) or might use pictures to help students pay attention to sounds.

Letter Knowledge on the Developmental Continuum

As literacy educators we know that all children must learn the letters, but how do we know when a student is in trouble with his/her letter acquisition? What exactly is normal and when should we intervene? The answer, of course, depends on exactly what we mean by *letter knowledge*. There appears to be clearer evidence about the level of letter knowledge that students should have by the end of kindergarten and end of PreK than at different points in between.

If we worked backward, we would say that by the end of kindergarten students should have mastery of almost all the facets of letter knowledge (e.g., naming upper- and lowercase forms automatically, identifying sounds automatically, and writing letters). The most important of these skills is the ability to automatically identify the sound that accompanies each visual symbol, because this is the skill that students use when they read. Information and evidence from a number of sources support this standard. See Table 4.1 for details.

TABLE 4.1. Standards for Letter Knowledge in Different Documents

Document	Standard
Kindergarten	
Common Core Standards for the English Language Arts (2010)	Kindergarteners should "demonstrate basic knowledge of one-to-one letter–sound correspondences by producing the primary or many of the most frequent sounds for each consonant" (p. 16).
	"Associate the long and short sounds with common spellings (graphemes) for the five major vowels (p. 16)."
Preventing Reading Difficulties in Young Children (Snow et al., 1998)	Kindergartners should be able to recognize and name letters, and know most one-to-one letter/sound correspondences.
I've DIBELed Now What? (Hall, 2006)	Hall specified the actual rate at which kindergartners should be able to name letters by stating, "If they cannot name 40 randomly arranged letters in a minute, they may need additional instruction and practice on their letters" (p. 173).
PreK	
State Standards	Name between 10 and 20 letters. Most states specified 10 letters.
Piasta et al., 2012	Name 18 uppercase letters and 15 lowercase letters.

In the United States, by the end of kindergarten students are expected to have mastered all letter-sounds. A clear indication that complete letter knowledge should been acquired by the end of kindergarten is the fact that first-grade standards do not even address letter-sound knowledge. In first grade the emphasis is on applying letter-sound knowledge to read new words (Snow et al., 1998). Thus, if a first grader at the beginning of the school year cannot quickly and accurately identify the sound for almost 100% of letters, intervention is needed.

Many children are attending PreK, and some states are even offering it in public schools. There are also clear guidelines about the level of letter knowledge that children should have by the end of PreK. In 2012, researchers Piasta, Petscher, and Justice (2012) informally analyzed the number of letter-names required in several standards documents. Most states required PreK students to learn 10 letters, a prescription that was likely influenced by *Preventing Reading Difficulty in Young Children* (Snow et al., 1998). Some states set 20 letter names as the standard, and others specified that fewer than 10 letters were adequate. Recent evidence suggests that although children who can name less than 10 letters are definitely *at risk* of developing later reading difficulty, children who can name at least 10 are not necessarily out of the water (Piasta et al., 2012). A recent study suggested that PreK students should be able to name 18 uppercase letters and 15 lowercase letters (Piasta et al., 2012). PALS, a screening instrument in Virginia, found that of the PreK children who scored exactly 12 on uppercase alphabet recognition in the Spring of their 4-year-old PreK year, about 74% were reading on or above grade level in the spring of first grade—2 years later. That percentage goes up with every increase in letters known (PALS Office, personal communication, April 23, 2013). Although these criteria may seem a bit high for PreK students, the fact that they predict future success makes them useful goals to strive for when working with little ones on letter knowledge.

We were unable to find clear guidelines about the thresholds of letter naming or letter-sound knowledge that students at risk might have at the beginning of kindergarten. Based on the recent Piasta et al. (2012) study we suggest that at the beginning of kindergarten students should be able to provide about 18 uppercase letter-names and would recommend that students with levels below 10 be targeted for intervention in kindergarten rooms. We believe that it is very important to note the points along the continuum at which knowing *letter-names* is the measured skill and points at which the knowing *letter-sounds* is the measured skill. By the middle of kindergarten and at the beginning of first grade, the measured skill is letter-*sounds* and not letter-*names*, because letter-sound knowledge is the more difficult (and more important) skill. At the beginning of the continuum, in PreK and initial weeks of kindergarten, naming is the measured skill.

Diagnostic Assessments to Inform Intervention Goals

Teachers need to determine the focus of letter knowledge. What is it that the students really need to be able to do with letters? Does the student need to be able to quickly and automatically name letter-sounds, as required at the beginning of first grade? Or is the child in the early stages, such as PreK, when basic familiarity with naming some letters is the focus? In order to start letter interventions, teachers need to know exactly which letters and/or letter-sounds the student knows. This knowledge will ground the intervention and focus teaching on that which the student does not know. Letter intervention would begin with prekindergarteners who cannot name at least nine uppercase and seven lowercase letters by midyear, for kindergartners who cannot name 18 uppercase and 15 lowercase letters at the beginning of the year; and for first graders who cannot identify all letter-sounds. We recommend that all PreK and kindergarten teachers give diagnostic assessments of letter naming or letter-sounds and that first-grade teachers use letter-sound measures for students who have not passed the school's literacy screening benchmark. In this section we identify three types of diagnostic measures: (1) letter-name measures, (2) letter-sound measures, and (3) letter-naming fluency or speed measures.

Letter-Name Measures

Assessments of students' ability to name letters are among the most straightforward instruments that exist. Most have uppercase and lowercase forms with letters randomly arrayed on a blank sheet. Some include the Roman forms for the lowercase *a* and *g* as well as the ball-and-stick/manuscript forms (Clay, 1993). Letters are not placed in alphabetical order so that students cannot rely on memory of the order of the alphabet to help them in naming. The administrator asks the student to name each letter, giving him/her a prearranged time to name each letter (e.g., 3–5 seconds). Responses are written on a record sheet (see Figure 4.2). We recommend that letter-naming measures be administered in PreK and at the beginning of kindergarten.

▶ Lower-Case Alphabet Recognition: Student Progress Chart

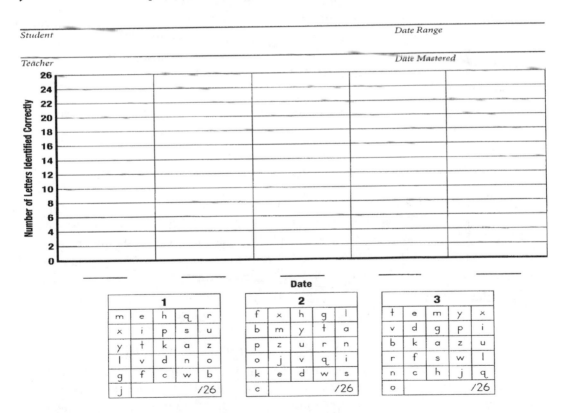

FIGURE 4.2. A sample progress monitoring measure for letter interventions. Copyright by PALS Marketplace. Reprinted by permission.

Letter-Sound Measures

Assessments of letter-sounds typically take the same form as the letter-naming measures, but the directions are different. The assessment administrator requests that the student provide the sound of the letter. Sometimes students get confused with this direction and provide letter-names. Most teachers will gently ask the student to provide the *sound* of the letter and not the name. For vowels, most letter-sound measures require students to identify the short-vowel sounds because the long-vowel sounds are replicated in the names, and knowledge of short-vowel sounds reflects more sophisticated learning. We recommend that letter-sound measures be administered at the middle of kindergarten, end of kindergarten, and beginning of first grade.

Letter-Naming Speed or Fluency

Although many teachers do not use a measure of letter-naming speed, we believe that in certain circumstances a letter-name fluency measure is helpful. The letter-naming fluency measure essentially identifies the number of letters that a student can name in a minute. Students with automatic recognition of letter-names should be able to identify at least 40 letters in a minute. We suggest administering a letter-naming fluency measure, such as DIBELS, when a student just barely meets letter/sound benchmarks and there is a desire to ascertain how strong and certain a student's knowledge of letter names is. Usually this kind of assessment occurs in the latter part of kindergarten or the beginning of first grade.

What to Do with Diagnostic Data

Once the diagnostic assessment data have been collected, teachers will have specific information about the precise letter-names or letter-sounds that students need to learn. This information will provide the content parameters for the intervention. We do suggest that teachers systematically plan the letters on which they will give focus each week and that they give attention to the sequence with which they teach this content. In the next section we describe how an interventionist used the diagnostic information, along with an established sequence, to plan her letter intervention.

Some teachers have questions about whether to focus on letter naming or letter-sounds. Although both are related to each other, letter naming is easier, and research shows us that with some phonemic awareness it can support letter-sound acquisition. The focus of the intervention should also be guided by the student's developmental level and the degree to which the student is lagging behind. Interventions in PreK are almost always focused on letter naming because prekindergarteners are so young and letter naming is the entry point for letter knowledge.

In the middle of kindergarten or at the beginning of first grade interventions are almost always focused on letter-sounds because letter-sound knowledge is the essential access skill for beginning reading instruction. The goal of kindergarten instruction is the acquisition of letter-sounds. However, some children will need help with letter-names at the beginning of kindergarten. If a student knows few letter-names, then we recommend beginning an intervention with letter-names, infusing some phonemic awareness instruction, and gradually increasing the focus on letter-sounds.

For each letter intervention group, we suggest recording the letters that each student knows on one sheet along with other pertinent information that we discuss in the next section. We provide a blank Letter Intervention Goal-Setting Sheet in Form 4.1 and a completed example in Figure 4.3. This sheet can be used to record students' letter-naming knowledge or letter-sounds, depending on their ages. In this example, you can see that the teacher has indicated that the measure was for letter-sounds and that she did not use the uppercase part of the sheet. The example shows information for a group of kindergarten students in the middle of the year who did not meet the literacy benchmark score. Any intervention teacher working with this group could easily pull out one page and see the letter-sounds that each student knows and the ones that each student needs to work on. In this example, students know between 9 and 14 letter-sounds. Note that many of the letters that the students need to learn overlap and that they roughly match the order of acquisition that we mentioned at the beginning of the chapter.

Determining the Focus of the Intervention

After collecting basic diagnostic information, the intervention teacher (along with the reading specialist, classroom teacher, and other involved parties) needs to identify the focus of the intervention, intervention strategies, and how the intervention will be evaluated.

Setting an Intervention Focus

Figure 4.3 shows the intervention focus and goal that the teachers selected for this letter intervention. Recall that the intervention focus is the content of the intervention lesson and the goal is the measurable behavior that indicates that the students have learned that content (see below for a more in-depth discussion of goal setting and progress monitoring). The content of the intervention should be guided by research and the teacher's knowledge of the students participating. We suggest that teachers plan the letters that they will give attention to each week and then identify two or three activities through which they may teach this content. If students know fewer than 10 letters, we suggest that teachers identify several letters that all students *know* and then target two additional letters that will be the focus each week (given a daily intervention time). In this way, the intervention will be balanced between the known and unknown and will not overwhelm or discourage younger learners (i.e., prekindergarteners). If students know more than 10 letters, we suggest a slightly brisker pace that targets three or more letters each week, with additional known letters included.

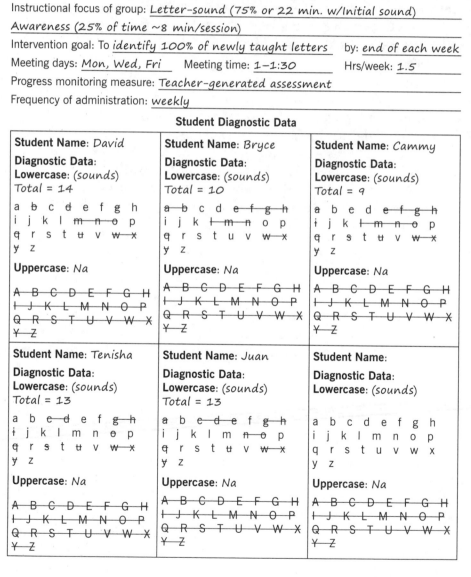

Letter Intervention Goal-Setting Sheet

Instructional focus of group: *Letter-sound (75% or 22 min. w/Initial sound)*
Awareness (25% of time ~8 min/session)
Intervention goal: To *identify 100% of newly taught letters*   by: *end of each week*
Meeting days: *Mon, Wed, Fri*   Meeting time: *1–1:30*   Hrs/week: *1.5*
Progress monitoring measure: *Teacher-generated assessment*
Frequency of administration: *weekly*

Student Diagnostic Data

Student Name: *David*
Diagnostic Data:
Lowercase: *(sounds)*
Total = 14

a b̶ c d̶ e f g h
i j k l m̶ n̶ o p
q̶ r s t u̶ v w̶ x̶
y̶ z

Uppercase: *Na*

A̶ B̶ C̶ D̶ E̶ F̶ G̶ H̶
I̶ J̶ K̶ L̶ M̶ N̶ O̶ P̶
Q̶ R̶ S̶ T̶ U̶ V̶ W̶ X̶
Y̶ Z̶

Student Name: *Bryce*
Diagnostic Data:
Lowercase: *(sounds)*
Total = 10

a̶ b c d e̶ f̶ g̶ h̶
i j k l̶ m̶ n̶ o p
q̶ r s t u v w̶ x̶
y̶ z

Uppercase: *Na*

A̶ B̶ C̶ D̶ E̶ F̶ G̶ H̶
I̶ J̶ K̶ L̶ M̶ N̶ O̶ P̶
Q̶ R̶ S̶ T̶ U̶ V̶ W̶ X̶
Y̶ Z̶

Student Name: *Cammy*
Diagnostic Data:
Lowercase: *(sounds)*
Total = 9

a b e d e̶ f̶ g̶ h̶
i̶ j k l̶ m̶ n̶ o̶ p
q̶ r s t u̶ v w̶ x̶
y̶ z

Uppercase: *Na*

A̶ B̶ C̶ D̶ E̶ F̶ G̶ H̶
I̶ J̶ K̶ L̶ M̶ N̶ O̶ P̶
Q̶ R̶ S̶ T̶ U̶ V̶ W̶ X̶
Y̶ Z̶

Student Name: *Tenisha*
Diagnostic Data:
Lowercase: *(sounds)*
Total = 13

a b e̶ d̶ e f g̶ h̶
i̶ j k l m n o̶ p
q̶ r s t u̶ v w̶ x̶
y̶ z

Uppercase: *Na*

A̶ B̶ C̶ D̶ E̶ F̶ G̶ H̶
I̶ J̶ K̶ L̶ M̶ N̶ O̶ P̶
Q̶ R̶ S̶ T̶ U̶ V̶ W̶ X̶
Y̶ Z̶

Student Name: *Juan*
Diagnostic Data:
Lowercase: *(sounds)*
Total = 13

a b e̶ d̶ e f g̶ h̶
i j k l m n̶ o̶ p
q̶ r s t u̶ v w̶ x̶
y̶ z

Uppercase: *Na*

A̶ B̶ C̶ D̶ E̶ F̶ G̶ H̶
I̶ J̶ K̶ L̶ M̶ N̶ O̶ P̶
Q̶ R̶ S̶ T̶ U̶ V̶ W̶ X̶
Y̶ Z̶

Student Name:
Diagnostic Data:
Lowercase: *(sounds)*

a b c d e f g h
i j k l m n o p
q r s t u v w x
y z

Uppercase: *Na*

A̶ B̶ C̶ D̶ E̶ F̶ G̶ H̶
I̶ J̶ K̶ L̶ M̶ N̶ O̶ P̶
Q̶ R̶ S̶ T̶ U̶ V̶ W̶ X̶
Y̶ Z̶

FIGURE 4.3. Completed example of a Letter Intervention Goal-Setting Sheet.

In addition to selecting the number of letters to teach, consider the guidelines that direct content choices. As described earlier, the letters with *transparent* names (e.g., *b, v, j*) are usually easier to learn than *opaque* letters, which in turn are easier than *ambiguous* letters (e.g., *x, h, y*). We certainly suggest that the *ambiguous* letters be taught near the end of mastery. Another important consideration is maximal visual and sound contrasts. Teaching the letters *b, p,* and *d* in the same set would present a challenge visually because these letters are essentially flipped or rotated versions of each other. They also are fairly close from a sound perspective. Say /p/, /d/, and /b/. The /b/ and /p/ sounds are both made by pushing your lips together and the manner is the same, a holding of air and then releasing it. The only thing that differentiates these two sounds is voicing. When you say /b/ there is buzz or voicing in your throat, and when you say /p/ there is not. Again the instructional implication is that you would not want to teach these at the same time. The authors of *Words Their Way* provide the following sequence for teaching letters:

1. *b, m, r, s*
2. *t, g, n, p*
3. *c, h, f, d*
4. *l, k, j, w*
5. *y, z, v, qu*

The interventions for letters focus squarely on naming letters and their sounds, but as the research suggests, letter-sound and phonemic awareness knowledge are best when combined. As described below, letter interventions might include a focus on phonemic awareness 20–30% of time, especially for students who are in late kindergarten/early first grade and need to solidify letter-sound knowledge. Some teachers assess initial sound awareness by using pictures and asking students to name the sounds or to orally identify the sound that they hear in a spoken word. These measures are not directly related to letter naming and are probably not necessary unless the intervention focus is firmly on letter-sound. They will provide information about the degree to which a student naturally hears sound differences, and they will be an indicator of the capacity that a student possesses to match letter names to sounds. If the scores on these measures are no greater than chance, then the student may take a longer time to learn letter-sounds, and pairing the letter intervention with *some* phonemic awareness instruction would be important. Remember, the intervention should be very clearly focused on letter knowledge, with 20–30% of the time, or 6–9 minutes, spent on phoneme awareness.

Figure 4.4, a sample Six-Week Letter Intervention-Planning Sheet, shows a teacher's content planning for the five-student intervention group in Figure 4.3. This teacher started by tallying the letters that all of the students in the group knew and all of the letters that *everyone* did not know. This information helped

Six-Week Letter Intervention-Planning Sheet

All students know the following letters: j, k, p, r, v, z   All students do not know the following letters: g, h, q, t, w, x, y

Week 1 B, M, R, S **Date:** Jan. 16–20 **Notes:** Everyone knows R. 4-day week MLK **Activities:** *Mon.* intro B and M: Model a picture sort. Students do the sort with different pictures. *Wed:* Add S–BMRS sort *Fri*—Short week **ABC Arcs:** Personalized baggies with all known letters and the new letters. Don't Forget: Name it, Sound it, Find it, Place it. (10–15 min.) **Spelling Test:** Dictate the four sounds/day /j/ /k/ /p/ /r/ /v/ /z/ (1 known) /b/ /m/ /s/ (3 unknown) **Progress Monitoring:** None—short week	**Week 2** T, G, N, P Jan. 23–27 **Notes:** Everyone knows P. **Activities:** **Picture Sorts:** *Mon.* intro T and N: Model a picture sort. Students do the sort with different pictures (3 min. demo, 5 min. sort). *Wed:* Add G–T, N sort. *Fri*—T, N, G **ABC Arcs:** Personalized baggies with all known letters and the new letters. (10–15 min.) **Spelling Test Day:** Dictate four sounds/day on dry erase: /j/ /k/ /p/ /r/ /v/ /z/ /b/ /m/ /s/ (1 known) /t/ /g/ /n/ (3 unknown) **Personalized Games:** Follow the path with focus letters (FRI) **Progress Monitoring:** Taught letter-sounds for B, M, R, S, T, G, N, & P; letter-sound fluency	**Week 3** Review Jan. 30–Feb. 3 **Notes:** Review by using progress monitoring measure to guide review and solidify **Activities:** **Letter-Sound Motions M–F:** Teach and review letter-sound motions for all letters (e.g., /b/, beating chest for heart beat). **Picture Sorts M–F:** Set up two sorts (B, M, R, S, & T, G, N, P). Switch sorts. **Letter Flash:** With partners. One partner shows letter and the other partner says the sound. **Spelling Test:** Dictate four sounds/day on dry erase: /t/ /g/ /n/ /b/ /m/ /r/ /s/ (4 unknown) **Progress Monitoring:** Letter-sounds for B, M, R, S, T, G, N, & P
Week 4 C, H, F, D Feb. 6–10 **Notes:** No knows H Challenging week **Activities:** **Letter-Sound Motions M–F:** Teach C, H, F, & D and review letter-sound motions for all letters (e.g., /h/, dog panting). **Picture Sorts M–F:** Set up two new sorts (C & H; F & D). If mastered, add review sorts (B, M, R, & S; T, G, N, P). **Letter Flash:** With partners. One partner shows letter and the other partner says the sound. **Spelling Test:** Dictate four sounds/day on dry erase: /t/ /g/ /n/ /c/ /h/ /d/ /f/ **Progress Monitoring:** Letter-sounds for B, M, R, S, T, G, N, P, H, C, F, & D; letter-sound fluency	**Week 5** L, K, J, W Review Feb. 13–17 **Notes:** Review week from Week 4. Everyone knows J and K & four know L. **Activities:** **Picture Sorts M–F:** Set up two sorts (C, H, F & D; L, K, J, W) *Wed:* Letter Stack Game with B, M, R, S, T, G, N, P, C, H, F, D, L, K, J. *Fri:* Two-person Follow the Path with C, H, D, & F; L, K, J, & W. **Spelling Test:** Dictate four sounds/day on dry erase: /j/ /k/ /l/ /w/ /c/ /h/ /d/ /f/ (4 unknown) **Progress Monitoring:** Letter-sounds for B, M, R, S, T, G, N, P, H, C, F, D, L, K, J, W; letter-sound fluency.	**Week 6** Y, Z, V, QU Feb. 20–24 **Notes:** Everyone knows Z. No one knows qu, y. **Activities:** **Meaningful Motions M–F:** Y, V, QU **Picture Sort and Label M–F:** Do sort and then label each picture card with letter-sound. Three sorts (Y, V, QU, Z; C, H, F, & D; L, K, J, & W) **Letter Flash:** With partners. One partner shows letter and the other partner says the sound. **Spelling Test:** Dictate four sounds/day on dry erase: /j/ /k/ /l/ /w/ /c/ /h/ /d/ /f/ /y/ /v/ /qu/ (4 unknown) **Progress Monitoring:** Letter-sounds for B, M, R, S, T, G, N, P, H, C, F, D, L, K, J, W; letter-sound fluency.

FIGURE 4.4. Sample Six-Week Letter Intervention-Planning Sheet.

her to know when the pacing of her instruction needed to speed up or slow down. She used a modified version of the *Words Their Way* sequence but also took into account the knowledge of her students. For example, she turned Week 3 into a review week because she knew that most of the students in the group did not know the previous week's letters. The progress monitoring measures were planned for each full week and included a direct assessment of the letters that were targeted in the intervention and assessment of letter-sound fluency. In our experience, schools are often not in session for 5 full days per week, and for this reason we usually suggest that teachers plan to do progress monitoring weekly but to adjust this when there is not a full instructional week. Note that this interventionist planned to use the results of the progress monitoring measures to review letters in subsequent weeks.

Teachers must decide exactly what behavior they will target with students, be it letter naming or letter-sound identification. In the example in Figure 4.3, the intervention focus is letter-sound knowledge. Students are asked to name the sound that accompanies each letter. The intervention lessons also include a supportive skill that will build students' capacity for the target goal. We know from research that letter-sound interventions are best when combined with some phonemic awareness instruction (National Reading Panel, 2001). So the focus in this intervention will also include some initial sound phonemic awareness instruction that will target hearing the initial sounds in spoken words. About 75% of the intervention time, or 22 minutes, will focus on letter-sound instruction and about 25%, or 8 minutes, will focus on initial sound awareness. Because these students were kindergarteners in the middle of the year, the focus of the intervention is solidifying letter-sounds by the end of the year when they should have automatic command of the letter-sounds.

Letter Intervention Activities

As we state earlier, the design of interventions should be highly routine and consistent in their content but the activities can change to keep students motivated. For letter interventions this means that the teacher is focusing on a consistent set of letters but may use different activities to keep the lessons interesting for the children.

Tasks should mirror what is required in the progress monitoring assessments and in actual reading. In the case of letter knowledge this means that students should have practice looking at letters and naming the letter-sounds themselves (vocalizing). Although it seems obvious, this is a detail that can easily be overlooked. We once worked with a teacher who had been doing a letter intervention for 3 weeks and was not getting results. When we observed, we understood why. The three mainstays of her intervention were a computer program that had students tracing letters and participating in a matching game for lower- and uppercase letters, and an activity of coloring alphabet sheets (i.e., students colored an outline of the letter and the pictures that began with that letter on the sheet). The students could write the letter forms but didn't know the associated sounds. They could discriminate and match upper- to lowercase, but again they had not learned to associate the name or sound with the visual symbols. In fact, they could have learned just as easily to do the same thing with Cyrillic alphabet letters, given the activities that the teacher was using.

As we emphasized previously, craft projects that involve cutting, coloring, and gluing generally are not suited to intervention time because such ancillary activities take up too much time and do not focus on the target behavior. Interventions should be targeted to one clear objective, such as identifying the sounds represented by the letters or naming letters. A well-developed letter-sound intervention specifies the focal letter-sounds, contains two or three engaging activities that allow students to practice the target skill, and includes corrective feedback from the teacher about the accuracy of responses (e.g., "Yes, that letter [*j*] represents the /jjjj/ sound. No, that letter [*p*] represents the sound /ppppp/, not /bbbb/. It's easy to confuse with *b* but look—in the letter *p* the tail faces down. Now you tell me, what is the sound that this letter makes? [*p*].") Activities that do not provide practice with the target skill will not help students and instead become time-consuming distractors. After all, the focus of the intervention is not cutting or coloring or pasting.

We have seen hundreds of wonderful letter activities that are targeted; that is, they prioritize letter-sound knowledge. Here we describe five letter activities that incorporate the components of a successful letter intervention.

Alphabet Arcs

We are real fans of the alphabet arcs (see Figure 4.5). These mats provide a template for students to place and manipulate plastic letters. We have found that both teachers and students respond favorably to the alphabet arc. Here we provide an overview of a series of alphabet arc activities. There are many professional resources that describe activities to do with alphabet arcs, the most detailed of which is a professional resource book entitled *Reading Readiness Skills* by Neuhaus Education (available at *http://neuhaus.org/online-store*). We strongly suggest that teachers interested in using alphabet arcs purchase this comprehensive resource.

Alphabet arcs can be used to practice both letter naming and letter-sound knowledge. They can also be carried into a decoding intervention. We find that the alphabet arcs are very useful for interventions because they are engaging, simple, and repetitive. We highlight two very simple arc activities here, but there are many more, including games, mentioned in the *Reading Readiness Skills* book.

The first activity is naming and placing all 26 letters on the arc. Students are given a pile of letters and asked to follow the routine detailed in Figure 4.5. A student will take a letter and first say its name, "*F*." Then the student is asked to

1. Name it.
   Student names the letter.

2. Sound it.
   Student says the sound of the letter.

3. Find it (on the arc).
   Students run the letter underneath each letter outline on the arc until they find the matching one.

4. Place it (on the arc).
   Students place the letter within the letter outline on the arc.

5. Check by singing and touching.
   Student slowly sings the alphabet (using a tune such as "Mary Had a Little Lamb") and touches each letter.

FIGURE 4.5. Alphabet arc routine.

"sound" the letter by saying its sound /fffff/. To find the letter on the arc and place it in the right space, students run the plastic letter under the arc of letters until they find a match. When using the alphabet arc for intervention, it is essential that students follow the routine of naming the letters and saying the sounds. If students do not follow the routine, then the activity amounts to little more than an intricate puzzle. After all of the letters have been placed, the student checks his/her work by singing the alphabet and touching each letter. We suggest *not* using the traditional alphabet song since this speeds up the "*lmnop*" part of the alphabet. Some teachers use the "Mary Had a Little Lamb" tune, or something else, so that students have enough time to touch each letter and say the name. In addition, letters must exactly match the outlines on the alphabet arc, otherwise the activity does not work. Do not run out to the dollar store and try to match the size and exact specifications of the arc. (We tried this and it did not work!) Neuhaus provides a very inexpensive set of letters to use that *do* match the letter outlines, and this detail is important. We like the alphabet arc as an intervention tool because it allows each student to have many practice opportunities, it does not create any paperwork, students love handling the brightly colored letters, and they treat it as a game.

Despite these advantages, however, we have found that the entire arc is overwhelming for students who know less than 10 letters or who are prekindergarteners. We are sure many PreK teachers can imagine the mess that would ensue if they turned their students loose with 26 plastic letters and alphabet arcs! Instead, teachers can use what are called "pre-arc" cards, which have only five or six letter outlines on them. Students follow the same procedures but only with five letters. We worked with a school that used the pre-arc cards in a PreK intervention with great success.

Picture Activities

Activities with pictures are most often used to help students focus on the sounds in words as opposed to the visual forms of the letters. Pictures require students to listen to sounds and match those sounds to a target letter or set of other pictures that share the same beginning sound. Picture–letter matching and picture sorts are two ways in which we can use pictures to help students focus on letter-sounds.

In the picture–letter matching activity, students match alphabet letters to a picture that has the same sound at the beginning. To do this activity, students need to isolate the initial sound of the word represented in a picture, recall the letter that represents that sound, and then put the two together. Although picture–letter matching seems simple, it is actually a multistep task for young learners. To utilize the picture–letter match activity for an alphabet intervention, each student is given sets of pictures to match with three to five letters. In the text box *Picture–Letter Matching*, we provide step-by-step directions for this activity.

Picture sorts are a bit easier because they remove the letter matching portion of the task. With a picture sort students must simply isolate the initial sound of the word in a picture and then match it with other pictures of words beginning with that sound. Picture sorting builds initial sound awareness that is the basis for learning and retaining letter-sound information.

In a picture sort, students match pictures to a target sound, creating columns, instead of matching each picture to a separate letter. The difference between picture–letter matching and picture sorts is that the picture sorts focus more on listening for sounds in words and specifically address initial sound awareness. Picture sorts are a good step backward if a teacher is trying to teach letter-sounds and students are not retaining the information. By doing picture sorts, teachers can determine if students can hear sound differences and are beginning to become phonemically aware. Without basic phonemic awareness students will not benefit from phonics instruction or learn letter-sounds.

Picture sorts were popularized with *Words Their Way* (Invernizzi, Bear, & Templeton, 2011). Detailed instructions and premade sorts can be found in the *Words Their Way* materials. These materials save teachers precious time when preparing intervention lessons. Of course, teachers may also create their own picture sorts using clip art. Picture sorts can be more hands-on and add an element of excitement for students when they are asked to sort actual objects based on beginning sounds.

To conduct a picture sort intervention, start students off with a set of pictures and a set of header pictures with letters. *Header pictures* are well-recognized images that are used to identify the content of columns for the picture sort. They remind the student of the sound that goes in a column. For example, if they see a picture of a cat as the header picture, students will know that words with the same sound as *cat* go under that picture. At the top of their workspace students place the header pictures with letters and then match picture cards to the correct picture or letter in the header column.

PICTURE–LETTER MATCHING

Materials

Clear pictures for each target letter-sound
    Cards with target letters to be matched to each picture.*

Step 1: Review Letter Sounds and Name Pictures

Bb		Mm		Rr

                               Picture
                               Cards

Start by asking students to put their letter cards in three separate piles and their picture cards underneath. There will be multiple copies of each letter card in each pile. Then review the letters' names and sounds with the top letter from each pile as a group. For example, the teacher might say, "Okay, so let's name and sound each of our letter cards. *B*, /b/, *M* /mmm/, *R*, /rrrrr/. Now you name and sound the other letter cards by yourself." As a whole group identify/name each picture in the picture pile and replace them.

Step 2: Model the Matching Process and Do Guided Practice

Bb		Mm		Rr

Demonstrate how to match the picture to the correct letter. For example, flip the first picture card and explain: "I will say the name of a picture and then match it with the letter that has that sound at the beginning. Here I go: *bear*. That has the sound /bbb/ at the beginning—it goes with the letter *b*." Put the picture card right next to the letter. Then have the group do a guided practice item by holding up a new picture and asking the students to match it to the correct letter. We ask students to work quickly and put their completed pairs at the top of their space.

(continued)

---

*For PreK and early kindergarten students we would put both the upper and lowercase letters on the cards. In late kindergarten first grade we would put just the lowercase, since students are reaching the point at which they should have letters mastered.

Step 3: Independent Practice and Corrective Feedback

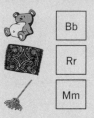

Students create "matches" with the pictures and letter cards as shown above. As students finish, the interventionist can check their work. If there is an incorrect match, the first correction is usually a very generic comment. If a generic comment does not result in a correct match, then more specific scaffolding is offered. For example: "Let's see, this is the letter *S*. It makes the sound /sssss/. You have matched it with a picture of a *fffffan*: ssssss/ /fffffan/. Do they match?" If the student is still having difficulty, the feedback gets even more specific.

Figure 4.6 shows the routine that we use for picture or word sorts. First, we ask students to name each picture. Often we do this as a whole-group activity to make sure that everyone is referring to the pictures with the same labels. Sometimes what is supposed to be a *pail*, for instance, gets called a *bucket*, which can cause confusion if the sort is focused on "*P*" words.[1] Second, we set up the header pictures. These are the pictures with the letter/sounds that create the categories or columns into which the students will sort their pictures. Third, we ask them to use a specific strategy to sort. Students are instructed to say each picture and then say each header picture. Verbalizing the picture's name is very important because the activity is focused on sound awareness, and if students do not say and hear the sounds, they are missing the most important part. Verbalizing each header picture and sort picture allows students multiple opportunities to focus on and hear the initial sounds in each category. In addition, to do sound matching you must *hear* the sounds.

After all the pictures are placed, we ask students to take the header picture card and move it down the column, placing it next to each picture and saying the header and the picture—for example, "*Jam/jar, jam/jack, jam/jail*." The final step of a picture sort and the most often forgotten by both teachers and students is the reflection step. At this step the students must say *why* the pictures are placed in each column. For example, students might say, "These pictures are all together because they all have the /j/ sound at the beginning. These pictures are all together because they have the /t/ sound at the beginning."

---

[1]Like many similar examples, the preference for one of these words over the other can be traced to regional dialect differences. The word *pail* is traditionally a Northern dialect term, whereas *bucket* is Southern.

- Name the picture.
- Set up the column headers.
- Say each picture, say each header picture.
- Place the picture in the right column.
- Check for mistakes.
- DECLARE and REFLECT.
  - These pictures went here because . . .

FIGURE 4.6. Picture sort routine.

Games

Teachers worth their salt can tell you that if you tell students that they are going to "play a game," it can change the energy and motivation that are behind the activity. We share several games that we have found useful for letter-sound and letter-naming practice (see the text box *Games for Letter Activities*). As we described in Chapter 3, there are certain parameters to choosing and using games. There are a number of games that can provide students with meaningful opportunities for practice.

Meaningful Pictures and Motions for Retaining Sounds

Because letter interventions must include different strategies, we share a strategy that was brought to our attention by Dr. Bruce Murray at Auburn University (see Dr. Murray's Reading Genie page for many examples: *www.auburn.edu/academic/education/reading_genie*). Teachers often tell us that although they have worked and worked to teach a letter-sound, a student is not retaining that particular letter-sound. When basic phonemic awareness or other issues can be ruled out as a possible explanation, we suggest using pictures and motions to help solidify the association. (Remember, "Do something different!" is an important principle for delivering intervention.) When children are having trouble retaining the sound that is associated with a particular letter, teaching motions and using pictures can help (see Table 4.2). These are called "sound analogies" (Murray, 2012). For example, as described below in a description of a letter intervention, some students were having difficulty retaining the sound of /g/. Using the motions, a teacher would show students how to get their mouth, tongue, and throat ready for that sound. For the /g/ sound, the mouth is open, tongue at back of mouth, and the throat and voice box are open. Lifting a glass as though you are gulping milk is the motion and mnemonic for this sound. Many teachers will also obtain pictures that show someone gulping milk with a *Gg* next to it. We really like the motions and the mnemonics because the motions that we have seen closely match the target sounds, are memorable to children, and are fun.

GAMES FOR LETTER ACTIVITIES

Games are a wonderful way for students to practice skills in a lively, engaging format. However, as we describe in Chapter 5, games that do not allow maximum practice opportunities are not optimal for a brisk, 30-minute intervention lesson. Whenever possible, we suggest finding ways to keep all students participating in the game, even if it is not their turn to roll the dice or move a player.

Board Games

There is certainly magic to putting any content into a board game format, giving students dice and game pieces, and letting them go at it. With young students we suggest very simple board game formats that allow maximum turns and practice. Find a colorful game board with a fun theme and blank squares. Laminate the board so that you can write in the letters that you want students to practice. We use permanent markers and then erase the ink with nail polish remover. We have two basic formats: one with picture cards and one without. For the one without picture cards, students roll the dice, land on a square, and pronounce the sound that matches the letter. The other students are thinking the answer in their minds and confirm if the student is correct. The format with picture cards also requires a dry erase board for each student. There are no dice in this format. The student flips a card, names the object (a very important step), and identifies the next space on the board with the letter matching the sound. The other students listen to the object being named and then write down the target letter on their dry erase board. We found great templates for these games at *http://donnayoung.org/homeschooling/games/game-boards.htm.*

Letter Stack

This is an ingenious and simple game sure to appeal to active boys (see *http://stayathomeeducator.com/abc-letter-stack-game*). Essentially, two students each take a group of 20–30 small letter tiles (Scrabble size) and work cooperatively to build a letter tower. Each player takes a turn by naming a letter, identifying the sound, and then placing the letter in a tower. The students go back and forth, taking turns. If a letter name or sound is not correctly named, it does not go on the tower. The object of the game is to build the tallest tower of correct letters without it falling. The reward at the end of the game is knocking the tower down—a real delight for students. To keep the intervention on track, carefully monitor the earliest runs with this game to remind students to name letters and sounds. They can get carried away with stacking. (Teachers can also use an old Jenga game with letters written on the wooden pieces. We have also seen teachers use dominoes.)

(continued)

PowerPoint Games

There are a number of templates in Microsoft Word's PowerPoint that allow teachers to build fun, whole-group games. The trick to these games is to keep the whole group participating by having students write down their answers or whisper them to a partner. We like to use the templates to display letters and then ask students to quickly name the sounds that accompany the letters. The initial investment of time to get these ready is a little bit high, but once the game is in place it can be used over and over. We found great templates at *http://people.uncw.edu/ertzbergerj/ppt_games.html*.

Kinesthetic Games

Many teachers have learned that active games in which students participate in gross motor movement can be highly rewarding (especially if your intervention block is at the end of the day). We have seen teachers use old Twister games with letters written on them and beach balls to help students rehearse letter-sounds. With these games, it is important to very clearly stipulate the rules and routines so that the action part is used for the purpose of rehearsing letter-sounds. Keep tight control on the game when it is being introduced and gradually release this control as students learn to play it.

TABLE 4.2. Meaningful Associations for Letter-Sounds

Phoneme	Mouth feel	Gesture	Meaningful representation
/a/	Jaw and tongue are down.	Rub eyes with fists.	Crying baby
/b/	Lips start out together, then they open and a puff of air comes out. Voice box on.	Pat chest.	Beating heart
/c/	Tongue is humped in the back of your mouth.	Pull index finger to click camera.	Click
/d/	Tip of tongue touches above your top teeth. Voice box on.	Knock on table.	Door knock
/e/	Mouth open, tongue behind bottom teeth.	Hand cupped behind ear.	Hard to hear
/f/	Top teeth touch your bottom lip.	Swirl open hand.	Electric fan
/g/	Mouth is open, tongue humped at back of mouth. Voice box on.	Raise glass.	Gulping milk
/h/	Air comes out of mouth.	Pant.	Hot dog
/i/	Mouth is open, tongue is slightly lowered.	Mouth open, tongue out.	Icky sticky

Note. Reprinted by permission of Bruce A. Murray.

For some students a similar strategy using mirrors helps illustrate the physical motions for creating a specific sound (Lindamood & Lindamood, 1998). Teachers have students use mirrors to check their musculature for making a sound. For instance, with the /b/ sound a teacher might say:

> "Okay, this is a sound where my lips start together and then they are going to explode open, like 'Boom!' and my throat will buzz. We are going to say this sound. Get your mirror out. Are your lips together? On the count of 3, we are going to say 'Boom.' When you say that /b/ sound watch your mouth open. Here we go—1, 2, 3, *boom*! Did your mouth open? Now let's do it again, but we are going to say '*Boom*' without the *-oom* part. We are just going to say /b/. Can you do it? Get your mouth together—1, 2, 3 /b/!"

Although this might seem tedious and unnecessary, we have found that for some students this type of specific, physical instruction is really helpful.

Dictating Letters, or "Spelling Test"

Although the focus of most letter interventions is not on the writing of letters, we believe that adding some dictation to the end of a letter intervention can be great practice. With the kids we call this activity "spelling test." Kindergartners especially feel cool and grown-up doing a spelling test, like the big kids. We like to do this with dry erase boards and colorful markers, and we like to ask students to do it as quickly as possible to practice fluency with letters. Usually this section of a lesson is only about 5 minutes.

Children divide their dry erase boards into six sections and number the sections. In some cases we use permanent markers to subdivide the board ahead of time. (Nail polish remover or some other acetone product can take off the lines later.) For each of the items, we ask the students to write the letter representing the target sound. We say the sound in isolation (e.g., /v/), a sample word, then the sound again, and finally ask the students to write the letter. Such a routine would sound like this:

> "Okay, I want you to listen for #1. I am going to say a sound. Watch my mouth, listen, and then write down the correct letter for that sound. If you can write both the upper- and lowercase letters, you get 2 points. Here we go: /vvvvvvvv/ like the /v/ in *violin*, /vvvvv/. Write the letter that matches the sound /vvvv/."

At the end we all flip our boards and do a group check. Often the teacher has her own board and walks the students through checking their letters. They get a point for each one they get correct and a bonus point for each one in which they can write both the upper- and lowercase letters. Reversals are correct unless the reversed letter creates a new letter (e.g., a *b/d* reversal).

Once students have about five out of six correct, we intersperse items whereby we isolate the letter-sound with items in which we provide only the name of something with the target sound and the students have to isolate that sound. So we might say:

> "Now this time, I am going to see if you can do the hard work and figure out the letter that matches the first sound in *mmmmmmmmat*. Write down the letter for the first sound in *mmmmmmmmat*."

This is a slightly more difficult skill that tells us if students have acquired some level of initial sound awareness rather than merely memorizing answers. If they can hear initial sounds, then we know that they are well on their way to reading. Some students want to show us that they can hear other sounds in the words. We allow them to show us their knowledge and praise them for it, but we do not add bonus points to their scores, since it is that we are interested in only initial sound knowledge at this time.

Goal Setting and Progress Monitoring

As we discussed in Chapter 2, there are two ways in which student progress can be monitored. MM allows us to evaluate the impact of instruction directly on the skill at the center of the intervention. GOM allows us to assess reading improvement more broadly and can be measured over a longer period of time. When letter naming or letter-sound knowledge is the focus of intervention, the two different forms of progress monitoring may result in the evaluation of very similar skills.

Assessing the impact of letter interventions on letter knowledge is usually very straightforward and consists of having students identify letters that are presented in random order. Of particular importance, the letters that are assessed should match the letters that have actually been instructed as part of the intervention. Although additional letters may also be assessed, the interventionist specifically wants to know if the intervention is resulting in the student's identification of the taught letters. Figure 4.4 shows that each week the intervention teacher introduced four letters to her students (three of which were not already known). In its simplest form, progress monitoring toward mastery requires the intervention teacher to assess the three newly taught letters at the end of each week. Following each assessment the teacher would want to note how many letters the student correctly identified. Importantly, if certain letters were not mastered, then these letters could be the focus of ongoing instruction in the future. The goal for the students in this group would be to accurately identify 100% (3/3) of the newly taught letters each week and to retain those letters during subsequent weeks. Thus, the MM measure would include three letters during Week 1 of intervention, but this would increase to six letters after Week 2 and would continue to increase as new letters were introduced.

In addition to monitoring whether students were learning newly taught letters or newly taught sounds, the intervention teacher would also want to know if students were generally moving toward important end-of-the-year goals. As suggested earlier, students who are in a Tier 2 group that is focused on letter skills should have automatic command of letter names-sounds by the end of the year. Although accomplishment of this goal would be most common for kindergarten students, it is possible that some struggling students in first or even second grade may be working toward this goal as well. A commonly used GOM for students at this level is a measure of letter-sound fluency. Students are presented with a sheet of random letters and asked to identify the sound that each of these letters makes. The task is timed; students are asked to identify as many sounds as they can in 1 minute. This factor of timing is helpful because teachers can tell whether students are becoming more automatic with this skill over the weeks of intervention. Measuring automaticity is a wonderful way of documenting even small amounts of reading growth over extended periods of time.

Evaluating Interventions

As described in Chapter 3, we suggest that teachers use three tools as they deliver and evaluate interventions: (1) intervention logs, (2) progress monitoring results, and (3) fidelity checklists. We provide examples and discuss how these three tools might look for a letter intervention using the group introduced in Figure 4.3.

The sample intervention log in Figure 4.7 shows the interventionist's plans and notes for one week of intervention. As described in Chapter 3, this is a simple form upon which the interventionist tracks student attendance and makes anecdotal records that will guide future decisions and instructional planning. When we see a high-quality intervention log, we can almost see the wheels turning inside the brain of the interventionist, who is continually forming hypotheses about a child's progress. On this intervention log we note that the interventionist is pleased with the progress for Cammy and Juan. She did make a comment that she believes Juan's confusion with the /b/ and /p/ sounds is the result of his first language, since the articulation of these sounds in Spanish is not always clear, but she is not concerned about his progress. With Bryce, she has recorded an absence on Wednesday and wonders if he was absent the previous week. We can see that she is hypothesizing that his lack of progress might be due to attendance issues. With both Bryce and David the interventionist has concerns and notes that they are both having problems with G. Her comments suggest a shift to sound analogies and associated pictures, which reflects her hypothesis that new strategies are needed for these students.

Intervention Log

Instructional focus of group: _Letter-sound and phonemic awareness—reviewing and solidifying B, M, R, S, T, G, N, P—lots of review needed on G—all saying /j/ for sound._

Week of: _January 30–Feb. 3_ **Intervention teacher**: _____

Curriculum/materials: _Picture sorting B, M, R, S, & T, G, N, P (later mix the sort for letters that are not mastered). Alphabet arc with just these letters. (Don't forget "Sound it" in arc routine. Personalized follow-the-path games with these letter-sounds._

Attendance and Observation Records

Student Name: _David_	Student Name: _Bryce_	Student Name: _Cammy_
Attendance: (Circle if absent) M T W Th F	**Attendance**: (Circle if absent) M T (W) Th F	**Attendance**: (Circle if absent) M T W Th F
Notes: _Still struggling with G—gets right 1/2 of the time. Need a new strategy for that sound (Orton motion pictures?) Picked up ~ ☺_	**Notes**: _Has B, S_ _Others struggling—N, M, G—more pa? Motion pictures?_ _Did he miss last week?_	**Notes**: _Wow. She has all but P._
Student Name: _Tenisha_	Student Name: _Juan_	Student Name:
Attendance: (Circle if absent) M T W Th F	**Attendance**: (Circle if absent) M T W Th F	**Attendance**: (Circle if absent) M T W Th F
Notes: _Tired at intervention._ _Is she bored? She already knew all but G prior to intervention. Speed up? Exit?_	**Notes**: _Doing well—confusing B/P sounds._ _This is probably a 1s language thing. Not concerned._	**Notes**:

FIGURE 4.7. Sample Intervention Log.

Figure 4.8 shows the progress monitoring data for David, which indicate that David is progressing and improving, responding well to the intervention. During the initial diagnostic test, he knew 10 letters and after 6 weeks of intervention he knew all letters taught and all letters of the alphabet as indicated on the post-test. Between the diagnostic test and the posttest, the MM data demonstrated that David consistently learned and retained the letters taught to him. The results indicate that he has learned this skill and that instruction was effective. It is also positive to note that David's letter-sound fluency scores also improved during the time of the intervention. This suggests that the intervention was having a positive impact on this broader outcome. As David moves on to a new skill that will be

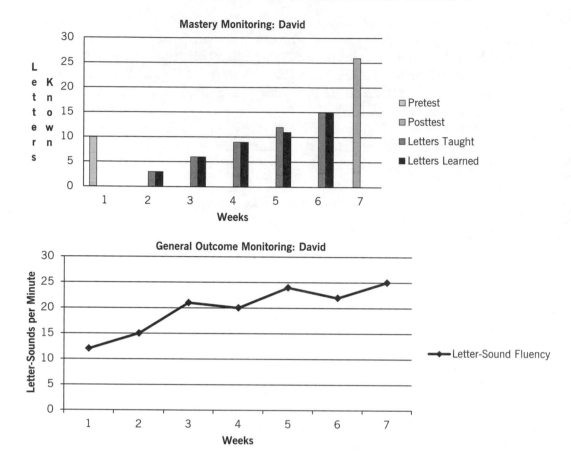

FIGURE 4.8. Progress monitoring data for David.

taught to him, his letter-sound fluency scores will continue to be monitored to ensure that this skill continues to improve.

Bryce, on the other hand, is not responding quite as well. As shown in Figure 4.9, he began the intervention knowing 12 letters and then in the subsequent weeks he demonstrated difficulty learning new letters. At the end of 6 weeks he only knew 11 letters. This pattern shows inconsistency and a lack of retention. In addition, Bryce has not made progress on letter-sound fluency. When comparing his progress on this measure to that of two of his peers also working in his instructional group, it is clear that his peers are responding much more positively. The intervention does not appear to be working as well for him, and the movement toward using sound analogies is probably a good idea.

A third tool that can be helpful for evaluating an intervention is the Fidelity Checklist for Letter and Letter-Sound Interventions in form 4.2. As described in earlier chapters, the fidelity checklist captures the "active ingredients" of the intervention and helps teacher and student stay on track. In terms of letter interventions, the active ingredients are really quite simple: The intervention must specifically focus on one of two behaviors—letter naming or letter-sound identification. When observing a letter intervention, we like to see that the majority of the time is spent on activities in which the students look at the letters and produce their sounds or names. As with all interventions, we like to see 2–3 weeks of planning that reflect a series of letters that will be taught. The letters selected should reflect diagnostic information and should be ordered based on the types of letter-sounds, as discussed earlier (e.g., similar sounds and or visual symbols would not be taught in the same group—*b*/*p*, *t*/*d*). The plans should also reflect progress monitoring data. Lastly, we believe that the intervention log should contain very specific comments about what students are or are not retaining.

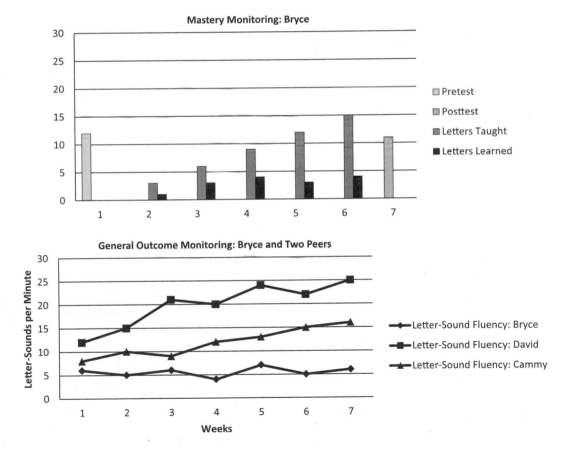

FIGURE 4.9. Progress monitoring data for Bryce.

Conclusion

In this chapter we have provided an overview of letter interventions. Although instructional interventions with letters represent high-quality teaching, they are unique. Within an RTI framework, the teaching is brisk and well planned but different. More specificity is offered, more practice opportunities are available, different ways to associate letters and sounds are used, and more individualized feedback is offered. Our experience tells us that letter information is very teachable, and often students take far less time to learn this information than initially projected. When letter-sound instruction slows down, the issue is almost always phonemic awareness. Although letter-sound knowledge does not guarantee the eventual acquisition of reading proficiency, it is essential and children who do not have it are at a disadvantage.

FORM 4.1

Letter Intervention Goal-Setting Sheet

Instructional focus of group: _____

_____

Intervention goal: To _____ by _____

Meeting days: _____ Meeting time: _____ Hrs/week: _____

Progress monitoring measure: _____

Frequency of administration: _____

Student Diagnostic Data

Student Name:	**Student Name:**	**Student Name:**
Diagnostic Data: **Lowercase:** a b c d e f g h i j k l m n o p q r s t u v w x y z **Uppercase:** A B C D E F G H I J K L M N O P Q R S T U V W X Y Z	**Diagnostic Data:** **Lowercase:** a b c d e f g h i j k l m n o p q r s t u v w x y z **Uppercase:** A B C D E F G H I J K L M N O P Q R S T U V W X Y Z	**Diagnostic Data:** **Lowercase:** a b c d e f g h i j k l m n o p q r s t u v w x y z **Uppercase:** A B C D E F G H I J K L M N O P Q R S T U V W X Y Z
Student Name:	**Student Name:**	**Student Name:**
Diagnostic Data: **Lowercase:** a b c d e f g h i j k l m n o p q r s t u v w x y z **Uppercase:** A B C D E F G H I J K L M N O P Q R S T U V W X Y Z	**Diagnostic Data:** **Lowercase:** a b c d e f g h i j k l m n o p q r s t u v w x y z **Uppercase:** A B C D E F G H I J K L M N O P Q R S T U V W X Y Z	**Diagnostic Data:** **Lowercase:** a b c d e f g h i j k l m n o p q r s t u v w x y z **Uppercase:** A B C D E F G H I J K L M N O P Q R S T U V W X Y Z

Fidelity Checklist
for Letter and Letter-Sound Interventions

Date:						
Goals						
A. Measuring Intervention Goals[1]						
• Does the intervention goal state specifically what students are to do as a result of the intervention?						
o Naming letters? Or sounds?						
o By a specific date?						
o Specific criteria for success (e.g., 24/26 lowercase letters)?						
B. Intervention Content						
OBSERVATION						
• List activities observed during one intervention:						
• Do the activities provide practice with the behavior that is being measured in A (e.g., naming letters? naming letter-sounds?)						
• Is the majority of time being spent on the major goal of letter naming[2] or letter-sound[3] (70–80%)?						
• Is each student getting at least three opportunities to individually practice each target letter or letter-sound?						
PLANNING						
• Is there long-term planning across weeks that reflects a scope (e.g., specific letters) and sequence (e.g., the order for teaching those letters)?						
• Are the specific letter-sounds being targeted a reflection of diagnostic data?						
• Are dates for progress monitoring shown?						

(continued)

[1]Place a check in the box if the answer to the question is yes.

[2]Appropriate for PreK and beginning of kindergarten.

[3]Appropriate for midkindergarten and beginning of first grade and beyond.

INTERVENTION LOG							
• Are there specific comments reflecting letter-sound learning? (e.g., specific letters learned, not too many generic comments—*Nice!*)							
• Do the comments show that plans are being altered as a result of progress monitoring data?							
ADDITIONAL NOTES:							

CHAPTER 5

Interventions for Decoding and Phonemic Segmentation

- What research is available on decoding and phonemic segmentation instruction?

- As children learn to read, what are the phases of decoding through which they progress?

- Why do beginning struggling readers experience difficulty in transitions between decoding phases?

- How are diagnostic assessments helpful tools to inform intervention instruction focused on decoding and phonemic segmentation?

- What elements of planning and assessment make decoding interventions the strongest?

- What are some specific decoding and phonemic segmentation interventions that provide students with multiple, engaging and meaningful opportunities to practice decoding skills?

- What items should be on a fidelity checklist for decoding interventions?

What Does the Research Say about Decoding Instruction?
• •

By the end of first grade students should have a store of 300–500 words that they know automatically (Snow et al., 1998). These words should include both high-frequency words—which are the words that occur very often in the English language and that sometimes contain irregular letter-sound relationships (e.g., *the, is, come, do*)—and decodable words that they can "sound out," independently. As any first-grade teacher will tell you, the ability to analyze an unknown word and blend together the sounds to produce a fully pronounced word is a major milestone. When students decode words, they are showing that they are able to apply the letter-sound content that they have learned. Application of letter-sound information is pivotal, and in our experience, a skill that most often trips up struggling readers.

As a mature reader, you probably rarely need to sound out and blend together words because most of the words that you read are ones that you have seen hundreds, if not thousands, of times. These words were decoded or sounded out by you some time ago and have been fused into your memory so that you currently access them by sight. However, if you come across a challenging word that you have not seen before, such as *redacted*, you could apply your knowledge of letter-sounds and meaning patterns to help you. Then, with subsequent encounters with a word such as *redacted*, you would access the word automatically, by sight.

A great deal of research documents the development of decoding and why learning to decode is so important. Adams (1990) and many others explain that English is fundamentally an alphabetic language with symbols (letters) representing speech sounds (phonemes). Thus, reading English requires students to "break the code" of letters to pronounce words. As it turns out, readers go through a process whereby they first decode words slowly and sometimes with a great deal of concentration, but after doing so three or four times they learn the words automatically and can recall them promptly without an arduous decoding process (Ehri, 2005).

When learners decode words by using letter-sound information and blending together sounds, they are using an independent strategy for reading that bootstraps their acquisition of more and more words. Share (2008) called this the *self-teaching hypothesis*; he explained that application of the code enables readers to independently decode words during reading that are eventually added to their sight vocabulary. The ability to accurately decode and then automatize words precedes fluent, efficient reading (see Figure 3.2). If students cannot decode accurately, then they will struggle with fluency.

Decoding on the Developmental Continuum

Developmentally, decoding takes place after students have acquired most letter-sounds and are aware of initial phonemes. The ability to decode also takes place within a particular developmental sequence that has been well researched (Ehri, 2005). Figure 5.1 shows the developmental phases that readers go through as they gradually learn to apply what they know about the letter-sounds in words. The

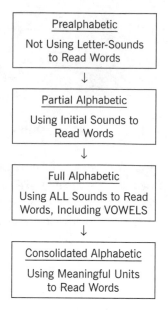

FIGURE 5.1. Development of decoding ability.

names of these phases all have the word *alphabetic* in them because each phase represents a new insight about, and level of application of, alphabetic information. At the prealphabetic phase readers are not actually using letter-sound information to recognize words. Instead they might use salient features of words to help, like the two *o*'s in *look*, or the length of the word *elephant*. Note that although they might be paying attention to letters, they are not making use of the letter-*sound* information. In the example of *look*, the reader does not know the sound that the two *oo*'s make and would likely identify other *oo* words (e.g., *book, took, cook*) as *look*.

Once readers have entered the partial alphabetic phase, they have gained the insight that letters represent sounds and they can use this information to help them, especially at the beginnings of words. For example, if presented with two words, *cat* and *bag*, a partial alphabetic reader would be able to identify which of the two was *cat*. This is possible because the reader is using initial sound associations to recognize the word. However, when partial alphabetic readers are faced with two words beginning with the *same sound*, they may become confused. What partial alphabetic readers lack is knowledge of vowels and how they work. Because all words have vowels, they are only able to partially use letter-sounds when reading.

At the full alphabetic phase, readers are able to apply what they know about vowel sounds to fully decode a word. The very first application of letter-sound information occurs with the simplest of words, where there is a one-to-one letter-sound correspondence (e.g., *get, hit, tap, bat, cup*). Although these words seem very simple to the mature reader, it is no small task for a beginning reader to sound out each letter and then to blend the sounds together in a cohesive whole. Many first-grade teachers have watched a reader who can sound each letter but not blend them together. It might sound something like this: "/b/, /a/, /t/ . . . /b/, /a/, /t/ . . . *apple?*" In this example, the reader has trouble retaining all three sounds in memory and putting them together. The task of blending the letters in a word together can be very challenging for many readers, and decoding interventions close this gap. Once readers can decode short-vowel words with the CVC pattern, they seem to take off and become more efficient at reading. The transition from the partial alphabetic phase to the full alphabetic phase is a transition with which many readers struggle, and it is this transition that many reading interventions in the area of decoding are aiming to facilitate.

Eventually, readers move into what is called the *consolidated alphabetic phase*, in which they move beyond making simple, one-to-one associations to seeing groups or units of letters that typically occur together. Through their experience decoding, consolidated alphabetic readers begin to notice that words can be seen in parts (e.g., *str-ip, b-eat-ing*). They also become acquainted with common multiletter units such as long-vowel patterns (e.g., *ea, a__e, oa*), simple inflections (e.g., *-ing, -er*), blends (e.g., *str-, gr-, sl-*), and digraphs (e.g., *th, sh, ch*). When readers consolidate letter units, they are able to read more fluently and efficiently, and they are propelled into the next step on our developmental continuum, fluency (see Figure 5.1).

As they apply letter-sound information in full alphabetic decoding, readers are using phonemic segmentation skills (Lemon & Fuchs, 2010; Nation & Hulme, 1997). Phonemic segmentation is the ability to *hear* a word and break that word down into each of its *sounds*. This skill undergirds or supports decoding. A reader who can segment phonemes would be able to tell you that the sounds in *got* are /g/ + /o/ + /t/. If a student cannot hear or identify the individual sounds in a word, he/she will not be able to apply letters to these sounds when decoding. Notice that this oral competency is very similar to the analysis that takes place when readers decode words as they are reading. Students who successfully navigate the transition from partial to full alphabetic reader are most likely acquiring phonemic segmentation skills in the process of learning to blend words together. These readers are able to segment sounds (phonemes) without direct instruction and appear to self-teach the phonemic segmentation that supports decoding. Readers who are struggling, like many of those who will need decoding interventions, may not be able to segment sounds (phonemes) and will likely require explicit instruction in phonemic segmentation. We suggest pairing phonemic segmentation instruction with decoding instruction when diagnostic data indicate that phonemic segmentation skills are lacking.

Diagnostic Assessments
to Inform Intervention Goals

For most decoding interventions in the primary grades, the major focus is supporting students in blending words with the short-vowel CVC pattern. Several pieces of research indicate that first graders should be able to blend together a short-vowel CVC word by at least the middle of the first grade year (Riedel, 2007). If students have reached the end of first grade or the beginning of second grade and cannot do this, then they are in need of an intervention that is focused on decoding short-vowel CVC words. Teachers working with struggling readers first need to determine if a reader who has not met the benchmark is in need of decoding help and then to identify which letter-sounds (usually vowels) require attention. Many students may also require support with phonemic segmentation skills. Literacy screening assessments typically include a decoding measure, especially in the first grade, but schools that are not using a decoding measure can quickly determine if a student is in need of decoding help by administering one of the simple decoding measures described in the following paragraph. Prior to administering a diagnostic decoding measure, make sure students are solid in automatic letter-sound recognition of consonants.

We have encountered students in the second or third grade who have struggles in fluency that can be traced back to decoding issues. In these cases students have difficulty with consolidating letter patterns (e.g., long-vowel patterns, *r*-controlled vowels) and/or struggles with multisyllabic words. However, in PreK through second grade, common decoding issues do not include consolidated letter patterns or multisyllabic words. In fact, it is in late first grade and early second grade that increased attention is given to teaching these patterns to everyone. In this book, therefore, we do not focus on consolidated alphabetic decoding issues. We place our attention on the transition from partial to full alphabetic decoding.

Decoding Assessments

There are a number of simple decoding measures that we recommend using to identify the specific vowels and other letter-sound patterns (e.g., blends and digraphs) that students cannot decode. The text box *Sources for Free Decoding and Phonemic Segmentation Assessments* lists a number of measures. Most contain lists of words that include each of the five short-vowel sounds as well as short vowel words with consonant blends (e.g., *grip, slap*) and digraphs (e.g., *ship, chap*). Often these measures include "nonsense words" or "pseudowords" that follow common English spelling patterns (e.g., *vun, shep, lan*). Pseudowords are sometimes used in decoding measures instead of real words because the ability to read pseudowords assesses a reader's skills in decoding and blending together unknown words. A test administrator can be sure that the reader has not seen the word if it

SOURCES FOR FREE DECODING AND PHONEMIC SEGMENTATION ASSESSMENTS

Cool Tools: Informal Reading Assessment
www.paec.org/itrk3/files/pdfs/readingpdfs/cooltoolsall.pdf

Click steps:
- Go to *www.paec.org/itrk3/files/pdfs/readingpdfs/cooltoolsall.pdf*

This set of free assessments contains assessments in the areas of phonological aware-ness, phonics, fluency, vocabulary, and comprehension. The set has a full complement of assessments covering many skills, including rhyming, initial sound recognition, sylla-ble awareness, blending, and segmentation. The phonics survey assesses letter-sounds and contains 80 words to evaluate students' abilities to read words with short vowels, blends, digraphs, silent-e, long vowels, *r*-controlled vowels, prefixes, suffixes, and mul-tisyllabic words.

Diagnostic Decoding Surveys at Really Great Reading
www.rgrco.com

Click steps:
- Tools for Beginning Readers
- Assessments
- Diagnostic Decoding Surveys

This 20-page booklet contains two decoding measures, one at the beginning level and one at the advanced level. The beginning level contains three sections: real words, sentences, and nonsense words. The tool contains five sight words and 15 read words containing short-vowel patterns, blends, or digraphs. There are also three sentences containing both regular and irregular words. The nonsense word section contains 10 words that represent short vowels and short vowels with blends and digraphs. There is a high-quality scoring protocol that breaks out the students' error patterns by letter-sound.

Sylvia Greene's Informal Word Analysis Inventory at LINCS
http://lincs.edu.gov/readingprofiles/index.htm

Click steps:
- Word analysis
- Assessments paragraph: Download a free copy of Greene's Informal Word Analy-sis Inventory from this site.

(continued)

Abecedarian Reading Assessment at Balanced Reading
www.balancedreading.com/assessment/abecedarian.pdf

Click steps:

- Balancedreading.com
- Get a free copy of the Abecedarian (K–1) Reading Assessment

This assessment set contains a battery of tools that cover letter knowledge, phonological awareness, phoneme awareness, alphabetic principle, vocabulary, and decoding. The decoding measure has two parts.

is a pseudoword. (See the textbox *Advantages and Disadvantages of Using Pseudowords in Assessments.*) Figure 5.2 shows the results of a decoding measure for Sakeela, a second grader at the end of the year. The results of this sample reflect the profile of a student who needs a decoding intervention. Although Sakeela knows some high-frequency words by sight, she is confused by short vowels. The data in both the Real Words section and the Nonsense Words section intersect to indicate her inconsistency in this area. She pronounced some sounds correctly in the Real and Nonsense Words sections (e.g., *lid, rag, zin*) but others incorrectly (e.g., *dot, hum, bet, yud, vop, keb*). About 14 of her errors, the highest proportion of errors, involved short vowels and short-vowel–long-vowel confusions. Sakeela has begun to transition into the full alphabetic phase of word recognition but has not solidified his knowledge of short vowels. He needs greater attention and help in this area.

Phonemic Segmentation Assessments

If the students whom you are teaching do not have strong decoding skills and you suspect that they might require some support in phonemic segmentation, both the Cool Tools and Abecedarian assessments listed in the text box *Sources for Free Decoding and Phonemic Segmentation Assessments* contain phonemic segmentation assessments. During these assessments the test administrator pronounces a word and then asks the student to break the word down into its parts. The assessment is completely oral, and there are no word cards or other visual stimuli for the student to use. For example, the administrator might say the word *moo*, and the student would be required to break the word into its two parts: /m/ + /oo/. Depending on the assessment, the student either receives a point for each segment that he/she correctly identifies (e.g., *moo*—2 points), or the student receives only 1 point if the word is correctly segmented in its entirety. Most phonemic segmentation assessments progress from simple, two-phoneme words to three- and

ADVANTAGES AND DISADVANTAGES OF USING PSEUDOWORDS IN DECODING ASSESSMENTS

Pseudowords are madeup words that conform to typical English patterns. The following are examples of pseudowords: *vun, rop, stip*, and *heth*.

There are both advantages and disadvantages to using pseudowords in decoding assessments. It is possible for readers, especially those who struggle, to memorize whole words without decoding them, and this can be problematic in a decoding assessment. For example, a reader could learn holistically or remember the word *hot*. Perhaps the reader grew up in a bakery, saw that word on an oven door, and learned the word but did not know how the letter-sounds /h/ + /o/ + /t/ mapped onto the word. If this word were used in a decoding measure and the student read it accurately, then the test administrator would incorrectly assume that the student could decode the sounds in the word. When we use pseudoword tests with students, we usually model reading pseudowords, emphasizing that the words are not "real" and will not sound like real words. We sometimes even say, for example: "*Jom. Jom.* What's a *jom*? How do you *jom*? You don't know, do you, because *jom* is not a real word. The words you are going to read are silly like that. They are not real words, so don't try to make them sound like real words." Some testers will tell students that they are learning a new language called *robot talk*. This makes the new secret pseudolanguage playful and funny. We just remind students that they want to get the words right so that the other robots will understand them.

The disadvantage of using pseudowords is that readers have no recognizable target against which to test the accuracy of their pronunciations. Part of what helps readers decode is their vocabulary and knowledge of words. For example, Tresha was trying to decode the word *got*, but she was having trouble with the vowel sound. She checked her decoding attempts with her knowledge of words. We could hear her checking her decoding attempts against known words: "/g/ + /o/ + /t/. *Gat*? No that's not a word. /g/ + /o/ + /t/. *Gooooot*? *Gooot*? Say it fast, *got*! Yeh, *got*! That's a word."

We suggest using decoding assessments that include both real and pseudowords because the data from each type of assessment will inform a high-quality decoding intervention. Assessment of both real and pseudowords will create a clear picture of the letter-sounds that the student knows and those that must be learned.

four-phoneme words. In addition, most phonemic segmentation tests provide a number of examples for teacher modeling. Because phonemic segmentation can be an unfamiliar skill, it is important to make sure that students understand the task. Providing different examples can help. If the student is unable to segment words after several examples, proceed with the assessment. Because students who need decoding interventions often have difficulty with phonemic segmentation, we always suggest that teachers record students' attempts at segmenting the words by writing down what they said.

The results of James's phonemic segmentation assessment are very similar to those of many students that we have seen. Figure 5.3 shows James's responses to

Error Column Totals

Student __Sakeela Student__

Grade __2__ Date __July 9, 2008__

Examiner __Susan Doe__

BEGINNING DECODING SURVEY RECORDING FORM **A**

Observations
Check the appropriate boxes:
- ☑ Reads sound by sound, then blends word
- ☑☑ Possible b/d or b/p reversal
- ☐ Quick to guess
- ☐ Slow

	Real Words	No Try	Sight Word	Sound Added or Omitted	Consonant Initial	Consonant Final	Short Vowel	Consonant Digraph: ch, sh, ck, wh, th / Letters qu	Blend
Sight Words	1 see ✓								
	2 one ✓								
	3 they ✓								
	4 you ✓								
	5 are and		X						
CVC Words	6 rag ✓		NA						
	7 lid ✓		NA						
	8 dot don't		NA	X			X		
	9 hum him		NA			X			
	10 bet best		NA	X					
Digraphs & Short Vowels	11 rich ✓		NA			NA			
	12 shop ✓		NA		NA				
	13 tack take		NA			NA	X		
	14 quit quite		NA		NA		X		
	15 moth mother		NA	X		NA	X		Blend
Blends & Short Vowels	16 dust ✓		NA				NA		
	17 step ✓		NA				NA		
	18 trip tip rip		NA	XX	X		NA		XX
	19 pond bond SC		NA		X		NA		
	20 brag ✓		NA				NA		

Sentences (irregularly spelled sight words are italics)	No Try	Sight Word	Sound Added or Omitted	Initial	Final	Short Vowel	Digraph & Letters qu	Blend
21-26 *The* a ✓ cat ✓ hid ~~in~~ on ~~a~~ the ✓ box.		XX				X	NA	NA
27-35 *The* ✓ fresh ✓ fish ✓ ~~is~~ was ✓ still ✓ on ✓ *the* ✓ wet ✓ ~~grass~~ glass.		X						X
36-42 Six ✓ flat ✓ shells ✓ ~~were~~ are ✓ in ✓ my ✓ ~~bath~~ bathtub.		X	XXX					

	Nonsense Words	No Try	Sight Word	Sound Added or Omitted	Initial	Final	Short Vowel	Digraph & Letters qu	Blend
CVC	43 vop vope		NA				X	NA	NA
	44 yud yude		NA				X	NA	NA
	45 zin ✓		NA					NA	NA
	46 keb kept		NA	X		X		NA	NA
Digraphs	47 shap shape		NA		NA		X		NA
	48 thid ✓		NA		NA				NA
	49 chut ✓		NA		NA				NA
	50 weck wreck		NA		X	NA			NA

29 Words Read Correctly (out of 50 total)	Error Column Totals	0	5	9	3	1	9	0	3
		No Try	Sight Word	Sound Added or Omitted	Initial / Consonant	Final	Short Vowel	Digraph & Letters qu	Blend

FIGURE 5.2. Sample decoding results. Copyright 2008 by Really Great Reading. Reprinted by permission.

the Yopp–Singer Test of Phoneme Segmentation. He was able to correctly segment, or break, eight of the 22 words into sounds on the assessment. Five of his correct answers were two-phoneme words (e.g., *no, me, lay, at,* and *do*) and three were three-phoneme words. In several of his attempts James segmented the word into the onset (beginning sound) and rime (vowel with ending). This suggests that he is aware of and can segment beginning sounds, but is challenged by remembering three sounds. In several cases he simply repeated the word. Students will do this when they are making attempts to segment. They start out with every intention

Yopp-Singer Test of Phoneme Segmentation

Score (# correct) ___7___

Name ___JAMES___

Date ☐ fall _____
☐ winter _____
☐ spring _____

Directions: Today we're going to play a word game. I'm going to say a word and I want you to break the word apart. You are going to tell me each sound of the word in order. For example, if I say old, you should say /o/ /l/ /d/. Let's try a few together.

Practice items: (assist in segmenting, if necessary)   ride (3)   go (2)   man (3)

Test items: (Circle those items that the student correctly segments; incorrect responses are recorded on the blank line following the item.)

1. dog   _d - og_
2. keep   _k - eep_
3. fine   _f - ine_
4. no (circled)   _____
5. she   _she_
6. wave (circled)   _____
7. grew   _g - oo_
8. that   _th - at_
9. red   _r - i - d_
10. me (circled)   _____
11. sat   _sat_

12. lay (circled)   _l - ay_
13. race   _r - ace_
14. zoo   _zoo_
15. three   _t - ea_
16. job   _j - ob_
17. in   _in_
18. ice   _ice_
19. at (circled)   _____
20. top (circled)   _____
21. by   _by_
22. do (circled)   _____

FIGURE 5.3. Sample test of phonemic segmentation. Copyright 1995 by Hallie Kay Yopp. Reprinted by permission from Yopp (1995).

to segment, but just don't know where the breaks should occur. Often students who are transitioning into the full alphabetic phase could benefit from phonemic segmentation instruction to build their capacity for decoding. If James's phonemic segmentation scores had been closer to 15 or 16 correct items, we would not suggest pairing phonemic awareness instruction with decoding instruction. Given his profile, however, we believe that some phonemic segmentation instruction would support James in his transition into full alphabetic decoding.

What to Do with Diagnostic Assessment Data

Once the diagnostic assessment data have been collected, teachers will have specific information about the degree to which students are able to fully decode words and the vowel sounds they know. The phonemic segmentation data will indicate if students possess the ability to break down words orally into sounds, a skill that supports decoding. The diagnostic data guide the intervention by informing its content. If students are weak in both phonemic segmentation and decoding, then about 20–30% of intervention time should be devoted to phonemic segmentation because it builds capacity for decoding. If students have some phonemic segmentation but are weak in decoding, more of the intervention time should be devoted to decoding practice. The decoding data will indicate which vowel sounds students are able to decode in words. Within a decoding intervention group we usually find that knowledge of vowels is spotty, with some students decoding a few vowels accurately and other students having very little knowledge of vowels. Unless there is a consistent pattern of need with the intervention group, we suggest teaching the vowel sounds in a specific order. Occasionally, all of the students in a group will show mastery of a few short vowels, but this is usually not the case. If there is a short vowel that a group *does* know, it is usually the short *a*. In the next section we describe how an interventionist used the diagnostic information, along with an established sequence, to plan her intervention.

For each intervention group, we suggest recording the decoding score and short vowel(s) that each student knows on one sheet along with other pertinent information that we discuss in the next section. We provide a blank template for recording these scores in Form 5.1. This sheet can be used to record students' decoding knowledge on both real and pseudowords. If a teacher or school does not use pseudowords, then this section can be ignored. There is also space to include phonemic segmentation results, if given. The completed sample form in Figure 5.4 shows a fairly typical group of students. Notice that this group exhibits some differences in short-vowel knowledge but enough intersections to support focused instruction in a small group. Taylor has the least knowledge of short vowels and Damon is the strongest, but all of the students show inconsistencies in their performance, especially when the pseudoword and real word performance is contrasted. These inconsistencies, reflected by the ability to read the vowel sound correctly in

Diagnostic Data Template for Decoding

Instructional focus of group: _Blending together short-vowel, CVC words with some phonemic segmentation for support._

Diagnostic measure used: _Beginning Decoding Survey (Really Great Reading)_

Intervention goal: _MM—to accurately read 7/8 short-vowel pseudo- and real words GOM—to improve reading rate toward 25 wcpm._

Meeting days: _Mon.–Fri._   Meeting Time: _11:10–11:20_   Hrs/week: _2.5_

Progress monitoring measure: _MM—teacher designed: 4 real & 4 pseudowords. GOM—reading rate grade 1 passage_

Frequency of administration: _MM—weekly, GOM—biweekly_

Student Name: _James_	**Student Name**: _Taylor_
Diagnostic Data: **Real CVC words.** Score: _2/5_ ⓐ ⓔ i ⓞ u (circle unknown sounds)	**Diagnostic Data**: **Real CVC words.** Score: _1/5_ a ⓔ ⓘ ⓞ ⓤ (circle unknown sounds)
Pseudo CVC words Score: _1/8_ ⓐ ⓔ i ⓞ ⓤ (circle unknown sounds)	**Pseudo CVC words** Score: _0/8_ ⓐ ⓔ ⓘ ⓞ ⓤ (circle unknown sounds)
Phonemic Segmentation Score: _7/22_ _Repeated words or said initial sound and then vowel + consonant (e.g., c-at, d-ad)._ **Notes**: _Not very solid on short vowels. Seems to know short i. Can segment some two-phoneme words._	**Phonemic Segmentation Score**: _2/22_ _Unable to segment. Gave first sound or repeated word._ **Notes**: _May know short a but may not. All other sounds are weak. Not able to segment phonemes._
Student Name: _Damon_	**Student Name**: _David_
Diagnostic Data: **Real CVC words.** Score: _3/5_ a ⓔ ⓘ o u (circle unknown sounds)	**Diagnostic Data**: **Real CVC words.** Score: a ⓔ ⓘ o ⓤ (circle unknown sounds)
Pseudo CVC words Score: _5/8_ a ⓔ ⓘ o ⓤ (circle unknown sounds)	**Pseudo CVC words** Score: a e ⓘ ⓞ ⓤ (circle unknown sounds)
Phonemic Segmentation Score: _9/22_ _Could do all two-phoneme words._ **Notes**: _Can segment some, needs to segment three phonemes. Is really solid decoding short o and u._	**Phonemic Segmentation Score**: _5/22_ **Notes**: _Knows short a, inconsistent with others. Segmentation of both two- and three-phoneme words— mostly short a._

FIGURE 5.4. Completed example of Diagnostic Data Template for Decoding.

one form but not the other, are very common. When students show such inconsistencies, they do not fully possess the skill. In a nutshell, this form allows a teacher to look at the data for all students and see which short-vowel sounds require focused instruction.

Determining the Focus of the Intervention

What elements of planning and assessment make decoding lessons strongest? Well, after collecting basic diagnostic information, the intervention teacher and the RTI leadership team need to identify the *focus* of the intervention, the associated goal, how that goal will be *monitored* on a weekly basis, and *when* the intervention will be delivered.

When planning interventions for decoding, there are five principles to keep in mind (Stahl, 1998):

1. *Focus on decoding.* Interventions should be simple and should focus only on decoding.
2. *Be systematic.* Specify the content to taught and the logical sequence in which that content will be taught.
3. *Do not abandon instruction too soon.* Make sure to give systematic decoding instruction *at least* 6 weeks to work.
4. *Keep instruction clear of extraneous activities.* Make sure that all the activities require students to *decode* words. Avoid cutting, coloring, pasting, worksheets, or even high-quality instructional activities that *do not relate* to decoding.
5. *Use novel strategies.* Identify research-based strategies that have not been applied *consistently* with students before and try them.

First, decoding interventions need to be focused on decoding. Anyone should be able to walk into the room and know immediately what the teacher is trying to do—teach students to blend together sounds in written words.

Second, the decoding intervention must be systematic, meaning that the content being taught is specified and the sequence of that content is logical. Decoding interventions that are not systematic usually include short-term plans or activities with contents that are not organized for any particular reason. For instance, a teacher might teach the -*at* word family for 2 days of intervention with a flip book and then on the third day shift to teaching the -*ot* word family with a picture matching game. No consideration of what will be taught the next day or the next week is given—the intervention is only about today. When ad hoc, unsystematic decoding instruction is being offered, we often hear comments like, "Well I have taught him those -*ot* words and he just hasn't retained them." We like to ask, "How long did you teach those words? What did you teach before and after?" Answers to these kinds of questions indicate the degree to which a scope and sequence are present in the intervention. Effective decoding intervention is purposeful and well organized.

Third, be careful not to abandon the intervention instruction prematurely. Often students in a reading intervention need more practice, more explanation, and more repetition, particularly with decoding interventions. Although many students in reading intervention are very smart, they need more time. Stopping a strategy too early will yank the rug out from under their feet when they might just be on the verge of "getting it."

The fourth feature of good decoding instruction is that it is clear of extraneous ideas or activities. Sometimes teachers have great instructional ideas that are better suited to a guided reading group, a center, or a word study group. For example, we observed a teacher asking students to alphabetize their collected word cards as they played a game. The intention of keeping the students busy while their peers were playing a game was a good one, but it derailed the focus of the intervention. Some of the students had collected words such as *bat, bit*, and *bug*, which confused them and required the teacher to sideline the game in order to explain alphabetizing using the second letter in a word.

Fifth, use novel strategies. We often see teachers select the very same strategies and techniques that have *not* worked for months over and over again. For example, we know one teacher whose decoding instruction focused mostly on teaching word families and switching the initial consonants at the beginning. The strategy had been very effective with most of the class, but not for the students receiving intervention in January. When we watched her with intervention students, this strategy consumed about 75% of the intervention time, and the students still were not able to decode novel words. She needed to do something different with these students and give it enough time to work. The strategy was not working for this group of students. Please note that there *are* times when students can and should be provided with more exposure to a strategy that has been used in the classroom. If, for instance, students have not had *consistent, focused* exposure to the strategy, then continuing it during intervention might be helpful. However, if students have been taught using a particular strategy for weeks or months, then trying something new during intervention is probably best. Also keep in mind that *novel* does not mean an untested or unproven idea used impulsively; it simply means something that has not been tried with a particular student before in a consistent way.

Setting an Intervention Focus and Goal

High-quality interventions are well planned and focused. Teachers know exactly what they are trying to teach students and exactly what the students are expected to do as a result of the intervention. The focus of the intervention is set and a specific mastery monitoring (MM) goal for the intervention is planned before instruction begins. Figure 5.5 shows the intervention focus and MM goal that the teachers selected for this decoding intervention. The intervention focus is decoding short-vowel CVC words. The goal, the measurable behavior, is accurately decoding seven of eight pseudo- and real words containing each of the short-vowel sounds. The teacher designs her own progress monitoring measure consisting of four real and four pseudowords for each target vowel. Because the diagnostic data show inconsistency in performance, we believe that these students should not be exited from an intervention too early.

The purpose of decoding instruction is for students to generalize or apply that knowledge to connected text reading. Thus, we want decoding instruction to eventually transfer to accurate, automatic decoding in passage reading. A general outcome measure (GOM) would be a reading rate measure on a passage at the students' instructional reading level. However, reading rate and fluency are not the focus of the intervention, and teachers should not spend time teaching fluency during the decoding intervention. The purpose of the GOM is simply to help determine whether a student's decoding skills are improving in such a way that they are more broadly or generally impacting connected text reading—an important goal of reading instruction.

Figure 5.5 shows a sample planning sheet for 6 weeks of instruction for this decoding group, and Form 5.2 provides a blank template. The content of the intervention includes both the short-vowel sounds that are the focus of the intervention and the research-based learning activities for the students. These students do not have consistent patterns in what they appear to know about short vowels. There are two students who are solid with short *a* and one student who knows short *i* in both the pseudoword and real-word contexts, but there are no short vowels that all students know. The goal of the intervention—to decode all short vowels in real and pseudowords—indicates that all of the short vowels must be taught in this 6-week intervention plan.

Teachers often ask a very important question about the sequence that should be used when teaching short vowels. When teaching short-vowel sounds, sequence is very important because certain short-vowel sounds are very similar and teaching them in succession may confuse students. Figure 5.6 shows the vowel wheel (found at *www.musicedted.info/SingingBetter2/Vowels.html*) illustrating where each vowel sound is made in the mouth. This figure has all of the vowel sounds in English, including long-vowel sounds and diphthongs. If you start at the top of the vowel wheel and say all the sounds, you can feel your mouth open and close and the sounds generate from the high front to the high back. Sounds that are adjacent to each other are very similar and should not be taught in close sequence. It is best to separate similar sounds in the sequence. For example, both short *a* and short *e* are made in almost the same the place in the mouth, and this is also true for short

Decoding Intervention Group Template

Intervention goal: _MM—to accurately read 7/8 short-vowel pseudo- and real words. GOM—to improve reading rate toward 25 wcpm._

Meeting days: _Mon.–Fri._   Meeting time: _11:10–11:40_   Hrs/week: _2.5_

Progress monitoring measure: _MM—teacher designed, 4 real & 4 pseudowords. GOM—reading rate grade 1 passage_

Frequency of administration: _MM—weekly. GOM—biweekly._

All students know the following short vowels: _No vowels are known by all students but two students are solid on short a and one_

Week 1 _Short a_	Week 2 _Short o_
Date: _Jan. 28–Feb. 1_	**Date**: _Feb. 4–8_
Notes:	**Notes**:
Activities: _Phoneme segmentation_: _Two-phoneme words (at/am, an/ad, as)_ _How to read a word_: _Take off the final consonant, blend initial consonant and vowel, add final. Do every day.*_ _Roll–Say–Keep_: _bag, bat, hat, ham, ram, mat, tap, gap, lap, map, rap, yap, fat, cat, rat, mat, sat, gag, hag, nag, rag, tag, wag, am, ham, jam, Pam, Sam, yam_ _Reading pseudowords_: _rad, kad, pag, jat, yan, bam (two/day)_	**Activities**: _Phoneme segmentation_: _Three-phoneme words with flow sounds (continuants—lot, mob, sob, lock, sock, mock)_ _Review how to read a word one time._ _Read It, Break It, Make It_: _hot, dog, cop, cot, fog, hop, not, log, pot_ _Follow-the-Path_: _Words from Roll, Say, Keep Week 1 + log, hog, bog, dog, fog, jog, cot, got, hot, lot, not, rot, cob, mob, job, rob, sob_ _Reading pseudowords_: _gog, rog, fod, mot, wot, dod (two/day)_
Progress Monitoring: _None—short week_	**Progress Monitoring**: _two short a, six short o_

(continued)

FIGURE 5.5. Sample Six-Week Intervention-Planning Sheet for Decoding.

Week 3 *Short i* **Date**: *Feb. 11–15* **Notes**: **Activities**: Phoneme segmentation: *Three-phoneme words with stops (tip, bit, pin, tin, dim kit)* Read It, Break It, Make It: *bin, fit, hip, fin, dip, bit, kin, lip, sit* Roll–Say–Keep and Follow-the-Path: *For Valentine's stickers, words from Roll, Say, Keep Weeks 1 & 2 + bin, fin, in, kin, pin, tin, clip, dip, hip, lip, nip, rip, ship, sip, tip, trip, zip, bit, fit, hit, it, kit, lit, pit, sit* Reading pseudowords: *jit, dit, bim, yim, vit, rin (two/day)* **Progress Monitoring**: *two short o, six short i*	**Week 4** *Review a, i, o* **Date**: *Feb. 18–22* **Notes**: *Reevaluation of students' needs after this week* **Activities**: Activities: Making Words: Set 1: *(b, a, g, i, t, c, o, l) bag, big, bit, bat, cat, cot, lot, lit* Set 2: *(h, t, l, b, c, o, i, a) hot, lot, lit, bit, hit, hat, cat, cot* Set 3: *(b, g, t, f, p, i, o, a) big, bag, bat, fat, fit, pit, pot, rot* Vowel star with u, a, e: *b__g, j__g, h__t, g__t, p__t.* Reading pseudowords: *jit, gam, biv, hod, wap, vot* **Progress Monitoring**: *President's Day, short week*
Week 5 *Tentative* **Date**: *Short u & e Feb. 25–March 1* **Notes**: *Check needs. Who needs review?* **Activities**: Reading pseudowords: *yut, vun, zun, jep, bep, hep (two/day)* Quiz, quiz, pass: *Mon—just short-u and -e words. Wed & Thurs—all vowel sounds* **Progress Monitoring**:	**Week 6** *Tentative* **Date**: *Contrast e/a & i/e March 5–8* **Notes**: **Activities**: Mouth moves, e and a: *Review the place and manner of articulation for these sounds.* Making words: Set 1: *bet, bat, pat, pet, let, met, mat, hat* Set 2: *bet, bit, hit, lit, mit, met, set, sit* Set 3: *mat, mit, pit, pet, set, sat, sit, pit* Three in one game: *Use all five vowel sounds for review.* **Progress Monitoring**:

FIGURE 5.5. *(continued)*

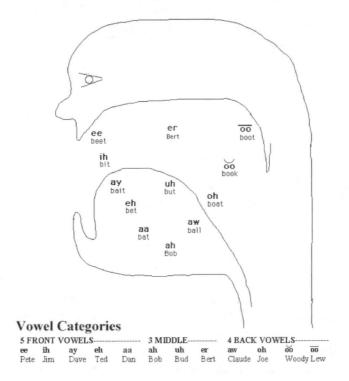

FIGURE 5.6. Vowel wheel. Reprinted by permission of Edgar R. Norton, *www.musicedted. info*.

e and *i*. This is why children often substitute short *e* for short *a* when writing or decoding words.

With this information in mind, the interventionist has structured the sequence of vowel sounds beginning with short *a* in Week 1, then moving to short *o* and then short *i* in Weeks 2 and 3. Note that she does not teach short *i* and *e* in subsequent weeks or short *a* and *e*. The interventionist has the students review all three sounds during Week 4 and then adds short *u* and *e* in Week 5. At the beginning of a decoding intervention, we usually recommend that only one vowel be given focus each week, especially with students who are in a decoding intervention. However, as the plan reflects, students are still practicing and reviewing sounds from the previous weeks in both the games that they play and in the pseudowords that they are asked to read. Once students gain some momentum, it may be possible to teach two sounds in one week, as this plan does in Week 5.

Some teachers prefer to have a "new" sound each week and a "review" sound so that students can have something that is known to which they can compare the unknown or new sound. The review in Week 4 provides important practice time and consolidation of known information, and Week 6 reviews and solidifies all sounds. The timeline for meeting the intervention goals is reasonable but brisk, and it is possible that one student within the group of four might need a week or 2 of additional time.

More discussion of decoding intervention activities is provided in the next section. The intervention activities for decoding emphasize sounding out and blending together short-vowel CVC words. As research suggests, decoding is enhanced by phonemic segmentation activities, which might include 20–30% of time dedicated to phonemic awareness (NICCHD, 2001). Note that although the plans include some light phonemic segmentation instruction, the intervention accentuates decoding. In addition, the students will practice decoding pseudowords (about two per day) to ensure that they are comfortable with these in an assessment and to guarantee that they are able to transfer their decoding knowledge.

Decoding can be a significant hurdle for some children, and so consistency, practice, and modeling are particularly important. For example, students need to be told how they should approach decoding words, and this approach should be used throughout the intervention. This teacher sets expectations during the first week by introducing a consistent procedure for "How to Read Words." She asks students to decode many words during their intervention lessons, and this procedure will provide them with a consistent strategy for doing so. Sometimes without realizing it, teachers offer many different approaches, thinking that they are giving students options, but those who are in a decoding intervention are likely to be confused by a panoply of strategies.

For instance, on one day a teacher might say, "Look at that word, *cat*. Do you see a small word in that word? A word that we had on our word list?" Another day the teacher might say, "Okay, what's the first letter? C. What sound does it make? /k/. Now what's the second letter? *A* What sound does that make? /a/. Now what's the last letter? *T*. What sound does that make? /t/. Put it all together. Say it fast." The strategy for decoding words needs to be the same strategy every day, which, in this case, is blending the first two sounds and then adding the final letter-sound. In addition to giving attention to consistency, teachers need to remember the fifth intervention principle, "Do something different!"

Decoding Intervention Activities

We have found so many engaging and lively decoding activities to use with students that it is difficult to choose just a few to highlight in this chapter. In selecting decoding activities, keep three points in mind. First, as described in Chapter 3, activities should be motivating and exciting to the students. The content of the decoding intervention stays fairly stable and focuses on pronouncing written words with target short-vowel sounds. However, the way that the content is practiced and repeated need not be boring and dry. Clever teachers can keep students practicing in lively ways. Second, for decoding interventions, students need to practice *decoding* words, paying close attention to the order of sounds and letters in words. Activities should require students to build words by paying attention to each letter-sound build decoding skills. Third, simplicity is the key with interventions. Too many materials, too many procedures, and too many details distract from practice and can easily get the intervention off track. Because interventions are often delivered in a short amount of time, KISS (Keep It Simple, Sweetheart!) is our motto.

Sound Boxes: A Strategy for Phonemic Segmentation

One of our favorite strategies for developing skills in phonemic segmentation is called *sound boxes*. Although it is very similar to the Elkonin boxes strategy that Reading Recovery teachers use, there are a few differences. We like Patricia McCarthy's approach (2008), which is detailed in an article in *The Reading Teacher*. Sound boxes provide younger children with a way to make an abstract element—phonemes—concrete. Each sound in a word is represented by a box and students push a counter or penny into the box for each sound of the word.

We provide examples and details about how to do sound boxes using an instructional sequence that we call MaGIC. The MaGIC acronym stands for the standard parts of a lesson: modeling, guided practice, independent practice, and corrective feedback (see Figure 5.7). We like this acronym because it is easy for teachers to remember and can easily be embedded into any teacher content. When we use sound boxes for decoding interventions, we stick with short-vowel sounds because those are the sounds that we are trying to get students to decode. We find that doing a few phonemic segmentation items at the beginning of a lesson segues nicely into decoding practice.

The types of words that a teacher chooses to segment can make or break the activity. Use words with a maximum of three phonemes. We do not suggest using words with beginning or ending consonant blends (e.g., *st-, gr-, fl, -nd, -mp*) because the focus of the decoding intervention is on the short-vowel sound. If students struggle with three-phoneme words, then use two-phoneme words (e.g., *at, it, in*). McCarthy (2008) describes three different levels of words. Level 1 words are those that begin with an initial sound that can be sustained. These sounds might be called "flowing" sounds because you can start them and continue to make the sound for a period of time: The sound is fluid. In the research literature these sounds are called *continuants* because you can continue them (e.g., *s, z, l, m, n, f, r, v*). Usually these consonant sounds are made with a partially open vocal track. In contrast, stop consonants, or what we might call *pop sounds*, cannot be held. Sounds like *d, t, p,* and *b* cannot be continually sounded and are not fluid

<u>M</u>odeling: Show the students what you want them to do. **Do** an item as if you were a student. Think aloud. Make typical mistakes and then correct them.

Watch me decode this word (bag). I cover the ending sound, the /g/. Then I say the /b/ and the /a/ and then I say it again /b/ /a/. Then I put them together /baaa/, /baaa/. Then I take my finger off the end and say it /baaaag/. /Bag/

<u>G</u>uided Practice: Lead the entire group in doing a practice item together. Identify students who did it correctly or who corrected mistakes. Describe what these students did.

Now I want you each to look at the word card you have sat. We are going to do this together. Everyone cover the ending sound, the /t/. Now say the first sound /ssss/ and then next sound /a/. (Follow sequence above.) Did you see how Glenn put the sounds together and then put a /d/ sound at the end? But that wasn't right. He looked again and made it /t/.

<u>I</u>ndependent Practice: Give each student an item with which to practice the skill by him/herself.

<u>C</u>orrective Feedback: Ask each student to share his/her independent practice item *just with you.* If the item is not correct, show the student how to do it correctly and then ask him/her to do it again.

Avery, I like that you got the /saaa/ part of that word. The ending sound is not quite right. Watch me /sssaaaa/ and then /t/. That's t /t/. So if I put it together it's /ssssaaaaat/ sat. Now you try.

FIGURE 5.7. MaGIC instructional sequence (Modeling, Guided Practice, Independent Practice, Corrective Feedback).

because they quickly begin and end. Because fluid sounds can easily be stretched for a period of time, they are good first-level words. Level 2 words begin with pop or stop consonants, such as *d, t,* or *p,* and are not easily stretched. Level 3 words have blends; we do not suggest using these for the purposes of the decoding interventions in this book. When doing phonemic segmentation exercises, keep in mind that the instruction should be brisk and short (no more than about 8 minutes). Research supports the pairing of phonemic awareness instruction with decoding, but it is not the main course—more like a salad or an appetizer to the intervention!

Strategies for Decoding Words

If you have worked with enough beginning readers, you know that they can say all the sounds in a word but still may not be able to blend those sounds together to actually read the word. Moving from identifying the letter-sounds in a word to blending them together is a milestone. We have watched students say the letter-sounds in a word and then struggle to come up with a word. Take Carl, for example. His initial attempts at blending sounds together sounded like this for the word *let*: "/llllll/, /eeeeeee/, /t/ . . . *table*?" In this example, Carl can clearly match letters to sounds, but he seems to have difficulty remembering the first two sounds of the word, /l/ and /e/, and just seized on the last sound and a word that he remembered. We have seen other students focus on the vowel and articulate a word beginning with the target vowel sound. For example, such a child would read *let* as "/lllll/, /eeeee/, /t/ . . . *egg*?" In both cases the reader is having difficulty maintaining all three sounds in memory. We have two strategies to help: one is called *Take Off the Ending* and the other is called *Start with the Vowel*.

For our first strategy, Take Off the Ending, students are asked to cover the final consonant, say the first two sounds, blend the sounds together twice, and then add the ending. Figure 5.8 illustrates this strategy. As with the phonemic segmentation exercises, we like to model this strategy with beginning consonant sounds that are continuants, or sounds that can be articulated and held for a period of time (e.g., *l, m, n, s, f, r*). If this does not work, we suggest our other strategy, Start with the Vowel. Some students find that beginning with their mouth open in a vowel sound and then closing down to make the consonant sound is an easier process when they are first blending. This process feels more natural—it's as if you can't help but blend the sounds together if you do it this way. The student covers the initial consonant, says the vowel and the consonant sounds, blends them twice, and then adds the beginning sound.

Whichever strategy you choose, we suggest that you consistently use it. Students who have not successfully blended words together need one good strategy, and they need to know exactly what to do when they come to an unknown word.

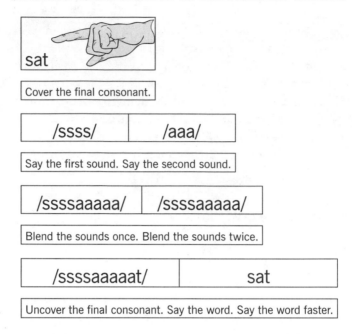

FIGURE 5.8. Take Off the Ending strategy.

Many students are unsuccessful because they are wildly stabbing at a word and are not sure what kind of approach to take.

Vowel Stars

We are big fans of the resources and materials provided on the website of the Florida Center for Reading Research at Florida State University. Almost every time we visit that website, we are sure to find engaging activities to support instruction. The Vowel Star can be found in a packet of materials for Decoding and Encoding (see Figure 5.9) available at *www.fcrr.org*. As the picture indicates, this strategy is a great one to use once students know from three to five vowel sounds. (As indicated in our planning guide in Figure 5.5, we altered a Vowel Star to include only three vowel sounds.) Students get a word frame with only the vowel left out, for example, *p__t*, and then they replace the blank in the center with different vowel sounds, pronounce the word, and then write it. We also ask students to put a star next to words that they create that are pseudowords. If a student *knows* that a word is not a real word, then we can see if he/she has arrived at an accurate pronunciation of the word. Many teachers have used flip books or blending wheels with word families, in which the initial sound of the word is changed to create words with endings, such as *-at*, *-an*, *-it*. We especially like the Vowel Star

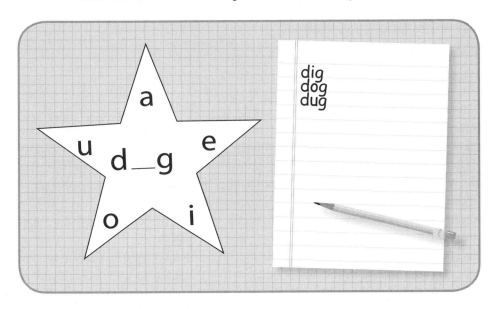

FIGURE 5.9. Vowel Stars. Copyright by the Florida Center for Reading Research at Florida State University. Reprinted by permission.

because it places emphasis on the *vowel* in the middle of the word. Many students who are receiving decoding intervention have used flip books or blending wheels and slip into an autopilot mode with them, just paying attention to the beginning sound, when they need to attend to the middle sound. The Vowel Star requires students to attend to the medial vowel sounds, and for this reason it is a perfect intervention activity. Devices like this have been used for many years, but the key is *how* teachers use them. All too often we see students assembling flip books or slides that change the medial vowel as an independent activity. The students never practice blending words, which is the entire purpose of the activity. We also see teachers asking students to "read the words to a partner." Although reading to a partner is great, students in decoding interventions need to have a teacher listen to (and correct) their decoding, if need be. After all, the reason that students are in intervention is because they need more support.

We also found a lively game, Quiz, Quiz, Pass, at *www.readingresource.net*. We like this game because it provides opportunities for self-checking. Students must read a word, and the picture is printed on the back of their card. They find a buddy, read their word for the buddy, check the word with the picture, and then listen to their buddy's words (Quiz, Quiz). After each buddy has read his/her words, they pass (Pass) the words on to another group. Once again, this is a simple game that does not require a lot of preparation but gives students ample practice decoding words.

Read It, Break It, and Make It

This strategy provides an engaging, focused routine with magnetic letters as students practice decoding words and *encoding them*. Although the primary focus during a decoding intervention is analyzing words and then pronouncing them, students will benefit from also practicing encoding, or spelling, words. Encoding is the mirror image of decoding, and the skills used during encoding will complement and support decoding. Think about it. When we ask students to spell a word, they must break it down into its component sounds, recall letters that correspond to those sounds, and then cross-check their spelling by reading the word. During the Read It, Break It, and Make It strategy, students first read a word, then break it up, and then remake it. Figure 5.10 shows the steps of this strategy and includes a sample word with magnetic letters.

When teachers hear about this strategy, sometimes they feel it is too simple. Many cannot imagine that a child would not be able to reassemble a simple CVC word immediately after seeing it together. They are surprised when students find this task challenging. It is the order of letter-sounds, especially in the middle of a word, that is not getting attention from struggling readers. Students who are struggling to decode vowels and move into the full alphabetic phase are not paying attention to *all* parts of the word and the order in which sounds occur. Often they are giving attention to the beginning and/or ending of the word and guessing the rest, with no analysis taking place. Their confusion in reassembling words is due to the lack of attention they are giving to the vowels in words and their own insecurity about which sounds each vowel letter represents.

1. **Make the word with magnetic letters.**
2. **Read the word.**
3. **Break the word up (scramble it).**
4. **Put the word together.**
5. **Read it.**
6. **Is it right? Yes? No?**
   Teacher remodels steps 1–5.
   Child does the same word again.

red
Read the word, *red*.

d r e
Break the word.

r d e
Put the word together.
Read the word, *rde*.
Teacher models steps 1–5.
Child does the same word again.

red
Read the word, *red*. That's right!

FIGURE 5.10. Routine for Read It, Break It, and Make It.

Building Words

Another decoding strategy that we like to use is very similar to Cunningham's Making Words (Cunningham & Hall, 2008). Generally, the teacher dictates words to the students, who will use letter cards or magnetic letters to make words by manipulating the letter cards. In our example in Figure 5.5, the teacher dictates six words in a particular sequence and then changes only one letter in the word at each subsequent turn. Students build the words and read them after each change.

The strategy requires teachers to specify the words that they will use *prior to the lesson* for two important reasons. First, you can only change one letter at a time, and second, when you are running a decoding intervention you cannot throw in vowel sounds that have not been taught. Trying to select words on the fly usually results in asking students to complete tasks they are unable to accomplish, such as reading words that have complex vowel or consonant patterns, rather than basic CVC words. Below is an example of a sequence that was thrown together, resulting in some problems.

- *lit*
- *mit*
- *mat*
- *mot*

In this sequence, the teacher wanted to move to a short-*o* sound, but because she could only change one sound in the word, she was forced to create a pseudo-word when that was not her intention. With some preplanning this could have been avoided. In Figure 5.5, the interventionist has specified a series of six words that students will build in sequence: *bag, big, bit, bat, cat, cot, lot, lit*. Note that each word alters only one letter at a time, and the plan shows the letters that will be needed for the word building in parentheses. This last step allows the teacher to quickly ask students to pull out specific letters at the beginning of the lesson. There are many wonderful resources with sequences that have already been specified, but we suggest that teachers who are using these resources for decoding interventions check the word sequences to make sure that the letter-sounds match those that their students are learning.

Games for Decoding

As described in Chapter 3, we are big proponents of games, but they need to be teacher supervised and focused on providing students with many opportunities to practice the target skill. In fact, that is our litmus test for a game: Does it provide each child with multiple opportunities to practice the target skill in an engaging and lively format? We like games such as Bingo, Roll–Say–Keep, and Follow the Path for practicing decoding. Roll–Say–Keep is a really simple game that we found at The School Bell (*www.theschoolbell.com*). All you need to play this game is a set of words on cards, a die, and the Roll–Say–Keep game board, which is downloadable from the website. Players put an equal number of cards face down on each of the six squares which each have the corresponding number of a dice side in the corner. Each player rolls the die, flips the card on the corresponding space, and says the word. If the word is pronounced correctly, the player gets to keep the card. If the word is not pronounced correctly, the team members or teacher pronounces it correctly, asks the player to pronounce it, and then puts the card at the bottom of the pile. The player with the most cards wins.

We also like simple Follow-the-Path games wherein students get to practice word reading. We suggest starting with a simple board with a path and fun theme. Some teachers like to change these with the seasons. The other materials required include a stack of many words, game pieces, and a die. At their turn, each student rolls the die and then picks up the number of cards that matches the face of the die. For example, if a student rolls a 5, he/she picks up five cards. The student reads each card and moves a space for each correctly read word. If a word is not correctly read, the student cannot move that space. The word is then read by the teacher, repeated by the student, and put back in the pile. We like this routine because the students are required to read more than one word per turn and because their movement on the board is directly tied to the number of words that they read correctly instead of simply the number that is rolled on the die. The traditional format of roll the die, read one card, and then move that number of spaces provides fewer practice opportunities than this alternate routine. One teacher also told us that she numbered the spaces in the top left-hand corner so that she could see how many words the children had read by simply looking at their place on the board. She recorded the number of practice words they read in her intervention log to make sure that the students were practicing. Another game we identified on the Florida Reading Research Center site is called Three-in-One. This is a very simple game in which the teacher creates three piles of cards: one for consonants, one for vowels, and a third for consonants. Each student has a record sheet and a pencil. When given a turn, a student flips a card from each pile, writes the word, reads the word, and then decides if it is a real word or a pseudoword. Students like to practice reading words, and the preparation for this game is very easy.

Goal Setting and Progress Monitoring

As noted previously, there are two ways to monitor progress: mastery monitoring (MM), which allows teachers to measure the impact that instruction has had on the skill being taught, and generalized outcome monitoring (GOM), which focuses on the degree to which reading improvement is impacted more broadly by the intervention and can be measured over a longer period of time.

The MM goal for decoding interventions involves students' decoding the target vowel sounds taught in the intervention. During the planning phase for an intervention, teachers identify a progress monitoring measure that will be used to assess the skill being taught. With decoding interventions, the progress monitoring measures usually consist of lists of simple CVC words that contain short-vowel sounds. Figure 5.5 shows that progress monitoring measures were planned for most weeks of the intervention. One week was shortened due to the Presidents' Day holiday, and so during this week progress monitoring did not take place. Note that this interventionist planned to use the results of the progress monitoring measures in Week 4 to review sounds. To do this she would analyze the results of progress monitoring to see if there are patterns in the data. For example, she might find that the entire group needs additional practice on specific sounds or that individuals need practice on different sounds. Word lists and games can be customized to include vowel sounds that match students' practice needs.

In this sample intervention, the progress monitoring assessment was teacher-designed. (See the text box *Designing Your Own Progress Monitoring Measures* for details.) The basic structure of the progress monitoring measure included four real words and four pseudowords in each measure. The teacher wanted to include pseudowords to see if the intervention was helping students apply letter-sounds and decode vowels in truly novel words. In choosing words to put into the progress monitoring measures, the teacher included three real words representing the current week's short vowel and one from the previous week, and the same for pseudowords. For example, the measure for Week 2 included the words *cot*, *cob*, *not*, and *hag* and pseudowords *bov*, *tob*, *sot*, *gab*. Many CVC words, such as *sot* and *gab*, though real are essentially pseudowords to children because their spoken forms are unfamiliar. In selecting words for the progress monitoring measure, the teacher also tried *not* to repeat many of the words that were used during intervention instruction for assessment. The teacher wanted to make sure that students were not just memorizing words but were able to apply their knowledge when encountering new words. The goal of the intervention is for students to accurately read seven of eight words with target sounds that were previously taught.

In addition, to the above goal and decoding progress monitoring measure, we also believe that a GOM for a decoding intervention can provide useful information. As we mentioned earlier in the chapter, a good GOM measure for decoding is an oral reading fluency measure. There are no reading rate benchmark scores before first grade. The very first reading rate goal found on any oral reading fluency measure is about 25 words correct per minute (WCPM). If a student's decoding is improving, then we would see an impact on oral reading fluency (see Chapter 6 for guidance on administering a measure of reading rate). So, the GOM measure for a decoding intervention like the one described here would be a measure of reading rate and the expected target would be 25 WCPM.

DESIGNING YOUR OWN PROGRESS MONITORING MEASURES

We have occasionally found that the teachers and schools may need to develop their own progress monitoring measures. We do not encourage this as a regular practice because we find that most schools and teachers do not have the time to invest in putting together a series of measures. However, if all resources have been exhausted, progress monitoring measures can be created. We worked with one school that did not have enough alternate forms of a measure to provide progress monitoring each week. So we needed to develop more forms. In this sidebar, we describe a process that we used to develop some word lists to monitor progress for decoding interventions with students. In this case, we were developing measures to the monitor progress of intermediate students learning to decode long vowels, but we provide an example here that is relevant to short vowels.

Step 1: Assemble a Team

First we put together a small team of people (three to four) that could share the work in developing a measure. The team consisted of two university faculty members, one reading specialist, and one teacher. We knew that we wanted different levels of expertise in the group and that we needed people who could be relied upon to complete tasks in a timely fashion. We really recommend using a team approach, because a group of people can divide the work and can troubleshoot mistakes better than individuals.

Step 2: Identify the Content, Format, and Structure of the Progress Monitoring Set

We had two problems. First, we did not have enough lists of short-vowel words and did not think that we would be able to monitor progress for 6 weeks. Second, we didn't have enough words on each list. We felt that at least 10 words would be necessary for each list.

When developing a progress monitoring measure teachers must be very clear about what they are assessing. We asked ourselves, "What do we want students to be able to do as a result of intervention?" Our answer was *decode short vowels*, and so our progress monitoring measure consisted of lists of words representing short-vowel patterns. We identified the content of the measure (e.g., what exactly would be tested), the format of the assessment (e.g., fonts, visual organization, student materials/teacher materials), and the structure (e.g., number of items, number of items per vowel sound). The content that would be assessed through the progress monitoring tools consisted of short-vowel patterns for different sounds with mostly real words for each short vowel (e.g., *bag, hat, can*) but also some pseudowords (e.g., *jav, yat, rab*).

(continued)

The teachers felt that having all the measures look the same would make them more usable. An interventionist trying to score an assessment would be able to find all the items in the same place for each assessment. Consistency in format makes tasks efficient and less time-consuming. Below is our format.

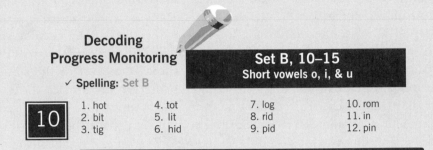

Decoding Progress Monitoring

✓ Spelling: Set B

Set B, 10–15
Short vowels o, i, & u

10

1. hot
2. bit
3. tig

4. tot
5. lit
6. hid

7. log
8. rid
9. pid

10. rom
11. in
12. pin

Lastly, we determined a structure for each list. It was important to establish a systematic and consistent approach to the lists. We created lettered sets of lists. (e.g., Set B—short vowels *o, i,* and *u*). We decided that the lists would consist of 12 words and that four of the words for each week would be a review of patterns that had been taught in the previous week (e.g., *hot, tot, log,* and *rom*). The remaining eight words would represent patterns taught during the week (e.g., *bit, lit*). Twenty-five percent of the words, or three words, would be pseudowords with short vowels.

After establishing the content, format, and structure of the measures, we assigned each person a particular content.

Step 3: Work Individually to Develop Pieces of the Progress Monitoring Set

We each took our task and completed it individually. Then we exchanged lists with each other to check for mistakes, inconsistencies, or other problems.

Step 4: Pilot the Assessments and Make Adjustments

The last step was to simply use the assessments and to keep notes about them so that we could make adjustments if parts of the assessment were not working. We decided to use the assessments for a month and then come back together to consider any changes that needed to be made. Most of the lists worked really well, but when we came to together, one teacher noted that one of the patterns on the list was somewhat unusual and that we probably didn't need as many items for that pattern as planned. In another situation, one teacher noted a word that was not in the students' vocabulary and which seemed to confuse them at different points. After the meeting we made these slight adjustments, duplicated the measures, put them into a spiral booklet format, and then shared them with the faculty at the school.

Evaluating Interventions

. . . .

To evaluate interventions, teachers can use three tools: (1) intervention logs, (2) progress monitoring results, and (3) fidelity checklists. Below, we provide examples of how these three tools might look for a decoding intervention using the group introduced in Figure 5.4.

Figure 5.11 is an intervention log for 1 week of intervention. This log shows students' attendance and anecdotal records of the detail of their responses to the intervention instruction. This intervention log shows that two of the students, Damon and David, are responding very well to the intervention. In fact, the teacher believes that Damon has really caught on to the intervention and internalized the processes. Her notes indicate that he is able to quickly decode the short-o words and does not need to use the decoding strategy of covering the final consonant in order to accurately read the words. These are hints that he may be able to exit the intervention soon. David is also doing well; he knows the short o already, but he is not as efficient as Damon in decoding, as the comments indicate.

What is important about the intervention log is that it provides information that would not otherwise be available through simply looking at the progress monitoring results. David and Damon would likely have the same levels of accuracy on a progress monitoring measure, but the interventionist's comments indicate that Damon is further along because he no longer relies on the decoding strategies and reads words more quickly. Intervention logs provide a window into the clinical judgment of the person delivering the intervention. The notes in the intervention log indicate that both James and Taylor are not easily decoding new sounds and are less skilled at phonemic segmentation. Taylor is having particular difficulty in reassembling words (in Read It, Break It, Make It) and seems to be struggling to put the letters in the correct order. This suggests that he is not exactly sure where vowels fit into words and may need additional help. The notes from the intervention log are invaluable for quickly communicating with other teachers and even parents about how interventions are going. Logs provide a complete picture that details responses to intervention. Considering intervention logs and progress monitoring assessments together is a good example of how quantitative and qualitative data can be used in tandem.

Figures 5.12 and 5.13 show progress monitoring data for two students, David and James. Figure 5.12 shows the MM measures for 3 weeks, detailing the specific words that these two students decoded correctly. The progress monitoring measure for this intervention was lists of words consisting of half pseudowords and half real words containing the vowel sounds being taught. David's progress monitoring data show that he is actually meeting the intervention goal of accurately reading seven of eight words for the vowels being taught. His error on the first progress monitoring check shows a substitution of short o for short a. Interestingly, on the

Intervention Log

Instructional focus of group: _To accurately read 7/8 short-vowel pseudo- and real_
words (a, e, i, o, u) in two successive weeks

Week of: _Feb. 4–8_   Intervention teacher: _____

Curriculum/materials: _Short o (short-a review) Phonemic segmentation sound_
boxes/reading pseudowords; Read It, Break It, Make It, Roll–Say–Keep

_____

_____

Attendance and Observation Records

Student Name: James	Student Name: Taylor	Student Name: Damon
Attendance: (Circle if absent) M T W Th F	Attendance: (Circle if absent) M T W Th F	Attendance: (Circle if absent) M T W Th F
Notes: _Can consistently segment two-phoneme words._ _Decodes the short-a words. Trying to transfer to short o. Can read real words but not pseudowords?._	Notes: _Still struggling with phoneme segmentation. On Break It and Make It needed several trials to make the word correctly. Not hearing/attending to three sounds? Look at journal for invented spelling. Does he have any vowels?_	Notes: _Wow! He knew short o at the beginning. He just sails right through them. His game went so fast—ran out of words. Seems to have internalized the process. Doesn't need to cover the ending to decode the words. Might be ready to exit in a week or 2?_
Student Name: David	Student Name:	Student Name:
Attendance: (Circle if absent) M T (W) Th F	Attendance: (Circle if absent) M T W Th F	Attendance: (Circle if absent) M T W Th F
Notes: _Already knew short o so I gave more practice items in short a. Did well but is not really quick. Needs more practice._	Notes:	Notes:

FIGURE 5.11. Sample Decoding Intervention Log.

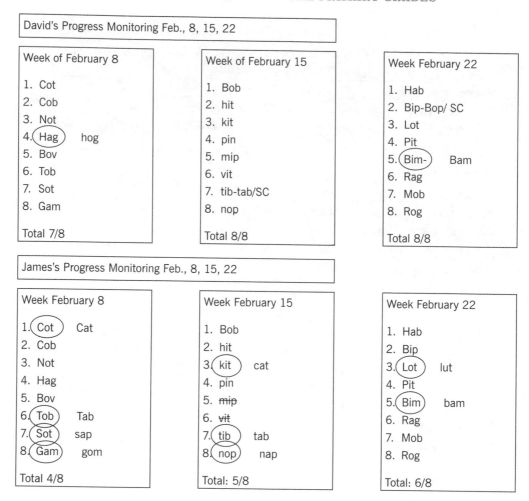

FIGURE 5.12. Sample progress monitoring.

other checks he self-corrects. The self-corrections reflect that he has a mechanism in place to read the words and that he knows when he is wrong. They show also that his knowledge is a little insecure, despite his meeting the goal of seven of eight words on the last two measures. He is not as efficient and confident in his decoding as Damon, who is "running out of words" when playing Roll–Say–Keep, and reading quickly (see Intervention Log Notes in Figure 5.11).

James's progress monitoring notes show a different picture. His scores show that he is improving across the three progress monitoring checks—they move from four to five to six of eight—but he has not yet met the goal of the intervention: seven of eight words read accurately. In the first check, he is interchanging short o- and short a-sounds and appears to default to a short-a sound when he does not know how to decode a word. James's difficulty with pseudowords is evident in the first progress monitoring check, but it then begins to fade. At some level, the reason that he is unsure about decoding pseudowords is that he is not fully secure in his understanding of letter-sounds. It is possible that even with some of the real words that he is decoding accurately, he is just making a stab, and sometimes his attempt is right and sometimes it is wrong. Whatever the reasons for his errors, James is making some progress, but may need additional support with segmenting three-phoneme words and solidifying his knowledge of the short-*a*, -*o*, and -*i* sounds.

Figure 5.13 shows both the decoding progress monitoring data and the GOM reading rate data in line graph form. The decoding charts include six data points, or 6 weeks of intervention, rather than the 3 weeks shown in Figure 5.12. The reading rate data show 4 weeks of data. David's graphs show that his acquisition of decoding—of blending sounds together—is impacting his fluency. He increased by 10 WCPM and is now reading about 25 WCPM. Although this progress is impressive, we do caution teachers that the impact of a decoding measure on reading rate data will not always be immediate. Often such data will not emerge before 10–12

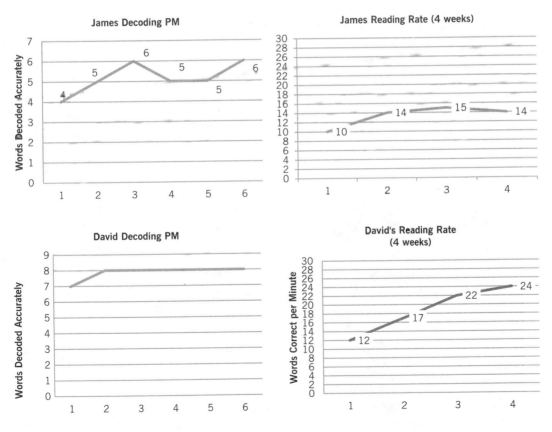

FIGURE 5.13. Progress monitoring for James and David (MM and GOM).

weeks because generalization and transfer take time. James's decoding skill has not improved much during the 6 weeks, and his reading rate has not changed much either, as expected. As discussed above, James would clearly require additional decoding intervention, possibly with some tweaking and modification.

In Form 5.3, we present a sample fidelity checklist for decoding interventions. This is an important tool that educators can use to determine ways to improve decoding interventions. Samantha, a reading specialist we worked with, explains: "When I am called into a situation and I am not exactly sure where to start, I will grab one of these fidelity checklists and use it so that I can focus myself. Instruction is so complicated, and it's nice to look down at a checklist to know what to pay attention to." Despite all the planning and assessment that go into instructional interventions, things can still drift. Decoding interventions should consist of activities that focus on sounding out words independently and of activities that complement or build capacity for decoding, such as phonemic segmentation or spelling words. In addition, successful decoding interventions also include planning and sequencing of sounds so that confusion can be avoided.

Conclusion

Decoding requires readers to *apply* their letter-sound knowledge. Decoding skills progress through various stages, and many struggling readers get stuck in the transition from the partial to the full alphabetic phase of decoding development. Diagnostic assessments for decoding, as well as phonemic segmentation skills, should be used to inform intervention instruction. Decoding interventions must be systematic and focused. With clear, targeted goals that can be monitored using equally clear measures, decoding interventions can be just the ticket to propel struggling readers to the full alphabet phase of decoding development. It is easy to get off track during interventions, so fidelity checklists serve as effective reminders and "self-checks" for staying focused on the goals of decoding intervention.

FORM 5.1

Diagnostic Data Template for Decoding

Decoding Intervention Diagnostic Data

Instructional focus of group: _____

Diagnostic measure used: _____

Intervention goal: To _____ by: _____

Meeting days: _____ Meeting time: _____ Hrs/week: _____

Progress monitoring measure: _____

Frequency of administration: _____

Student Name: **Diagnostic Data:** **Real CVC words.** **Score:** a e i o u (circle unknown sounds) **Pseudo CVC words** **Score:** a e i o u (circle unknown sounds) **Phonemic Segmentation Score:** **Notes:**	**Student Name:** **Diagnostic Data:** **Real CVC words.** **Score:** a e i o u (circle unknown sounds) **Pseudo CVC words** **Score:** a e i o u (circle unknown sounds) **Phonemic Segmentation Score:** **Notes:**
Student Name: **Diagnostic Data:** **Real CVC words.** **Score:** a e i o u (circle unknown sounds) **Pseudo CVC words** **Score:** a e i o u (circle unknown sounds) **Phonemic Segmentation Score:** **Notes:**	**Student Name:** **Diagnostic Data:** **Real CVC words.** **Score:** a e i o u (circle unknown sounds) **Pseudo CVC words** **Score:** a e i o u (circle unknown sounds) **Phonemic Segmentation Score:** **Notes:**

FORM 5.2
Decoding Intervention Group Template

Intervention goal: _____

_____ by _____

Meeting days: _____ Meeting time: _____ Hrs/week: _____

Progress monitoring measure: _____

_____

Frequency of administration: _____

All students know the following short vowels: _____

_____

Week 1 Date: Notes: Activities: Progress Monitoring:	Week 2 Date: Notes: Activities: Progress Monitoring:

(continued)

Decoding Intervention Group Template *(page 2 of 2)*

Week 3	Week 4
Date:	Date:
Notes:	Notes:
Activities:	Activities:
Progress Monitoring:	Progress Monitoring:
Week 5	Week 6
Date:	Date:
Notes:	Notes:
Activities:	Activities:
Progress Monitoring:	Progress Monitoring:

Fidelity Checklist for Decoding Interventions

Date:						
GOALS **A. Measuring Intervention Goals**[1]						
• Does the intervention goal state specifically what students are to do as a result of the intervention?						
o Decode words with short vowels (CVC)?						
o By a specific date?						
o Specific criteria for success (e.g., decode 90% of words)?						
OBSERVATION						
• List activities observed during 1 intervention:						
• Do the activities provide practice with the behavior that is being measured in A (e.g., decoding CVC words?)						
• Is the majority of time being spent on the major decoding (70–80%)?						
• Is each student getting at least 8–10 opportunities to practice decoding words independently?						
PLANNING						
• Is there long-term planning across weeks that reflects a scope (e.g., sounds) and sequence (e.g., the order for teaching those sounds)?						
• Are the specific letter-sounds being targeted a reflection of diagnostic data?						
• Are dates for progress monitoring shown?						
INTERVENTION LOG						
• Are there *specific* comments reflecting success with decoding? (e.g., Not too many generic comments—*Nice!*)						
• Do the comments show that plans are being altered as a result of progress monitoring data?						
ADDITIONAL NOTES:						

[1]Place a check in the box if the answer to the question is yes.

CHAPTER 6

Interventions for Fluency

GUIDING QUESTIONS

- What are the three main components of fluency?
- What is the important connection between fluency and comprehension?
- Students develop fluency along a continuum—what elements make up that continuum?
- What factors should be considered when developing fluency interventions?
- What are the components of high-quality fluency interventions in the primary grades?
- What are the guidelines for setting goals and timelines for fluency interventions?
- How can students' progress be monitored for fluency interventions?

In our work with schools we find that many teachers in the primary grades do not focus on fluency because they are often so fixated on helping students learn the alphabetic elements of reading. However, fluency is very important in the primary grades because the sooner readers become automatic and efficient with word recognition, the sooner they can read more text, and more complex text. We believe that early intervention in fluency in grades 1 and 2 could prevent a host of problems that occurs at the intermediate grades. We worked with a group of teachers in first grade who were doing a marvelous job teaching students to decode. However, toward the middle of the year, when they could have shifted their attention toward fluency, they were still focused on decoding. We encouraged them to "turn the fluency corner" as soon as they saw that their students were able to decode simple short-vowel words.

Fluency:
What Does the Research Say about Instruction?

Reading fluency generally refers to how efficiently and smoothly readers recognize words. As shown in Figure 6.1, it consists of three elements: (1) accuracy, (2) reading rate or speed, and (3) prosody or expression. *Accuracy* is the percentage of words read correctly; *reading rate* is the number of correct words read per minute; and *prosody* or *expression* refers to reading with proper intonation, rhythm, stress, and pausing (Kuhn & Stahl, 2003). Note that the measure for reading rate also subsumes accuracy because it addresses the words *correct* per minute. Accuracy, rate, and prosody influence comprehension (Kuhn & Stahl, 2003; National Institute of Child Health and Human Development, 2000). It does not matter how accurate, well-paced, or expressive a student is if she does not understand what she is reading. Therefore, we believe that in order for someone to be truly fluent, comprehension must be in place. For this reason, we consider comprehension to be a necessary component of fluency as well.

When readers are accurate and read at an appropriate pace, we say they have *automaticity*. This automaticity allows readers to devote attention to the *meaning* of what they are reading (Laberge & Samuels, 1974). Dysfluent readers find it difficult to focus on meaning, because their attention is at the word level. Thus, fluency is a necessary but not a sufficient ingredient for comprehension. More is needed. Students who are fluent do have a better chance of comprehending, but we cannot guarantee that they will comprehend.

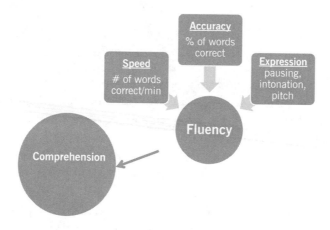

FIGURE 6.1. The three components of fluency that contribute to comprehension.

Have you ever heard someone say something like, "As long as students can read the words, as long as they get them right, how fast they read shouldn't matter"? We have heard this often, and it is a perfect example of how something can have intuitive appeal but be wrong. In an article in 2000, Rasinski (2000) identified three reasons *why* speed does matter in reading. First, slower readers read significantly less than their peers. Think about it. If there are two readers in your classroom and one reads 100 words per minute and the other reader reads 50 words per minute, it will take the second reader *twice as long* to read the same amount of material. Students who struggle to read fluently often fall behind by the middle and upper elementary school grades, as reading material becomes increasingly more difficult and reading is expected to be done silently (Worthy & Broaddus, 2002). These nonfluent readers are likely to read less than their fluent peers, putting their reading development even further at risk for delay. Second, excessively slow, expressionless reading is associated with poor comprehension. Those students who are putting so much effort into struggling through the words are actually not getting much meaning from the text. In essence, they are "barking at print" trying to get through the words, with little or no focus on meaning. Third, readers who struggle with fluency become frustrated, and their motivation declines as they advance in school.

The National Reading Panel (2001), as well as Kuhn and Stahl (2003), found that increases in fluency were associated with increases in comprehension and identified five facts about fluency intervention that should be considered during instruction. First, they concluded that what they called *guided oral reading* did improve students' fluency. Although the term *guided reading* is widely used to refer to small-group, balanced reading instruction, what the researchers meant by *guided oral reading* was any approach that included oral reading with a teacher. These approaches included repeated reading, impress reading (see below), shared reading, paired reading, or assisted reading. Second, effective, guided oral reading also was characterized by teachers' providing students with feedback about their performance and corrections for inaccurately pronounced words. Third, they indicated that successful fluency interventions included a *model* of fluent reading provided to students before, during, or after their reading, either through a peer, a teacher, or a digital version of the text. Fourth, the researchers found that high volumes of oral reading with either repetitive or nonrepetitive approaches were equally advantageous. Lastly, researchers indicated that good fluency instruction did not *just* focus on automatic word recognition but also gave attention to expression and rhythm.

In 2006, Hasbrouck and Tindal published an article in *The Reading Teacher* entitled, "Oral Reading Fluency Norms: A Valuable Assessment Tool for Reading Teachers." This article contained a listing of the oral reading fluency data (words correct per minute) for students in grades 1–8 (see Table 6.1). The document can be found at the Reading Naturally website (*www.readingnaturally.com*). The list

TABLE 6.1. Oral Reading Fluency Norms, Grades 1–8

Grade	Percentile	Fall WCPM[a]	Winter WCPM[a]	Spring WCPM[a]	Avg. weekly improvement[b]
1	90	–	81	111	1.9
	75	–	47	82	2.2
	50	–	23	53	1.9
	25	–	12	28	1.0
	10	–	6	15	0.6
2	90	106	125	142	1.1
	75	79	100	117	1.2
	50	51	72	89	1.2
	25	25	42	61	1.1
	10	11	18	31	0.6
3	90	128	146	162	1.1
	75	99	120	137	1.2
	50	71	92	107	1.1
	25	44	62	78	1.1
	10	21	36	48	0.9
4	90	145	166	180	1.1
	75	119	139	152	1.0
	50	94	112	123	0.9
	25	68	87	98	0.9
	10	45	61	72	0.8
5	90	166	182	94	0.9
	75	139	156	168	0.9
	50	110	127	139	0.9
	25	85	99	109	0.8
	10	61	74	83	0.7
6	90	177	195	204	0.8
	75	153	167	177	0.8
	50	127	140	150	0.7
	25	98	111	122	0.8
	10	68	82	93	0.8
7	90	180	192	202	0.7
	75	156	165	177	0.7
	50	128	136	150	0.7
	25	102	109	123	0.7
	10	79	88	98	0.6
8	90	185	199	199	0.4
	75	161	173	177	0.5
	50	133	146	151	0.6
	25	106	115	124	0.6
	10	77	84	97	0.6

Note. Data from Hasbrouck and Tindal (2006).

[a]WCPM, words correct per minute.

[b]Average words per week growth.

presents the reading rates of students at three points during the year (fall, winter, and spring). We describe how to use this chart in the section on diagnostic assessment, but we make note of it here because, in our opinion, these norms are invaluable to teachers as they intervene with students. These tables are necessary to interpret students' reading rates.

Although reading rates are important, fluency researchers have cautioned teachers recently about the dangers of focusing too much on speed. In an important article Rasinski (2012) described some of the issues that have occurred when fluency instruction is aimed only at increasing reading speed. He notes that students will equate being a "good reader" with being a "fast" reader and will leave comprehension in the dust as a result. Figure 6.2 illustrates the balance that should occur between speed and comprehension. If a reader has optimal speed, then he/she should be focusing on comprehension. Sometimes a student who is reading too fast will actually be sacrificing comprehension. One of the points that Rasinski makes is that a high-quality fluency program should include deep and wide reading that focuses on reading rate, accuracy, and expression in balanced proportions. He points out that expression, or the prosodic elements of reading, are actually very important. By asking students to pay attention to punctuation, the rise and fall of their voices, and the *way* that they read, we are helping them make an explicit link between word recognition and comprehension. Students must understand that they should read at an efficient pace and that they must put expression into their readings in order to reap the comprehension benefits from fluent reading. We purposefully like to use the term *efficient* word reading when referring to reading rate, as opposed to *fast, speedy,* or *quick* word recognition. The word *efficient* suggests doing something at a speed that would support reading with comprehension rather than simply doing something fast for the sake of doing it fast. Someone who is efficient is not rushed but also does not waste time. We all want students to be efficient in their word reading, but being fast for the sake of being fast is not the goal of fluency instruction.

In addition, fluency instruction can be dry and boring to students, but Rasinski (2012) cautions against allowing that to happen. We like the following quote, in which Rasinski reminds us that good fluency instruction integrates the science of reading with the art of teaching reading:

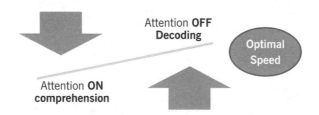

FIGURE 6.2. Optimal speed focuses on comprehension.

The science of teaching reading has shown us that reading fluency is a key component to proficient reading. . . . The art of teaching reading challenges all teachers to embed the science of reading instruction into their classrooms in ways that are authentic, engaging, and meaningful for students. (p. 520; emphasis added)

The *science of teaching reading* means that teachers are basing their lessons on content, knowledge, and strategies that are supported by research. The *art* means that teachers are using their inimitable skills with children to make fluency instruction purposeful, engaging, and meaningful. Both art and science are essential for effective teaching. A high-quality fluency intervention that integrates both the art and science of teaching begins with an understanding of how fluency fits into the developmental continuum.

Fluency on the Developmental Continuum

Fluency instruction fits into a predictable developmental sequence through which students progress. In general, this sequence explains *why* fluency is important and *what* proficiencies precede and follow it. We find Jeanne Chall's (1983) six stages of reading development useful for understanding how fluency fits into the literacy puzzle (see Figure 6.3). During the first stage (ages birth to 6), *Preliterate*, children are developing their oral language and vocabulary and becoming aware of the building blocks for traditional literacy instruction (e.g., concepts of print, letters, phonological awareness, story structure). Chall called this period of time *Stage 0* because reading itself does not formally develop, just the building blocks. At Stage 1 (grades 1 and 2), *Initial Reading and Decoding*, students are acquiring conventional literacy and developing their knowledge and application of the alphabetic principle. They are solidifying letter-sound knowledge and applying it as they decode. Because students are so focused on unlocking print, this stage is nicknamed "glued to the print," and the name fits because at this stage students are primarily focused on accurately decoding words.

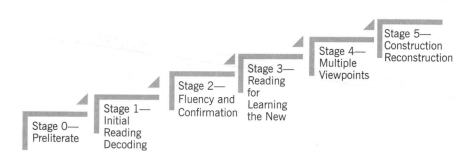

FIGURE 6.3. Chall's stages of literacy development.

Stage 2 (grades 2 and 3), *Fluency and Confirmation*, is when fluency becomes very important. This is all about ungluing the focus from the print and increasing fluency and automaticity. Students work on becoming more efficient in their word reading, more expressive, and acquire complex letter-sound patterns in multisyllabic words. In a sense, this stage prepares students for Stage 3, when texts increase in both length and complexity. At Stage 3 (grades 4–8), students are *Reading for Learning the New*, and the focus of their reading is learning information about science, history/social science. The average text also becomes much lengthier, gradually increasing from around 150 words in first grade to 2,000 words in fourth grade (Afflerbach, 1998). This increase in length at Stage 3 is why students must become more fluent in Stage 2—without fluency they will struggle to get through the volume of text required at the Stage 3. The importance of attaining fluency in a timely manner is all the more important in light of the Common Core expectation that children continually be exposed to texts of increasing complexity.

At Stage 4 (high school), *Multiple Viewpoints*, the focus moves beyond simply acquiring new information to encompass evaluating, critiquing, integrating, and comparing multiple perspectives. Stage 3, in which students build skill in reading and understanding information, lays the groundwork for the critical analysis necessary in Stage 4. In the final stage of literacy development, Stage 5 (adulthood), *Construction and Reconstruction*, learners read for their own purposes, be they professional or personal. The previous stages have equipped adult readers with the tools needed to read for a variety of purposes and to shift their strategies based on their purpose and the text. We believe that teachers need to understand what expectations follow Stage 2, *Fluency and Confirmation*. When teachers have an understanding of what they are preparing students to do with fluency work and see the big picture encompassed by Chall's (1983) stages of reading development, instruction becomes both urgent and meaningful.

Chall's stages and the ages and grades attached to them represent typical development. Although we can all learn about what is typical for development and fluency, most teachers know that fewer and fewer of today's students are "typical." Abby, a spirited, experienced teacher with whom we worked, challenged us once by asking:

> "Okay, well that may be typical, but I can tell you that I teach only about two 'typical' children per year. The rest of them are on two ends of the extremes. They're either struggling mightily or could get up and teach the class for me. Don't tell me what is typical; just tell me how I know when to help them."

She was right. Teachers need guidance about when to step in and offer fluency instruction. So, how can we tell if students need fluency intervention, especially in grades PreK–2? When should we intervene?

We find that teachers are not used to focusing on fluency in grades 1 and 2, and sometimes for good reason. After all, a great deal of energy is spent on helping students move from the early stages of literacy, in which they are acquiring foundational skills, to applying those skills in real reading. Students must be able to decode accurately before they can become more fluent. Accuracy precedes fluency, but we often find that some teachers focus on phonics and decoding beyond the point at which students have become accurate and do so to the exclusion of promoting fluent reading and rereading. As Chall's (1983) developmental continuum reflects, after students can decode all of the short vowels in CVC words, instruction should focus on fluency (see Figure 6.3).

As teachers provide support for fluency interventions, we also suggest that they bolster students' automaticity with the most frequently occurring words in English, sometimes called *sight words*. These are the words students will see over and over in print, and if they falter with these words, they will be slow and frustrated. These words sometimes have irregular spellings that can be complicated to students in the primary grades (e.g., *have, some, the*). We set a goal of 200 words that students should be able to recognize almost automatically—usually within less than 3 seconds—by the end of first grade. Teaching and rehearsing high-frequency, or sight, words contributes to fluent reading because these words make up a large proportion of print. If students can automatically recognize these high-frequency/ sight words, they will be "over the hump" with almost 25% of the words that they will encounter. There are many lists of high-frequency sight words, including the Dolch (1936) list, Fry (1980) list, and several more recent lists. Unlike many educational textbooks and materials, these word lists have not changed because the most common words are fairly stable over decades. (No one is inventing new prepositions, after all!) As we describe in the next section, there are many engaging websites that support high-frequency word learning.

Although the focus of this book is grades PreK–2, you will notice that our developmental continuum shows reading rates that go to the end of grade 1. We typically find that students in grade 2 who need intervention have not met the end-of-the-year benchmark for grade 1, which is virtually the same as the beginning of the year benchmark for grade 2. In the paragraph below we provide some additional targets that extend into grade 2.

Figure 6.4 provides reading rate (words correct per minute [WCPM]) guidelines through the second grade to guide teachers in knowing what is typical. (The inclusion of these reading rate standards is not to indicate that expression or comprehension is to be sacrificed for fluency. These standards simply provide clear goals that are easily measurable. As we describe in the following section, rubrics for evaluating expression should also be used.)

Accuracy must be considered first. At the beginning of Figure 6.4, we list accuracy in grade-level text because this is the first step in becoming fluent. Reading pace or speed does not matter if students are not reading the words accurately. If students are not accurate in grade-level text, then they must receive additional decoding instruction before a focus on fluency will assist them. If students are not

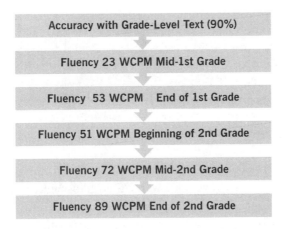

FIGURE 6.4. Fluency standards.

able to attain 90% accuracy on a passage for their grade level, then they need support in decoding the patterns and letter-sounds that are preventing accuracy. Only after this level of accuracy has been attained will focusing on other elements of fluency—namely, speed and expression—benefit students.

Diagnostic Assessments to Inform Intervention Goals

Fluency will not be a concern in PreK or kindergarten because the focus at these levels is on learning letter-sounds, decoding, and acquiring beginning words. However, as soon as the middle of grade 1, when benchmarks are first available, students may need fluency intervention. A teacher's first indication that intervention is needed comes when the student does not pass the universal, schoolwide literacy screener. The results would indicate that, for some reason, the student is not able to adequately recognize the words and comprehend grade-level text. If a student does not pass a literacy screener in first or second grade, we suggest first ruling out basic decoding and phonemic segmentation problems. If the student is able to decode at least four out of the five short vowels consistently, administering a fluency assessment would be in order. (If not, as we discussed in Chapter 5, difficulties with phonemic segmentation should be considered before providing a decoding intervention.)

Assessments of Reading Rate

An assessment of oral reading rate is a very common technique for identifying the need for fluency intervention. Assessing oral reading rate is very easy and provides results that can readily be compared to the norms in the text box *How to Use Reading Rate Norms.* Essentially, a student is asked to read several passages at grade level for 1 minute. For each passage, the examiner records the number of WCPM (see sample forms in Figure 6.5). We provide instructions for giving an assessment of reading rate in the text box *How to Give a Reading Rate Assessment.* A high-quality assessment will include three different passages at the same level. Because reading these passages takes only 1 minute each, the assessment is not overly taxing for the student.

In our work with schools, we have encountered a number of excellent questions about assessments of reading rate. We address many of these questions in detail in several text boxes. We often hear teachers talk about assessments of reading rate as "fluency assessments," but we prefer the term *reading rate* because it reminds everyone that the assessment is capturing only one component of fluency.

Assessments of Expression

As long-time fluency researcher and expert Tim Rasinski recently reminded us, speed cannot be the only goal of fluency instruction. For this reason, we suggest

---

HOW TO USE READING RATE NORMS

1. Obtain three estimates of the student's reading rate in WCPM using three passages.
   Example: 35, 33, 37 WCPM for a second grader

2. Identify the median score, which is the middle score.
   Example: 35 WCPM

3. Compare the median reading rate score to Table 6.1, Oral Reading Fluency Norms, Grades 1–8.
   a. Go to the section that matches the student's *grade* (i.e., second grade).
   b. Find the column that represents the time of the year that is nearest to the time that you administered the assessment (e.g., fall, spring, or winter).
   c. Look under the Percentile column. This column indicates the reading rate in WCPM that students at different percentile ranks read. For instance, the 20th percentile rank reflects that 20% of the scores were at the same WCPM or lower. We usually look at the 50th percentile rank by following along the column that shows that WCPM read at that level. We want students to be at least 10 words above or below the number of WCPM at the 50th percentile (Hasbrouck & Tindale, 2006).
      Example: In the fall of second grade the 50th percentile was 51 WCPM. Our student's score of 35 WCPM was more than 10 WCPM below that score (16 WCPM) and for that reason, we would recommend a fluency intervention.

Student Copy

Susan was nervous because it was her first day attending a new school.

She had just moved from a different state. She did not know anybody at her

new school. She was worried that the kids would be mean to her. Both her

mother and father had started new jobs, so Susan had to ride the bus to

school on her own that first day. This made her even more nervous. As Susan

was waiting for the bus, another girl about her age walked up to the bus stop

too. She said her name was Karen. She asked if Susan was going to River Park

School. Susan told her that she was starting school there that day.

Karen and Susan talked while they waited for the bus. Susan soon

found out that they were the same age and would be in the same class at

school. On the bus, Karen introduced Susan to a few of her friends. They

talked about what they both liked to do. Susan was happy to hear that Karen

also liked to read. She was excited to find out that Karen had a puppy, just

like Susan did. The two decided they should meet after school so their

puppies could play together. When they got to school, Karen gave Susan a

tour. She made sure to show Susan where the bathrooms were. Even before

the first school bell rang, Susan was starting to feel like she belonged. She

was so glad she had met Karen. She had a friend!

Assessor Copy

Student Name: _____ Date: _____

1. Place the Student Copy in front of the student. Point to the names on the Student Copy as you read them:

   "This is a story about <u>Susan and Karen</u>. I want you to read this story to me. You'll have 1 minute to read as much as you can. When I say "begin," start reading aloud at the top of the page. Do your best reading. If you have trouble with a word, I'll tell it to you. Do you have any questions? Begin."

2. Start the timer.
3. While the student is reading, mark errors with a slash (/).
4. At 1 minute, mark the last word read with a bracket (]).
5. When the student gets to a logical stopping place, say **"Stop."**

<u>Susan</u> was nervous because it was her first day attending a new school.	13
She had just moved from a different state. She did not know anybody at her	28
new school. She was worried that the kids would be mean to her. Both her	43
mother and father had started new jobs, so Susan had to ride the bus to	58
school on her own that first day. This made her even more nervous. As Susan	73
was waiting for the bus, another girl about her age walked up to the bus stop	89
too. She said her name was <u>Karen</u>. She asked if Susan was going to River Park	105
School. Susan told her that she was starting school there that day.	117
Karen and Susan talked while they waited for the bus. Susan soon	129
found out that they were the same age and would be in the same class at	145
school. On the bus, Karen introduced Susan to a few of her friends. They	159
talked about what they both liked to do. Susan was happy to hear that Karen	174
also liked to read. She was excited to find out that Karen had a puppy, just	190
like Susan did. The two decided they should meet after school so their	203
puppies could play together. When they got to school, Karen gave Susan a	216
tour. She made sure to show Susan where the bathrooms were. Even before	229
the first school bell rang, Susan was starting to feel like she belonged. She	243
was so glad she had met Karen. She had a friend!	254

Total Words Read: _____ − # of Errors: _____ = CWPM: _____

FIGURE 6.5. Sample reading rate passages (student and examiner copies). Copyright 2006 by the University of Oregon. Reprinted by permission.

HOW TO GIVE A READING RATE ASSESSMENT

. . . .

Materials

- Three passages of about 200 words at the student's grade level (unpracticed texts).
- One copy of the passage for the student to read (see Figure 6.5 for example).
- One copy of the passage for the examiner to use to mark errors (see Figure 6.5 for example).
- A stopwatch (preferably without a loud beeping sound).
- A pencil.

1. Preassessment Directions to the Student

Place a passage in front of the student and one for yourself, as the examiner. Tell the student that he/she will read the passage starting at the beginning. Explain that if the student has difficulty on a word, you will support him/her and that when you say "Stop," you would like him/her to stop reading. We also tell students that we will ask them questions about the passage after they have finished reading so that they understand that the speed reading is not the goal.

2. Beginning the Assessment

Say to the student, "Begin." As soon as the student reads the first word, start the stopwatch.

3. During the Assessment

As the student is reading, place a slash through words that are omitted or read incorrectly. (Resist the urge to write down the words that students substitute when they read words incorrectly. For example, if the word is *cat* and the student says "cab," *do not* try to write the word *cab* above the word *cat*. It will be a distraction and is not necessary for obtaining a reading rate. If the student pauses on a word, wait 3 seconds and if he/she does not pronounce the word, supply it *and mark it with a slash*.

The following are some guidelines for errors:

- If the student cannot read any words correct within the first five words, then stop and give a score of 0. (We recommend conducting the assessment with a new passage that is one grade level below the level of the attempted passage.)
- If a student correctly reads and then repeats a word, there is no error. However, increased repetitions will compromise a students' reading rate.

(continued)

- Do not count words incorrect for imperfect pronunciation due to second language, dialect, or articulation.
- If a student inserts a word, it is not counted as a error. Again, however, inserting words will impact reading rate.
- If a student reads a word incorrectly and then self-corrects, *within 3 seconds* the word is counted correct.
- All words must be read in the proper order to be counted as correct.
- The number of words that the student reads = the number of potential errors. For example, if you count a hyphenated word (e.g., *self-described*) as one word in your word count, then it may only be counted once as an error even if the student mispronounces both parts (e.g., *set-depth*).

4. Ending the Assessment

Once a minute has passed, say "Stop," and place a bracket after the last word that the student read (e.g., "The door closed] quickly.") Say to the student, "Tell me what this passage was about," or "Tell me what you liked about this passage."

5. Calculating Words Read Correctly per Minute

Count the number of words the student read in total and subtract from this number the errors that were made (e.g., 45 words – 4 errors = 41 WCPM). (See Figure 6.5.)

6. Repeat Steps 1–5 with Two Additional Passages

7. Use the Median Score

Use the median score—the one in the middle of the range (e.g., for scores of 120, 123, and 125 WCPM, 123 WCPM is the median score).

that teachers working with students in need of fluency interventions also conduct a separate assessment of students' expression. Many times students who are reading slowly are also struggling with expression. Because expression, or prosody, includes a number of elements such as pausing, changing intonation, and attending to the rhythm of text, we suggest that teachers use qualitative rubrics for evaluating it.

A *qualitative measure* is one that does not depend on counts of quantities, but instead relies on the judgment of a professional about the quality of reading. A *rubric* is a tool that consists of statements that describe a student's performance

Teachers use expression rubrics as a way to assess students' expression. Figure 6.6 shows an expression rubric designed by Rasinski (2004). It has four sections: Expression and Volume, Phrasing, Smoothness, and Pace. In the *Expression and Volume* section, teachers are to think about a volume and expression that would be comfortable in a conversation with a friend and to consider the degree to which the reading of the text matches these qualities. *Phrasing* refers to the extent to which readers pay attention to punctuation and use their voices to reflect it. A student who reads with phrasing will read a group of words together and then pause at an appropriate point, as opposed to reading word by word. *Smoothness* refers to the degree to which readers stop and start awkwardly or repeat words in

Name: _____

	1	2	3	4
Expression and Volume	Reads in a quiet voice as if to get words out. The reading does not sound natural, like talking to a friend.	Reads in a quiet voice. The reading sounds natural in part of the text, but the reader does not always sound like he/she is talking to a friend.	Reads with volume and expression. However, sometimes the reader slips into expressionless reading and does not sound like he/she is talking to a friend.	Reads with varied volume and expression. The reader sounds like he/she is talking to a friend with his/her voice matching the interpretation of the passage.
Phrasing	Reads word by word in a monotone voice.	Reads in two- or three-word phrases, not adhering to punctuation, stress, and intonation.	Reads with a mixture of run-ons, mid-sentence pauses for breath, and some choppiness. There is reasonable stress and intonation.	Reads with good phrasing; adhering to punctuation, stress, and intonation.
Smoothness	Frequently hesitates while reading, sounds out words, and repeats words or phrases. The reader makes multiple attempts to read the same passage.	Reads with extended pauses or hesitations. The reader has many "rough spots."	Reads with occasional breaks in rhythm. The reader has difficulty with specific words and/or sentence structures.	Reads smoothly with some breaks, but self- corrects with difficult words and/or sentence structures.
Pace	Reads slowly and laboriously.	Reads moderately slowly.	Reads fast and slow throughout reading.	Reads at a conversational pace throughout the reading.

Score _____

FIGURE 6.6. Fluency rubric. Scores of 10 or more indicate that the student is making good progress in fluency. Scores below 10 indicate that the student needs additional instruction in fluency. Modified with permission from Timothy Rasinski.

multiple attempts to read them correctly. Readers who are smooth will have few breaks and will self-correct easily with minimal loss of expression. Lastly, readers who are properly *paced* will read at a conversational pace as opposed to reading too slowly or quickly.

To use this rubric, we suggest that teachers ask students to read a passage at their reading level for several minutes. As the student is reading, the teacher can rate his/her expression in each of the categories with a maximum of 4 points per category. A score of 16 reflects a student who is very skilled at expression. Rasinski (2004) suggests that a score below 10 indicates that the student is struggling. Many teachers find it helpful to make notes as they are using the rubric, especially in areas where the student has difficulty. Often, teachers will apply this rubric over the course of a week, after listening to a student reading several passages. In these cases, the teacher simply keeps a clipboard handy with the rubrics and jots down notes during guided reading, reading workshop, or independent reading. As described below, notes from the rubric are also kept on the Intervention Goal-Setting Sheet to give attention to the expressive elements of fluency instruction required for each student.

Assessing Reading Level

We have found that in order to plan strong fluency interventions, teachers must have an estimate of each student's reading level. Without some knowledge of a students' reading level, teachers would be unable to select appropriate passages, Readers' Theatre scripts, or poems for fluency interventions. In addition, if a student is below grade level, then the level of the progress monitoring passages should be at the student's reading level as opposed to grade level (see the text box *Grade Level or Reading Level*).

There are many tools for estimating reading levels including informal reading inventories, the STAR tests, and other online tools. Table 6.2 provides word accuracy and comprehension rates for independent-, instructional-, and frustrational-level materials. There are some important clarifications to make with respect to both the accuracy and comprehension standards shown in this table. Originally, Betts (1946) suggested that students need to read independently at accuracy levels as high as 99%. However, recent analysis and review of the research suggest that this might not be necessary in all cases, especially when students are in the beginning stages of reading (Halladay, 2012). Thus, we have created a *range* for independent level. In addition, at times a students' comprehension and accuracy levels will not be aligned. For instance, a student might be reading a passage at levels that would suggest frustration and then comprehending at instructional levels. On the other hand, a student might have lower comprehension but higher accuracy. In the primary grades, especially with nonfiction passages, we often find that students have higher comprehension than word accuracy because they are reading simple

GRADE LEVEL OR READING LEVEL:
WHAT TO DO WHEN ASSESSING READING RATE?

When we are talking with teachers, we are frequently asked about the level of text for assessing reading rate. Teachers ask, "Should I use a text that is on the student's reading level or grade level to assess reading rate?" Fortunately, this very question is addressed in the article accompanying the oral reading fluency norms in Table 6.1 (Hasbrouck & Tindal, 2006). The answer lies in whether or not the assessment is being used for a *screening, diagnostic*, or *progress monitoring* purposes.

If the teacher has no information about the student's reading rate then, we first suggest a *screening* purpose. In other words, use the assessment to find out if the student is below accepted levels for fluency when compared to peers. Because we want to compare students to others who are in their same grade, we would use their grade level for passages. We are focused on comparing the students to other students and so for screening purposes we use a passage that is at the student's *grade level*. This will allow the examiner to compare the student's reading rate to the norms for his/her grade level. This recommendation follows the guidelines for using the oral reading fluency norms shown in Table 6.1: "Having students read for one minute in an unpracticed grade-level passage yields a rate and accuracy score that can be compared to the new ORF norms" (Hasbrouck & Tindal, 2006, p. 5). If the student's score is 10 words below the number of WCPM at the 50th percentile, then additional development of a student's fluency, both the reading rate and expression, *may* be in order. However, if a student's reading rate is significantly below level, than we suggest also making sure that the student has basic decoding skills, as described in Chapter 5. First graders who, at the end of the year, have a reading rate *below* 20 WCPM are at significant risk and those below 40 have some level or risk. In our experience, students reading below 20 WCPM usually are struggling with decoding.

If a teacher has determined that a student has basic decoding skills (can decode short vowels, at least) and still needs additional work on reading rate then, a *diagnostic* assessment of reading rate based on the student's *instructional reading level* is needed. Unlike in the screening purpose, we are not interested in comparing the student to others. Instead we want to compare the student to him/herself over a period of time to see if he/she improves. We want an assessment that is matched to the student's instructional reading level. The instructional reading level is the level of material that the student can read with 90% accuracy. Giving a student a reading rate measure on the instructional level would provide a baseline from which to assess *progress* in an intervention.

For example, let's say that a second grader was given a reading rate screening and had a score of 25 WCPM. The teacher ruled out decoding as an issue and decided to give a reading rate assessment on the student's instructional reading level: first grade. The reading rate may or may not change, but by giving a reading rate on the student's instructional level, the teacher could be sure that the assessment is appropriate to the intervention. Throughout an intervention, as the teacher is *monitoring progress*, passages level would continue to be selected at the student's instructional level.

TABLE 6.2. Standards for Independent-, Instructional-, and Frustrational-Level Materials

Level	Accuracy	Comprehension
Independent 　Reads without help.	100–96%	90–100%
Instructional 　May need support to read and some 　assistance with words.	95–90%	89–75%
Frustrational 　Material is too difficult to read 　under any conditions.	89% or lower	70% or lower

Note. In 1946 Betts set word accuracy levels at 99% for independent-level reading. However, for some time this stringent standard has been debated (see Halladay, 2012; Hunt, 1970; Powell, 1970).

narrative texts, for which they have strong background knowledge. In many cases the comprehension questions are ones for which they can access prior knowledge and answer.

Usually we use word accuracy as a gauge for students' reading level because in the primary grades students are acquiring the skills for accurate word reading. At the upper elementary level, we tend to encounter students who are accurate but not comprehending. If a student is accurate but slow (i.e., below reading rate expectations), then fluency instruction is warranted. In fact, this is a classic fluency case: a slow decoder whose cognitive energies are not being devoted to comprehension. If reading rate norms are being met and the student is not comprehending, fluency instruction is not what is needed. In general, we suggest that teachers identify the instructional reading level of students and use passages at this level for planning fluency interventions. There is some research that suggests that the level of reading materials for fluency instruction should be slightly above a students' independent level so that they are being challenged in the rereading that they do (Kuhn & Stahl, 2000).

Assessments of High-Frequency (Sight) Words

In grades 1 and 2, many students who are struggling with fluency also require additional support in learning the most frequently occurring words in English. There are literally hundreds of these lists, including Fry's (1980) Instant Word List, the Dolch list (1936), and many others. For the purposes of assessing primary grade students and knowing where to start an intervention with them, we like to use the Dolch list broken down into grade levels (see Figure 6.7). The list was designed quite some time ago by Edward Dolch (1936); it consists of 220 of the most common words found in reading materials at each grade level. For first-grade

Preprimer		Primer		First Grade		Second Grade		Third Grade	
a	look	all	out	after	let	always	or	about	laugh
and	make	am	please	again	live	around	pull	better	light
away	me	are	pretty	an	may	because	read	bring	long
big	my	at	ran	any	of	been	right	carry	much
blue	not	ate	ride	as	old	before	sing	clean	myself
can	one	be	saw	ask	once	best	sit	cut	never
come	play	black	say	by	open	both	sleep	done	only
down	red	brown	she	could	over	buy	tell	draw	own
find	run	but	so	every	put	call	their	drink	pick
for	said	came	soon	fly	round	cold	these	eight	seven
funny	see	did	that	from	some	does	those	fall	shall
go	the	do	there	give	stop	don't	upon	far	show
help	three	eat	they	going	take	fast	us	full	six
here	to	four	this	had	thank	first	use	got	small
I	two	get	too	has	them	five	very	grow	start
in	up	good	under	her	then	found	wash	hold	ten
is	we	have	want	him	think	gave	which	hot	today
it	where	he	was	his	walk	goes	why	hurt	together
jump	yellow	into	well	how	were	green	wish	if	try
little	you	like	went	just	when	its	work	keep	warm
		must	what	know		made	would	kind	
		new	white			many	write		
		no	who			off	your		
		now	will						
		on	with						
		our	yes						

FIGURE 6.7. All 220 Dolch words by grade in alphabetical order. Reprinted with permission from *dolchword.net*.

teachers who are working with students who require additional fluency instruction, we suggest using the grade 1 list to assess high-frequency knowledge and then targeting the unknown words during intervention. Often students in grade 1 who need fluency work will have gaps in the Preprimer and Primer lists as well. To assess student knowledge of these words, we create flash cards and a record sheet. The student is shown each word for 3 seconds and given credit for knowing the word if it can be given correctly within the 3-second time. *No corrections are offered by the teacher for incorrect words.* The purpose of this assessment is to identify the words that are known quickly and the ones that are not. For second graders, we suggest giving different lists based on the students' WCPM. If a student is slower than 50 WCPM, we suggest using the grade 1 list, because we have found that students at this rate will have gaps in the grade 1 list. Students in grade 2 who read faster than 50 WCPM would benefit from being assessed using the grade 2 list.

What to Do with Diagnostic Assessments

We are comfortable with using a multifaceted approach to assessing fluency that connects with the most recent research and thinking. These four assessments sample three types of fluency behavior that interventions should target. These include:

- A quantitative estimate of a student's reading rate that can be compared to national norms.
- A qualitative assessment of a student's prosody (expression, volume, smoothness, and pacing).
- An assessment of specific high-frequency words that the student needs to learn.
- An estimate of reading level for matching materials.

For each student, we suggest recording these four pieces of diagnostic data on a form that can then guide intervention goal setting and planning (see Form 6.1). The sample diagnostic data presented in Figure 6.8 pertain to a group of second graders who were assessed in the middle of the school year. Thus, their reading rate scores should be close to 72 ± 10 WCPM. We add ± 10 WCPM because this is the standard error of measure that Hasbrouck and Tindale (2006) specify in the directive about how to use the guidelines. Note that Darion's rate (63) is actually within 10 WCPM of the benchmark, but he was kept in a fluency intervention group because his expression was not strong. He stops and starts and is rather halting in his reading—qualities indicating that although his rate is close to target, he probably is not paying close attention to the meaning of what he is reading. Brenna has a reading rate of 60 WCPM and is highest in expression, suggesting that she is paying attention to the meaning of what she reads. However, her fluency would

Intervention Goal-Setting Sheet

Instructional focus of group: _____

Intervention goal: To *(a) increase speed by at least 6 WCPM and (b) fluency by 2–3 rubric points*

Meeting days: *Mon., Tue., Wed.* Meeting time: *M/12–12:30 T & W/1–1:55* Hrs/week: *1.5*

Progress monitoring measure and passage level: *MM & GOM: Rate—DIBELS 2nd Grade Oral Reading Passages Expression—Rubric Comprehension: Reading A–Z Comprehension Quick Checks Level K*

Frequency of administration: *Rate-weekly   Expression-biweekly   Comprehension: twice-week 3 and 6*

Student Diagnostic Data

Student Name: *Abe*	**Student Name**: *Brenna*
Reading Level: *2.1 (STAR)*	**Reading Level**: *2.0 (STAR)*
Reading Rate: *55 WCPM*	**Reading Rate**: *60 WCPM*
Fluency Rubric Score: *8/16* *2 on all levels.*	**Fluency Rubric Score**: *12/16* *3's on all levels.*
High-Frequency Word Score: *33/46* *(2nd grade list)*	**High-Frequency Word Score**: *30/46* *(2nd grade list)*
Notes: *Expression is really compromised. Having difficulty in oral reading.*	**Notes**: *Reading rate is slow, probably due to high-frequency word score, but expression is good.*
Student Name: *Caleb*	**Student Name**: *Darion*
Reading Level: *2.3 (STAR)*	**Reading Level**: *2.4 (STAR)*
Reading Rate: *59 WCPM*	**Reading Rate**: *63 WCPM*
Fluency Rubric Score: *10/16* *2 on smoothness, 2 on pace.*	**Fluency Rubric Score**: *9/16* *Score of 2 in phrasing and 1 in smoothness. Reads fast but stops and starts. Very halting.*
High-Frequency Word Score: *30/46* *(2nd grade list)*	**High-Frequency Word Score**: *35/46*
Notes: *Uneven with expression. Sometimes sounds just right and other times does not.*	**Notes**: *Has the fastest rate of all students but is not very expressive. Needs to work on expression.*

FIGURE 6.8. Sample Intervention Goal-Setting Sheet.

be bolstered by strengthening her high-frequency word knowledge. Like Darion, Caleb needs additional support with expression and also needs to increase his speed. Although these students have slightly different strengths and weaknesses, overall they can all be served in a fluency intervention group focusing on increasing speed, expression, and the number of known high-frequency words.

Determining the Focus of the Intervention

Prior to planning fluency interventions, teachers need to analyze diagnostic information to identify the focus and decide how the intervention will be monitored on a weekly basis (see Figure 6.8). Although we normally advocate for only one focus in most interventions, when it comes to fluency, we suggest two foci. We always include a measure of reading rate and either a measure of expression or high-frequency words. The reason we encourage a dual focus is that we have seen fluency interventions that focus only on speed. Typically, the students are doing repeated oral reading of one passage day after day, a practice that often results in students becoming bored and tuning out. The result is students who become excellent speed readers but who often pay little attention to meaning—the very purpose of fluency enhancement. High-quality fluency interventions consequently focus on both reading rate and expression.

We insist that knowing a student's reading level is important because without it, teachers cannot select the appropriate reading level of progress monitoring passages. As described in the text box *Grade Level or Reading Level*, passages used for monitoring the progress of a student's reading rate should match the student's *reading level*. In fact, on the Intervention Goal-Setting Sheet for Fluency, we ask that teachers specify the grade level of the passages (see Form 6.1 and Figure 6.8). In order to progress-monitor the reading rate, a teacher will need a set of passages that has been designed to assess reading rate. These sets of passages are usually around 200–300 words, have the same readability level, and often provide two forms, one to record reading rate and one for the students to read. Many of these look exactly like the reading rate assessments that we showed in Figure 6.5. Each time progress monitoring is planned, we suggest having on hand one or two extra passages in case a problem is encountered with the first passage. Several years ago, we found that students consistently struggled with a passage about Guatemala because of several difficult multisyllabic words. Although the passage was technically at the same difficulty level as the others we were using, it did not, in fact, prove to be similar in actuality. Free reading rate progress monitoring passages can be obtained at DIBELS (*www.dibels.uoregon.edu*) and at EasyCBM (*www. easyCBM.com*). We like these because they are well organized, easy to use, and have been empirically tested.

As we mentioned, we believe that fluency interventions have sometimes turned into speed drills, so we also suggest that teachers monitor expression and/or high-frequency word learning. To monitor expression, we suggest using the fluency rubric featured in Figure 6.6 to assess a student's reading of a passage that he/she has read one time before. The passage can be taken from any piece that is on the student's reading level. For monitoring growth in high-frequency words, we simply suggest that teachers keep a list of the words they are targeting as the progress monitoring measure.

As discussed in Chapter 2, in addition to MM measures such as those of reading rate and expression, teachers should also use a GOM measure. However, in the case of fluency in grades 1 and 2, the best GOM measure happens to be a measure of oral reading rate. Because this measure actually predicts strong reading in the future, it essentially *is* a GOM measure.

However, we do suggest that teachers keep an eye on comprehension for students in a fluency intervention so that the speed–comprehension imbalance does not take hold. We recommend using the Comprehension Quick Checks on the Reading A–Z website (*www.readinga-z.com*). These are simple passages on a variety of reading levels that include between 5 and 10 comprehension questions. There are multiple passages at each reading level that can be easily administered with some level of integrity from a comprehension standpoint. In other words, we believe that these Comprehension Quick Checks provide a reasonable estimate of a student's comprehension. However, keep in mind that they are not in-depth measures of reading comprehension.

Planning a Fluency Intervention

Figure 6.9 shows the four parts of a fluency intervention and the amount of time devoted to each part. We suggest dividing the time equally between reading for expression and reading to improve rate (about 10 minutes per activity, or about 70% of the entire intervention time). Activities that focus on improving reading rate often involve repeated oral reading with feedback and some type of timing of the reading. However, we have seen entire fluency interventions focusing on this kind of activity to the detriment (and boredom) of students. So we suggest that an equivalent amount of time be dedicated to reading for expression by repeatedly rehearsing poems, raps, and Readers' Theatre selections. By balancing these two purposes, interventions can stay lively, focused, and purposeful. We also suggest that 15% of the time (or about 5 minutes) be spent on high-frequency/sight words and comprehension follow-up. When fluency interventions fail to address comprehension, students get the idea that just reading to "sound good" or to "be fast" is the goal. When teachers incorporate comprehension into a fluency lesson, they are showing students that comprehension matters. Also, comprehension of a passage gives students an authentic reason to reread, a practice that also enhances

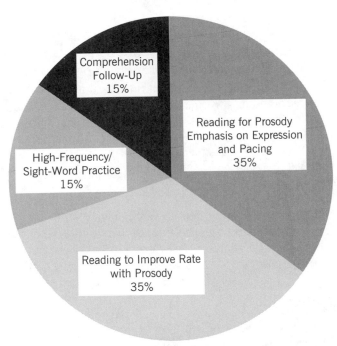

FIGURE 6.9. Parts of a fluency intervention.

their rate. (See the text box *How to Keep a Comprehension Focus in a Fluency Intervention.*)

In the primary grades, practice with high-frequency/sight words and high-frequency word phrases is also typically given too little time. We have found a number of lively games to use for learning high-frequency/sight words and phrases.

In *The Reading Teacher* Marcel (2011) uses the acronym REAL to remind students to focus on all elements of fluent reading: (1) rate, (2) expression, (3) accuracy, and (4) learning (comprehension). A lively graphic in the article reminds students of fluency goals. In the *R* square of the graphic the teacher identifies the student's current rate and the degree to which that rate needs to improve. In the *E* square, kid-friendly language is used to communicate with students about their expression in terms of three foci: intonation (voice goes up and down), phrasing (scooping or reading words together), and obeying punctuation. The *A* square refers to accuracy, which includes the student's percentage of word accuracy along with descriptors about self-monitoring. The *L* square helps students remember that reading is fundamentally about learning and remembering ideas, plots, and themes. Importantly, this graphic also supports an integrated approach to fluency instruction, in which all of four of the elements of fluency are integrated into most fluency practices. We agree, and, with the exception of high-frequency/sight-word practice, we emphasize each of the elements in suggested strategies.

HOW TO KEEP A COMPREHENSION FOCUS IN A FLUENCY INTERVENTION

We have seen many excellent fluency interventions that are lively, research-based, and multifaceted but which do not give adequate attention to comprehension. Part of the problem is that most interventions must be conducted in a short amount of time and must be focused on accuracy, reading rate, and prosody. Nonetheless, good fluency interventions must also send the clear message to students that comprehension cannot be compromised. Below are a few suggestions for integrating comprehension instruction into fluency interventions.

1. Model comprehension when you model fluent reading. Most fluency interventions include teacher modeling of accurate, efficient, and expressive reading. As teachers model these elements of fluency, they can also talk about comprehension. For instance, a teacher might say, "If I am going to read with expression, I really have to understand what is going on. For example, I need to understand that Tara is really hurt by Eric."
2. Follow initial readings of passages with comprehension questions. It's not what you say that matters, it's what you *do*. This could not be truer with the issue of comprehension. Telling students about the importance of comprehension is far less important than *showing* them. Consistently asking questions at the end of fluency practice demonstrates that you, as a teacher, do value you comprehension.
3. Use graphic organizers to record comprehension across the week. Many teachers tell us that part of the problem with comprehension activities is that they take too long during an abbreviated fluency intervention. We agree and suggest that teachers use graphic organizers throughout the week that can be developed. For instance, KWLs, story maps, fact–opinion, and cause–effect graphics allow students to add a little bit each day without turning the fluency lesson into a full-blown comprehension lesson.

Figure 6.10 provides a sample Six-Week Intervention-Planning Sheet showing a set of activities that emphasizes all four parts of the fluency instruction. Form 6.2 is a blank template. Having witnessed (and even guided) some pretty dreary, repetitive fluency interventions, we emphasize the importance of a lively, balanced plan that engages students. Although the fluency lesson contains four repeated sections, the activities in these sections can vary. Note, for instance, that the activities for improving reading rate include both repeated oral reading and a whole-class choral reading lesson (described below). Both include repeated reading but depart from the droning of purposeless rereading and provide teacher guidance and modeling of reading. In addition, the lesson integrates a mixture of strategies to improve expression, including phrase instruction, poetry, and Readers' Theatre. The lesson also reflects progress monitoring of both expression and reading rate to mirror the renewed emphasis on expression in the literature. Many of the strategies referenced in the lesson are described in detail in the following section.

Six-Week Intervention-Planning Sheet for Fluency

Instructional focus of group: _Increasing reading rate and expression_   Reading Level: _2.0–2.4_

Intervention goal: To _(a) increase speed by at least 6 WCPM and (b) fluency by 2–3 rubric points by April 1st_

Meeting days: _Mon., Tue., Wed., Thurs._   Meeting time: _M/TH, 12–12:30 T/W, 1–1:55_   Hrs/week: _2_

Progress monitoring measure and passage level: _Speed—DIBELS 2nd grade Oral Reading Passages & Expression—Rubric_

Frequency of administration: _Reading rate—weekly   Expression—biweekly_

Week 1 Feb. 18–22	**Week2** Feb. 25–March 1	**Week 3** March 4–8
Content: Rate (WCCR): To the Lake (Book) Expression (Phrasing): FRCC.org passage with phrase boundaries marked High frequency: Personal cards **Notes:** Introduce REAL Reader (Fig. 8.12) **Activities:** **Whole-Class Choral Reading (WCCR):** Tue.—model, listen, choral | Wed.—review hard words, echo read | Thur.—choral & paired **Comprehension:** At least two comprehension questions after WCCR. **Expression/Phrasing:** Mon.—model chunked phrases & read chorally | Tue.—choral read chunked phrases & discuss why phrases are chunked | Wed.—individual whisper read chunked passages | Thurs.—choral read passage without phrase boundaries. **HF Words:** Tue.—Read for teacher | Wed. & Thurs.—I Read, You Point, Roll–Say–Keep **Progress Monitoring:** None—President's Day, Mon.	**Content:** Rate (WCCR): Tata's Beat (Book) Expression (Phrasing): FRCC.org passage High frequency: Personal cards **Notes:** Review I am a REAL Reader **Activities:** **Whole-Class Choral Reading (WCCR):** Mon.—model, listen, choral (audiotape) | Tues.—review hard words, echo read | Wed.—choral & paired | Thurs.—choral audiotape & compare with Mon. reading Skip HF practice on Thur. **Comprehension:** At least two comprehension questions after WCCR. **Expression/Phrasing:** See previous week, but introduced passages without phrase boundaries on Wed. **HF Words:** Mon.—Add three new, I Read, You Point individual | Tue. & Wed.—I Read, You Point; Roll–Say–Keep; & Pig **Progress Monitoring:** expression rubric—FCRR passages without phrase boundaries. Rate—Tata's Beat	**Content:** Rate (WCCR): Over the Bridge (Book) Expression: Alexander and the Terrible, Horrible (200 words typed) High frequency: Personal cards + new phrase cards **Notes:** **Activities:** **Whole-Class Choral Reading (WCCR):** Mon.—model, listen, choral (audiotape) | Tues.—review hard words, echo read | Wed.—choral & paired | Thurs.—choral audiotape & compare with Mon. reading. **Comprehension:** At least two comprehension questions after WCCR. **Expression/Phrasing:** See previous week, but start with passages without phrase boundaries and have students mark and justify the phrase boundaries. **HF Words:** Mon.—Add three new words, add phrases with known words. Phrase; Haste Game | Tue. & Wed.—games with HF phrases. **Progress Monitoring:** Rate—Over the Bridge

(continued)

FIGURE 6.10. Sample Six-Week Intervention-Planning Sheet for Fluency.

Week 4 March 11–15	Week 5 March 18–22	Week 6 March 25–29
Content:	**Content:**	**Content:**
Rate: Leveled passage reading A–Z	**Rate:** Leveled passage reading A–Z	**Rate:** Leveled passage reading A–Z
Poem: "Who from Where the Sidewalk Ends"	**Poem:** From Poem for Two Voices	**Readers' Theatre:** Multilevel Readers' Theatre
HF: Add new words + phrases from FCRR.org	**HF:** Add new words + phrases from FCRR.org	**HF:** Add new words + phrases from FCRR.org
Notes:	**Notes:**	**Notes:**
Activities:	**Activities:**	**Activities:**
Repeated Reading: Mon.—Day 1, repeated reading procedures (Fig. 8.16) | Tue.—Day 2 (baseline rate) | Wed. & Thurs. Day 3–4—practice whisper reading	**Repeated Reading:** See previous weeks. Graph 2 readings (WCPM). Whisper reread other passages	**Repeated Reading:** See previous weeks. Graph 2 readings (WCPM). Whisper reread other passages
Comprehension: At least two comprehension questions after repeated reading.	**Comprehension:** At least two comprehension questions after repeated reading.	**Comprehension:** At least two comprehension questions after repeated reading.
Poetry Reading: Mon.—model choosing poem, model read, silent read | Tues.—read aloud, discuss mood | Wed.—read aloud, clues for expression | Thurs.—choral practice and then read for progress monitoring	**Poetry Reading:** Mon.—Poem for Two Voices, model read, silent read | Tues.—read aloud in divided groups | Wed.—read aloud in divided groups | Thurs.—choral	**Readers' Theatre:** Mon.—read, assign roles, review cueing (Figure 8.15) | Tues.—whole-group practice, review expression (Fig. 8.15) | Wed.—practice | Thurs.—tape (Share with classes via VIMEO)
HF Words & Phrases: Mon.—add three new words and phrases | Tue.—Thurs.—games with phrases and words	**HF Words & Phrases:** Mon.—add three new words and phrases | Tue.—Thurs.—games while checking HF individually	**HF Words & Phrases:** Mon.—add three new words and phrases | Tue.—Thurs.—games and flash phrase PowerPoint
Progress Monitoring:	**Progress Monitoring:**	**Progress Monitoring:**
Rate: Leveled A–Z passage	**HF:** Check personal cards and record accuracy on back of each card with date	**Rate:** Leveled A–Z passage*
Expression: Rubric on "who" poem	**Rate:** Leveled A–Z passage	**Expression:** Rubric on choice reading (take from repeated books and passages)

FIGURE 6.10. (continued)

Intervention Activities

Repeated Oral Reading and Other Strategies for Enhancing Reading Rate

Students who require fluency intervention have not built the level of automaticity with word recognition that other students have attained. They have not moved through the "glued to the print" stage to become efficient with decoding. In some respects these students simply lack depth in reading experiences. They have not had the volume of word recognition practice that other readers have had, and they have not consolidated and automatized commonly occurring patterns. They need large amounts of reading practice, which can be provided through both wide reading of many different texts and repeated reading of the same text (Kuhn & Stahl, 2003). In this section, we describe several strategies and practices for improving reading rate, including repeated oral reading. However, we begin with basic strategies to practice oral reading—strategies that avoid the common but ineffective method of round robin reading (RRR).

Even though teachers know that RRR is not the best practice, we find that it is very easy to slip into this habit, without realizing it. RRR is the practice of asking students to take turns reading aloud one after another. There are many problems with RRR. First, students do not receive a great deal of practice as they wait for their turn. Many students will skip ahead and practice only their section in anticipation of their turn. Second, the practice can be agonizing for students who are already dysfluent, as the rest of the group waits for them to finish struggling over words. Third, students who are more fluent grow bored and impatient as they wait, making the order less predictable does little to remedy these problems. Popcorn reading, for example, is a variation of RRR in which students take turns reading aloud, but are randomly selected. The amount of reading practice each child receives is still woefully small.

In this section, we provide an overview of strategies to support oral reading. When teachers provide fluency interventions, oral reading of text should be a significant part of their lesson. Teachers must hear students read orally during a fluency intervention. They must provide feedback to students about the words with which they are struggling. In the text box *Forms of Support Reading* are listed a number of different strategies for reading a book with students.

Repeated oral reading begins with the teacher selecting a book at the student's instructional level, introducing the book or passage, modeling fluent reading, asking the student to read, providing corrective feedback as he/she rereads, supporting continued practice of the passage or book, and timing the readings *intermittently*. Figure 6.11 provides guidelines for repeated reading with primary students. For those with fluency issues, a great deal of rereading is needed. We like to say that students at this stage should actually be rereading almost everything. For us adults,

FORMS OF SUPPORT READING

- *Echo reading*. Teachers read aloud a line of text and students repeat the line. Continue taking turns until the students are reading fluently and with expression.

- *Whisper reading*. Students all read at the same time, quietly in a "whispering" voice. In some cases students are given a "whisper phone," which directs their reading back into their own ear so that they can hear themselves.

- *Choral reading*. The teacher reads slightly louder than students, as they follow along and read with him/her. The goal of choral reading is for the entire reading to *be together*, to sound like one voice. Over time, the teacher slowly lowers his/her own voice and speed, allowing the students to take the lead.

- *Antiphonal readings*. This strategy is similar to choral reading except that the group is divided and one half reads one section and then the other half reads another section. This strategy can be used for reading poems for two voices.

- *Paired readings*. Teachers and students alternate reading together or independently (duet or solo). A signal should be determined for students to use when they are ready to switch from duet to solo, or vice versa.

- *Readers' Theatre*. Students assume roles and read a script aloud. Text should be interesting, contain dialogue, and have a strong plot. The meaning of the plot is conveyed through expression and intonation.

- *VoiceThread/podcast/Flip video recording*. Students record themselves reading and then play the recording back. They should work independently or with a partner to perform a quick analysis of their fluency skills by identifying something on which they are doing well and something they could work.

- *Interactive read-aloud*. Students listen attentively as the teacher reads a book and respond to and asks questions throughout. The purposes include modeling fluent reading with expression and appropriate phrasing; teaching new vocabulary; discussing and clarifying concepts; and making predictions, inferences, and connections.

the rereading may get a bit old and boring. However, for students who struggle with fluency, rereading provides them with support and opportunities for *success*, which is motivating and never boring.

There are several elements in this figure that differ from the typical method of repeated oral reading instruction. First, we do not suggest that every follow-up rereading be timed because students will assume that they should always read fast. Instead we suggest measuring a more naturally selected sample of reading rate by timing students intermittently. On Day 2, all students are timed to establish a baseline reading rate, and after that, only a few students are timed each day while the others practice rereading. Students find it motivating to have their reading rate visually graphed and to watch it improve, but we caution against making this too central a focus due to the risk of students' equating good reading with speed

---

Day 1
- Introduce a new book.
  - Preview.
  - Teacher reads.
- All students choral- or echo-read with the teacher.
- Each child individually rereads the book with corrective feedback (whisper read).
  - Listen for errors (but wait and allow the student to work on the word).
  - Return to problematic places.
  - Return to places where the child problem-solved (sounded out, self-corrected, repeated to get the word) and provide praise.
  - Don't encourage children to guess at words.
- Follow with comprehension activities.

Day 2
- All students choral-read the previous day's books.
- Each student reads about 100–200 words of the book for the teacher as the reading is timed. (Other students practice whisper reading the book until it is their turn.)
- Each child charts the number of words read per minute a fluency chart/graph.

Days 3–5
- The book is added to a collection of "Practice Reads."
- Students may be asked to read about 100–200 words of the book for the teacher about two to three times as the reading is timed. (This should not be every time the child practices.)
- Each child charts the number of words read per minute on a fluency chart/graph.

FIGURE 6.11. Repeated oral reading procedures.

reading. Second, we suggest that the students build up a small collection of books that are used only during the fluency intervention to practice rereading. Doing so provides a simple, individual activity for students to do while the teacher is organizing.

In a wonderful article in *The Reading Teacher*, Paige (2011) describes a strategy called "Whole-Class Choral Reading (WCCR)." For this strategy the teacher selects a 200- to 250-word text that could be read in about 2 minutes. Over the course of the week the teacher guides the students in reading the passage chorally, with the emphasis on a unified reading that, like a choir, sounds almost like one voice. On Day 1 of the sequence the teacher reviews difficult words. Paige describes how many teachers type the passage and use the bold font on troublesome words to visually cue students to be on the lookout for them. He also suggests that the teacher audiotape the class reading at the beginning of the week and again at the end of the week to show them how they improved. We like this suggestion because, like the visual display of reading rate, it is motivating. Unlike the visual display, however, it emphasizes how the reading *sounds*—the expressive, prosodic elements of fluency. The article also suggests that teachers use different approaches to reading as the week progresses to keep the choral rereading interesting and lively (e.g., antiphonal, echo, buddy, or paired reading). We particularly like the WCCR plan as a strong alternative to RRR. It is especially suited to primary readers, who might struggle with word accuracy and require lively repeated reading practice.

Practices to Enhance Prosody

It's a new day in fluency instruction and there are many, many creative and rich strategies to support the prosody elements of fluency. Building prosody (and rereading texts for authentic purposes) can be addressed through explicitly teaching phrasing, performing Readers' Theatre, reading poems and raps, and reading chorally. We suggest that during fluency intervention lessons teachers devote short amounts of time over the course of each week to a prosody project.

Text Phrasing

To read fluently, students must read words, but they must also mentally organize these words into phrases or meaningful groups. Rasinski, Yildirim, and Nageldinger (2011) write that "the phrase, in and of itself, is a textual unit worthy of explicit instruction. In many ways, it is the phrase and not the word that is the essential unit of meaning in a text" (p. 253). They introduce, in detail, a two-day phrased text lesson, in which they suggest teaching students to recognize the boundaries of phrases by modeling and practicing. Essentially, teachers model reading a passage in which the phrase boundaries have been marked, like this:

> On my way to the store yesterday / I saw a white rabbit / with big ears. // He looked at me quickly / and then darted into the bushes / before I could get close to him.

Teachers then practice reading the passages chorally with the students using the passages with the marked phrase boundaries. Gradually, students learn to read with the boundaries and graduate to passages without the phrase boundaries marked. There are several different sets of passages at the Florida Center for Reading Research (*http://fcrr.org*) in the fluency sections. Some of these passages mark the phrase boundaries by putting each phrase on a separate line like this:

> He knew he was late
> but Jimmy just couldn't hurry.
> "Come on!"
> said his mother,
> "We haven't got all day!"

This is a nice first step for younger students because the phrase boundaries can sometimes be difficult at first. Once students can read passages with phrasing using this system, then teachers can introduce the slashes to represent the phrase boundaries.

Many teachers are familiar with Readers' Theatre, the strategy in which students are assigned parts and then practice reading those parts expressively. The first step is finding an appropriate script. Reading A–Z has a number of scripts on its subscriber's website. For a yearly subscription fee, teachers can access down-loadable, printable materials that have been leveled. The website is convenient because teachers can have at their disposal ready-to-go materials at a designated reading level. We have discussed how fluency materials must be at an appropriate reading level because asking students to practice using materials that are too hard (or too easy) will not result in improvement. Although Readers' Theatre is a won-derful activity for building attention to the elements of prosody, including rhythm, intonation, pausing, and pacing, we find that many teachers become overwhelmed with all of the elements of fluency, and so we suggest using the list of Readers' Theatre guidelines in Figure 6.12.

Readers' Theatre

Because the purpose of Readers' Theatre is to *perform* the reading, students should always have an audience. Often students perform for parents or younger children. During an intervention lesson there is usually not enough time to travel to another classroom and perform. Many teachers use flip cameras, smart phones, tablets, or other devices to record the Readers' Theatre session and then play it back for the students. Such devices should be standard equipment for fluency intervention groups. These are truly essential measurement tools that move progress monitor-ing of fluency intervention away from sole dependence on counting the words read correctly per minute. In a sense, the students become their own audience. Students in fluency intervention groups find it especially helpful to see and hear how they

Goal	Guiding Assessment Question
Preparation	Has the student obviously rehearsed the piece?
Volume	Is the piece read at the appropriate volume?
	Is volume used purposefully to add emphasis or draw attention to part of the reading?
Cueing	Is the reader following along and prepared to read when it is his/her turn?
	Does the reader interrupt other readers or have to be reminded that it is his/her turn?
Punctuation	Does the reader pause at punctuation (e.g., period, comma)?
	Does the reader's pitch show attention to punctuation (e.g., exclamation mark, question mark)?
	Does the reader's voice change when he/she is reading something in quotation marks?
Accuracy	Does the reader accurately read all of the words? (Given extensive practice, near-perfect accuracy is expected.)
Pacing	Does the reader read the words at an appropriate pace (e.g., not too slow, not too fast)?
Oral Delivery	Does the reader convey the emotion in the piece using his/her voice?

FIGURE 6.12. Readers' Theatre guidelines.

are reading. The model of expressive reading provided by a recording of the reading and the fact that this reading is being done by the targeted students themselves are particularly reinforcing. Many teachers also ask students to create a podcast of their readings to share with others. Audio recording for a podcast, like video recording, creates an authentic audience for Readers' Theatre, a possibility that is quite motivating.

Poetry

Short texts such as poems or raps also tend to enhance expression and prosody. Figure 6.13 shows a simple set of guidelines that we have used with students to help them select, practice, and perform poems. The figure lists several sources for poems and provides the students with guidelines for selecting a poem. Students must be able to read most of the words in the poem and they must *like* the poem as well, because they will read it over and over. The second section of Figure 6.13 provides steps for students to follow in practicing their reading of the poem. At each reading students are asked to think about something slightly different as they practice, a technique that helps them accumulate layers of expression and prosody. Focusing on the poem in different ways also makes practice more engaging and motivating. We also like to use poems for two voices, with some lines assigned to one reader or the other while some are read in unison.

PICKING A POEM FOR PERFORMANCE
FINDING A "JUST-RIGHT" POEM FOR FLUENCY PRACTICE
1. Where to look:
   - *www.gigglepoetry.com*
   - *poetry4kids.com*
   - *Poets.org*

2. Read the poem.
   - Do you like it?
   - Can you read *most* of the words?
   - Can you see yourself performing it?

3. Read the poem a second time.
   - What is the poem's message? Why did the poet write it?

4. Is it a keeper?
   - YES—I like it. I can read it. I understand it. I CAN'T WAIT TO SHARE IT!!!!
   - NO—I don't like it. *or* There are some words that are too hard. *or* I don't "get" it. *or* I am not excited.

PREPARING FOR PERFOMANCE
STEPS FOR READING A POEM WITH EXPRESSION
1. First reading (silently). Find words you don't know. Learn the meanings and pronunciations of these words.

2. Second reading (aloud). Hearing it.

3. Third reading (aloud). Getting the mood.
   - This poem has a _____ mood (sad, quiet, happy, zany, angry).
   - How will that mood affect your reading?

4. Fourth reading (aloud). Text clues for expression.
   - Highlight text clues
     o Punctuation, repetition, onomatopoeia.

5. Fifth to seventh readings (aloud). Practice and flair.
   - What will you do to add to the poetry performance?
   - Pausing? Lowering your voice? Using your eyes?

6. Performance and evaluation
   - Perform the poem. Evaluate yourself, let a peer evaluate, or let a teacher evaluate.

FIGURE 6.13. Poetry performance for fluency.

Flash Phrases and Games
for Practicing High-Frequency/Sight Words

A small part of fluency interventions should include practice with high-frequency/ sight words and phrases. Because only 5 minutes of the intervention time is usually devoted to this, we suggest a selection of games and activities that can be quickly and easily accessed and implemented. The first step is to create a personalized selection of cards for each student. This selection of cards would be based on the assessment of high-frequency/sight words, described earlier in this chapter, where we also discussed The School Bell (*www.theschoolbell.com*), a great web source for word cards. There are sets in two formats for each of the lists. In creating a list, start with about 60% of words that the student knows and 40% that are in progress. If the word collection only contains the words students do not know, they can get discouraged and demoralized. A personalized word collection is an easy go-to at the end of a lesson: "Everyone, get out your word cards. Read them and put the ones that you have trouble with in a separate pile. I will work with each of you on these." Also, students can mark the cards with a star or a stamp each time they read the word correctly. These collections also become a handy set of words to incorporate into games such as Roll–Say–Keep, described in Chapter 5.

There are so many wonderful, creative games with which to practice high-frequency/sight words that it is difficult to cover them all. We appreciate very simple, premade games that require minimal cutting, pasting, coloring, or lamination from teachers. Several simple games for practicing individual words can be found at The School Bell website (*www.theschoolbell.com*). We like the premade Bingo cards that correspond to each of the lists and also the game Pig. To play Pig, students spread word cards out on the table along with four premade cards that say *Pig* and four that say *Stop*. A student begins his/her turn by declaring how many words he/she can read before getting a Pig or a Stop card. Cards that are read correctly can be kept. If a Stop card is picked, then the turn stops and the correctly read cards are kept. If the Pig card is picked, then the student has to put the correctly read cards back in the pile. The game continues until only the Stop and Pig cards remain. Additional games available at the FCRR site (*www.fcrr.org*) include Fast Match, a game in which students read and match high-frequency/sight words, and I Read, You Point, a game in which students identify high-frequency/sight words from a list as the teacher points. The latter game is especially good for new words or when the student is first learning a word, because the game requires receptive knowledge (simple identification) rather than expressive knowledge (reading the word).

Once students have developed some command of the individual words, we suggest practicing the words in phrases, because that is how high-frequency/sight words typically occur. Most high-frequency/sight words have no meaning or purpose in isolation; they must be grouped with other words. Phrase cards can be found at both the FCRR and School Bell websites. There are two games at the FCRR website, one called Fast Phrases and the other Phrase Speed Practice. In

Fluency

Objective

The student will gain speed and accuracy in reading phrases.

Materials

▸ YES and NO header cards (Activity Master F.004.AM1)
▸ Phrase cards (Activity Master F.013.AM1a – F.013.AM1h)
  Copy on card stock, laminate, and cut.
▸ Phrases correct per minute record (Activity Master F.013.AM2)
▸ Timer (e.g., digital)
▸ Pencils

Activity

Students read phrases in a timed activity.

1. Place the set of phrase cards face down in a stack and timer at the center. Provide each student with a phrases correct per minute record.
2. Working in pairs, student one sets the timer for one minute and turns the phrase cards over one at a time while student two reads the phrases as quickly as possible.
3. If all the words in the phrase are read correctly, the student places the card in a pile on the "YES" card. If one or more words in the phrase are read incorrectly, places it in a pile on the "NO" card.
4. Continue activity until the timer rings. Count the phrase cards in the "YES" pile and record the number on the phrases correct per minute record. Read phrases in the "NO" pile together.
5. Repeat the activity at least two more times attempting to increase speed and accuracy.
6. Reverse roles.
7. Peer evaluation

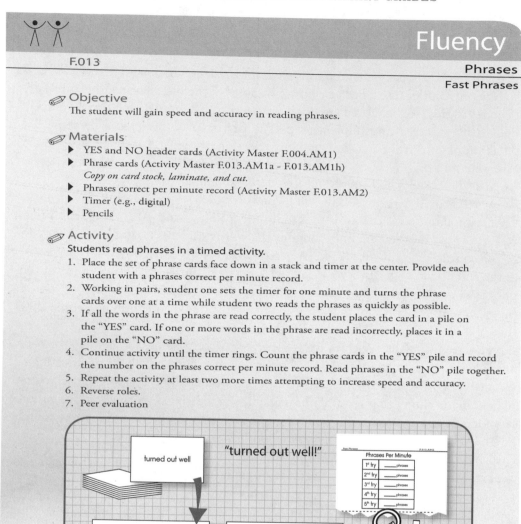

FIGURE 6.14. Fast Phrases game. Copyright by Florida Center for Reading Research. Reprinted by permission.

Fast Phrases (see Figure 6.14), students use cards with phrases on them and play to see how many phrases they can correctly name in 1 minute. They place the ones they've named correctly under a card that says "Yes!" and they place the others in a pile that says "No!" This is a very simple, low-maintenance game that can easily be played in the 5 minutes allocated for high-frequency/sight word practice in our fluency lesson. The second game, Phrase Speed Practice, is very similar in that students read a laminated list of phrases and use a Vis-à-Vis marker to cross out the phrases they read correctly within 1 minute.

In addition to these, we have seen teachers use PowerPoint to create "flash phrase" presentations. They put a phrase on each slide, followed by a blank slide. They then specify a timing for the presentation that allows about 3–5 seconds per slide. Students are able to practice the phrases with a partner as the teacher projects them on a screen or wall. The blank slides prevent the appearance of the next slide while students may still be working on a phrase.

We also recommend that you read more about fluency strategies. There is a wonderful book, *Good-Bye Round Robin: 25 Oral Reading Strategies* (Opitz & Rasinski, 2008), that offers an array of research-based practices to avoid RRR. We highly recommend it for detailed descriptions of a number of strategies.

Goal Setting and Progress Monitoring

Reading rate goals are informed by referencing the Oral Reading Fluency Norms in Table 6.1. We noted earlier that students at the 50th percentile rank increase about 1.2 words per week. Over 6 weeks, that would mean a cumulative increase of 7.2 words correct per minute, but because we are intervening in a targeted way with students, we expect better-than-average improvement. Consequently, we set a goal of at least a 10-word increase. With the fluency rubric, we expect an improvement of 2–3 points and plan to target the areas of smoothness and pacing. We suggest monitoring reading rate on a weekly basis and expression on a biweekly basis. Twice over the 6 weeks, we would also administer two Reading A–Z Comprehension Quick Checks on passages at the students' instructional reading levels.

Evaluating Interventions

To evaluate the impact of fluency interventions, teachers can use three tools: (1) intervention logs, (2) progress monitoring results, and (3) fidelity checklists. Next, we provide examples demonstrating how these tools can be used for the group in the context of the 6-week plan described earlier in the chapter.

Figure 6.15 contains an intervention log for 1 week of intervention. This log includes anecdotal notes and attendance records documenting students' responses

Intervention Log

Instructional focus of group: *Increasing reading rate and expression*

Reading Level: *2.0–2.4*

Intervention goal: To *(a) increase speed by at least 6 WCPM and (b) fluency by 2–3 rubric points by April 1st*

Progress monitoring measure and passage level: *Speed—DIBELS 2nd Grade Oral Reading Passages & Expression—Rubric*

Frequency of administration: *Reading Rate—weekly Expression—biweekly*

Week of *March 4–8*   Intervention Teacher _____

Curriculum/materials: *Passage from Alexander and the Terrible, Horrible, Over the Bridge leveled book, HF phrase cards FCRR.org*

Attendance and Observation Records

Student Name: *Abe*	**Student Name**: *Brenna*	**Student Name**: *Caleb*
Attendance: (Circle if absent) ⊙ T W Th F	**Attendance**: (Circle if absent) M T W Th F	**Attendance**: (Circle if absent) M T W Th F
Notes: *Still really slow . . . Maybe increased 2 words since Week 1.* *Accuracy is good but maybe he is "sounding" out in his head.* *Was sick this week?*	Notes: *Rate is increasing.* *Work with HF phrases seemed to help.*	Notes: *Does well with expression when there is a lot of modeling. Not independently.* *Not sure about how to mark phrase boundaries.*
Student Name: *Darion*	**Student Name**:	**Student Name**:
Attendance: (Circle if absent) M T W Th F	**Attendance**: (Circle if absent) M T W Th F	**Attendance**: (Circle if absent) M T W Th F
Notes: *Reads in phrases more after the phrase lessons.* *Still speed reading. Needs to work on expression. "Make it sound right, not fast." Knows HF words. Rate increased 5 words.* *May need a different group.*	Notes:	Notes:

FIGURE 6.15. Sample Intervention Log for fluency.

to the intervention instruction. The intervention log reflects notes taken during the third week of the fluency intervention. As the notes indicate, Darion is making good progress in reading rate but needs to concentrate more on expression. Notice that because most of the students in the group are experiencing reading rate issues, the interventionist questions whether it is the best placement for Darion, who is experiencing expression issues. Brenna appears to be making progress with her reading rate, due in part to increasing competence with high-frequency/sight words and phrases. Abe appears to be struggling and is not showing similar gains in reading rate, but he has been sick. Lastly, Caleb is increasing his skill with expression, but he needs a consistent teacher model in this area, indicating that he has not learned how and when to "color" his reading with expressive elements (phrasing, pausing, punctuation).

Figure 6.16 shows progress monitoring data (MM) for Darion, and Figure 6.17 shows progress monitoring for Abe. Note that even with the same intervention, these two students show different progress. The figures contain 5 weeks of reading rate data (baseline + progress monitoring), the latest expression rubric, and two comprehension measures. Darion, who was already on target with his reading rate, has shown an increase of 7 WCPM, and has almost met the goal for the intervention in terms of rate. However, he is a classic "speed reader" who has sacrificed expression in the race to get the words out faster and faster. Despite two weeks of phrasing instruction, his score on the phrasing section of the rubric is identical to his preintervention evaluation, and although he has become smoother and more consistent, as his score of 9 indicates, he probably needs more help with expression. The comprehension data suggest that Darion, for the most part, understands the meaning of the passages. However, he could improve, especially since he is becoming so much more fluent. He accurately answered five of six questions on each of the two comprehension measures, which is good but he could have done better.

Abe, in contrast, is struggling with both reading rate and expression, and his comprehension data reveal that his understanding of the passages is suffering. His reading rate has increased about 3 WCPM, and his scores on the expression rubric have not changed. During one of the weeks of progress monitoring, Abe was sick 2 days and so he may be suffering due to absences. His comprehension was not strong either. He answered four of six questions correctly on one measure and three of six on the second. During reading rate assessments Abe does not appear to sound out words or repeat them, but the interventionist surmises that he may be silently slogging through words, which might be slowing him down. Based on the progress monitoring notes at this point, Darion is very close to reaching the goals of the intervention and in fact may need a group that focuses more on expression and less on reading rate. Abe is struggling to meet the goals of the intervention, but because he has missed several sessions, his inconsistency may be the result of absences. He should be closely monitored because he may have an issue with accuracy that is hidden. If he does not improve in the next week, the intervention

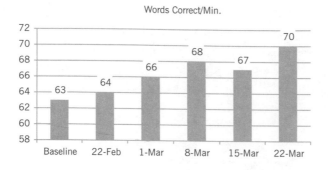

Words Correct/Min.

NAME _____

FLUENCY RUBRIC

	1	2	3	4
Expression and Volume	Reads in a quiet voice as if to get words out. The reading does not sound natural, like talking to a friend.	Reads in a quiet voice. The reading sounds natural in part of the text, but the reader does not always sound like he/she is talking to a friend.	Reads with volume and expression. However, sometimes the reader slips into expressionless reading and does not sound like he/she is talking to a friend.	Reads with varied volume and expression. The reader sounds like he/she is talking to a friend with his/her voice matching the interpretation of the passage.
Phrasing	Reads word by word in a monotone voice.	Reads in two or three word phrases, not adhering to punctuation, stress and intonation.	Reads with a mixture of run-ons, mid sentence pauses for breath, and some choppiness. There is reasonable stress and intonation.	Reads with good phrasing; adhering to punctuation, stress, and intonation.
Smoothness	Frequently hesitates while reading, sounds out words, and repeats words or phrases. The reader makes multiple attempts to read the same passage.	Reads with extended pauses or hesitations. The reader has many "rough spots."	Reads with occasional breaks in rhythm. The reader has difficulty with specific words and/or sentence structures.	Reads smoothly with some breaks, but self-corrects with difficult words and/or sentence structures.
Pace	Reads slowly and laboriously.	Reads moderately slowly.	Reads fast and slow throughout reading.	Reads at a conversational pace throughout the reading.

Scores of 10 or more indicate that the student is making good progress in fluency.   Score _____9_____

Scores below 10 indicate that the student needs additional instruction in fluency.

> **Comprehension**
> **Week 3:** 5/6 questions correct
> **Week 6:** 5/6 questions correct

FIGURE 6.16. Progress monitoring for Darion: Reading rate and expression rubric.

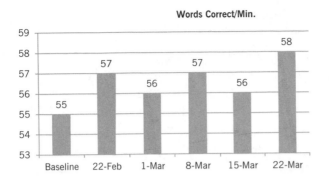

NAME _____

FLUENCY RUBRIC

	1	**2**	**3**	**4**
Expression and Volume	Reads in a quiet voice as if to get words out. The reading does not sound natural, like talking to a friend.	Reads in a quiet voice. The reading sounds natural in part of the text, but the reader does not always sound like he/she is talking to a friend.	Reads with volume and expression. However, sometimes the reader slips into expressionless reading and does not sound like he/she is talking to a friend.	Reads with varied volume and expression. The reader sounds like he/she is talking to a friend with his/her voice matching the interpretation of the passage.
Phrasing	Reads word by word in a monotone voice.	Reads in two- or three-word phrases, not adhering to punctuation, stress, and intonation.	Reads with a mixture of run-ons, mid-sentence pauses for breath, and some choppiness. There is reasonable stress and intonation.	Reads with good phrasing; adhering to punctuation, stress and intonation.
Smoothness	Frequently hesitates while reading, sounds out words, and repeats words or phrases. The reader makes multiple attempts to read the same passage.	Reads with extended pauses or hesitations. The reader has many "rough spots."	Reads with occasional breaks in rhythm. The reader has difficulty with specific words and/or sentence structures.	Reads smoothly with some breaks, but self-corrects with difficult words and/ or sentence structures.
Pace	Reads slowly and laboriously.	Reads moderately slowly.	Reads fast and slow throughout reading.	Reads at a conversational pace throughout the reading.

Scores of 10 or more indicate that the student is making good progress in fluency.   Score _____ **8** _____

Scores below 10 indicate that the student needs additional instruction in fluency.

> **Comprehension**
> **Week 3:** 4/6 questions correct
> **Week 6:** 3/6 questions correct

FIGURE 6.17. Progress monitoring for Abe: Reading rate and expression rubric.

teacher might want to assess his decoding skills, particularly his knowledge of common phonics patterns.

In Form 6.3, we present a sample fidelity checklist for fluency interventions. A fidelity checklist helps a reading specialist or instructional coach evaluate an existing fluency intervention in order to support a teacher in modifying instruction if necessary. The checklist reflects four areas: goals, observation of activities, planning, and intervention logs. The intervention goals should be explicitly stated and include both a reading rate measure and an expression measure. The activities observed during a fluency intervention should primarily cover both reading rate and expression. Keep in mind that some time should also be devoted to comprehension and, if necessary, to high-frequency/sight words and phrases. In particular, there should be ample oral reading in many different forms, including echo reading, choral reading, repeated reading, and whisper reading. The students should be actively reading and receiving corrective feedback from the teacher throughout the lesson. The planning for the fluency intervention should include the four areas described and should also identify passages or books to be read, which should be on the students' instructional reading levels. In addition, plans should specify progress monitoring based on passages at the students' instructional levels. Lastly, some type of intervention log with teacher notes should be kept, complementing the progress monitoring data. Notes in the intervention log are especially important when discussing the progress of students with colleagues or parents. We find that teachers rely on their notes to add depth to the numeric data.

Conclusion

In conclusion, facilitating fluency contributes to developmental progress by helping readers automatize decoding and focus on comprehension. Fluency is the bridge between decoding and comprehension. It is important to use what we know about this developmental continuum combined with various forms of student data to determine when and how we focus on fluency with our students. Fluency interventions should never resemble endless, meaningless rereading of passages with no attention to expression. Increasingly, researchers are emphasizing a balanced fluency lesson that is both cyclical and engaging. Students should know what to expect during a lesson and the parts of the lesson should be consistent. However, this does not mean that lesson activities need be monotonous. Instead, the lesson can build upon different elements of fluency when the activities are varied to optimize student attention and motivation. Of course, the progress of students in the fluency intervention must be monitored so that decisions about its impact can be made. In addition, teachers, reading specialists, and reading coaches can use fidelity checklists as reminders of the goals of their fluency intervention.

Intervention Goal-Setting Sheet for Fluency

Instructional focus of group: _____

Intervention goal: _____

_____

Meeting days: _____ Meeting time: _____ Hrs/week: _____

Progress monitoring measure and passage level: _____

_____

_____

Frequency of administration: _____

_____

Student Diagnostic Data

Student Name:	**Student Name:**
Reading Rate:	**Reading Rate:**
Reading Level:	**Reading Level:**
Fluency Rubric Score:	**Fluency Rubric Score:**
High-Frequency Word Score:	**High-Frequency Word Score:**
Notes:	**Notes:**
Student Name:	**Student Name:**
Reading Rate:	**Reading Rate:**
Reading Level:	**Reading Level:**
Fluency Rubric Score:	**Fluency Rubric Score:**
High-Frequency Word Score:	**High-Frequency Word Score:**
Notes:	**Notes:**

Six-Week Intervention-Planning Sheet for Fluency

Instructional focus of group: _____ Reading Level: _____

Intervention goal: _____

Meeting days: _____ Meeting time: _____ Hrs/week: _____

Progress monitoring measure and passage level: _____

Frequency of administration: _____

Week 1	Week 2	Week 3
Content:	Content:	Content:
Notes:	Notes:	Notes:
Activities:	Activities:	Activities:
Progress Monitoring:	Progress Monitoring:	Progress Monitoring:

(continued)

Six-Week Intervention-Planning Sheet for Fluency *(page 2 of 2)*

Week 4	Week 5	Week 6
Content:	Content:	Content:
Notes:	Notes:	Notes:
Activities:	Activities:	Activities:
Progress Monitoring:	Progress Monitoring:	Progress Monitoring:

FORM 6.3

Fidelity Checklist for Fluency Interventions

Date:						
GOALS **Measuring Intervention Goals**[1]						
• Does the intervention goal state specifically what students are to do as a result of the intervention?						
○ Increase reading rate in WCPM?						
○ Increase expressive elements (e.g., phrasing, pausing, rhythm?)						
○ Specific criteria for success (e.g., increase by 10 WCPM)?						
OBSERVATION						
• List activities observed during one intervention:						
• Do the activities provide practice with the behavior that is being measured in A (e.g., reading rate, expression?)						
• Is the majority of time (70%) being spent on the developing reading rate and expression?						
• Is each student practicing oral reading throughout the lesson in many different forms (e.g., echo, choral, repeated, and whisper)?						
PLANNING						
• Is there long-term planning across weeks that reflects four parts of the fluency intervention (e.g., reading rate, expression, comprehension, high-frequency word practice)?						
• Are the passages and books being read at the students' reading levels?						
• Are dates for progress monitoring shown?						

|(continued)

[1]Place a check in the box if the answer to the question is *yes*.

Fidelity Checklist for Fluency Interventions *(page 2 of 2)*

INTERVENTION LOG						
• Are there *specific* comments reflecting success with fluency? (e.g., not too many generic comments—*Nice!*)						
• Do the comments show that plans are being altered as a result of progress monitoring data?						
ADDITIONAL NOTES:						

CHAPTER 7

What to Do
When Interventions Don't Work

PROBLEM SOLVING

- What is Tier 3 intervention instruction?
- How does Tier 3 differ from Tier 2 intervention instruction?
- What are the two key assumptions underlying the problem-solving process?
- What are the procedural steps involved in problem solving?

You have referred to your fidelity checklists for Tier 2 intervention, and you have confidence that intervention instruction has been administered responsibly and appropriately. You have examined attendance records, and they look fine. Yet, your progress monitoring data indicate that a child exhibits little to no progress. Your intervention log likewise contains documentation that your student has struggled and exhibited frustration, even when adjustments were made to the intervention. What do you do next?

The primary purpose of Tier 3 within models is to ensure that *individualized* interventions are developed for those students who have not succeeded despite Tier 1 and Tier 2 supports. The development of these individualized interventions is based upon information that is gathered as part of a problem solving process. We believe that teachers should be aware of what occurs at Tier 3, the assumptions underlying the problem-solving process, and what teachers' roles are within this process. Before continuing with our discussion of Tier 3, we should note, however, that only a very small percentage of students (no more than 5–10%) should be referred for Tier 3 supports (Cook, Burns, Browning-Wright, & Gresham, 2011).

reading fluency skills. In particular, George is encouraged to quickly read passages that include vowel patterns recently reviewed in class. George's teacher notes that during this instruction, George reads slowly and easily becomes frustrated. After discussing this situation with the problem-solving team, his teacher notes that assessment data indicate that George has not yet become accurate in identifying short-vowel sounds. Thus, the focus of George's instruction is shifted to provide him with many opportunities to master or acquire short-vowel sounds, both in isolation and in reading simple CVC words.

A problem-solving approach that considers context also recognizes that other factors impact student learning. Some students, for example, may have mastered the necessary skills to be successful but may not be motivated. The problem-solving team would generate solutions to address this problem as well. In other situations the influence of peers or other classroom distractions may be significant. What is particularly important to understand is that team members discuss their beliefs about why a student is struggling and then test those beliefs by collecting assessment data to confirm or disconfirm those beliefs. If confirmed, the team is then able to develop interventions that address the reasons contributing to a student's difficulties.

Finally, the problem-solving approach addresses critical tenets of both the Individuals with Disabilities Education Improvement Act (United States Congress, 2004) (IDEIA) and No Child Left Behind. Both of these laws require the use of evidence-based instructional practices in meeting the learning needs of students. IDEIA, in particular, requires that inadequate or inappropriate instruction be addressed and that effective practices be employed prior to determining the existence of a learning disability. Similar to procedures used during Tier 2 of the process, the problem-solving approach addresses these issues by using data to (1) identify a student's learning needs, (2) develop interventions that have a research basis and are matched to a student's current stage of reading development, and (3) monitor student progress once these interventions have been implemented.

The Problem-Solving Team

Once it has been determined that a student is not responding to Tier 2 interventions (see Chapter 2), the grade-level team should make a referral to the school-level Tier 3 problem-solving team (PST). Unlike the grade-level teams discussed at the Tier 2 level, the PST is a school-level committee that receives referrals from *all* grade-level teams in the school. Although the focus of this book is on reading concerns, in most cases the PST will be constructed to address all types of academic concerns as well as behavioral issues. From a reading perspective, schools would be wise to ensure that the members of this team include faculty with expertise in the assessment of reading skills and reading instruction, in individualized reading interventions, progress monitoring, and decision making. Frequently, members of the school-level PST include an administrator, a reading specialist, a school psychologist, the referring teacher, the professional who has implemented the Tier 2 intervention (if not already on the team), a special education teacher, and the parents/guardians of the student.

We believe that each member of the team should fulfill specific responsibilities in order to ensure efficient and organized problem-solving efforts. Although some of these responsibilities are general in nature and could rotate from member to member across different cases, it is also likely that certain responsibilities will need to match the expertise and skills of a particular team member. At a minimum, we believe that there are at least four critical team roles needed to run these meetings. These roles also ensure necessary follow-up and coordination between meetings. Several of these roles were initially discussed by Rosenfield and Gravois (1996) and have since been widely adopted in many PST models. Note that the titles we use to describe each of these roles can be tailored to school preferences. The four team roles include the following:

1. *Timekeeper.* This individual is responsible for watching the clock as the meeting progresses and ensuring that the meeting stays on track to finish within designated time limits.

2. *Recorder.* The primary responsibility of the recorder is to take notes during each PST meeting and ensure that forms are properly completed. The recorder ensures that the coordinator has all completed forms for student files.

3. *Coordinator.* The coordinator has a number of significant responsibilities, such as receiving referrals from teachers, starting and storing case files, coordinating the meeting docket, inviting members, bringing required forms to the meeting, and running the meeting to ensure that all critical areas are discussed.

4. *Facilitator.* The facilitator meets with the referring teacher prior to the first team meeting and is responsible for conducting any additional recommended assessments, assisting with intervention implementation and progress monitoring, conducting fidelity checks, and generally ensuring that the problem-solving process stays on track between meetings.

The Problem-Solving Process and Phases

The problem-solving process is initiated with the completion of a referral form by the classroom teacher, the reading teacher, or the individual who has been implementing Tier2 reading interventions. The referral form should provide the PST with preliminary information about the supports that have been provided for the student to the point of this referral. In addition to basic demographic information, the referral form should include (1) the Tier 2 instructional group the student is in, (2) the frequency with which instructional groups have *actually* met, (3) the student's attendance in the group, and (4) progress monitoring data corresponding with Tier 1 instruction and Tier 2 intervention. In addition, the PST should have access to the intervention implementation logs.

Once the referral form has been given to the PST coordinator, the problem-solving process begins. There are four steps, corresponding to the phases of problem solving. These procedural steps and phases are highlighted in Figure 7.1. The problem-solving phases include (1) identifying the problem, (2) analyzing the problem, (3) determining an intervention, and (4) evaluating the intervention. These phases have characterized problem-solving models within psychology and education for many years (Bergan, 1977; Bransford & Stein, 1984) and have been widely incorporated into RTI approaches. Accomplishment of these four phases occurs through the procedural steps discussed next. For convenience, the major objectives of each of these procedural steps are included in Figure 7.2.

Procedural Step 1: PST Facilitator Meeting with Referring Teacher

Shortly after receiving the referral to the PST, the PST facilitator should schedule a meeting to discuss the reading concerns with the referring teacher. A main objective of this meeting is to define the reading problem that the team will address through intervention. This is accomplished through careful consideration of the

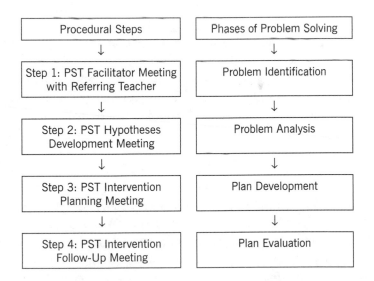

FIGURE 7.1. Problem-solving steps and phases.

Procedural Step 1: PST Facilitator Meeting with Referring Teacher

1. Review teacher concerns.
2. Discuss instructional methods and strategies.
3. Review curriculum objectives.
4. Discuss student behavior (i.e., level of engagement and presence of interfering behaviors).
5. Conduct brief assessment of reading skills.
6. Generate problem statement.

Procedural Step 2: PST Hypotheses Development Meeting

1. Develop hypotheses regarding identified problem
   a. Skill versus performance deficit
   b. Instruction and curriculum, learner, and classroom
2. Determine how hypotheses will be assessed
3. Assess hypotheses
   a. Review records and products
   b. Conduct additional interviews
   c. Conduct classroom observation
   d. Conduct additional direct assessment of student skills

Procedural Step 3: PST Intervention Planning Meeting

1. Use data collected in Step 2 to develop a step-by-step intervention plan.
2. Review research-based interventions to ensure the potential effectiveness of the plan.
3. Determine who will implement the intervention, when, and how frequently. Determine what materials will be needed to implement the intervention.

Procedural Step 4: PST Intervention Follow-Up Meeting

1. Collect progress monitoring assessment data on a weekly basis.
2. Evaluate progress monitoring data by comparing progress to designated goals.
3. Collect intervention fidelity data.
4. Determine effectiveness of intervention and make necessary changes.

FIGURE 7.2. Overview of procedural steps in the PST process.

skills the student has already attained versus those that need to be acquired. Another important objective of this meeting is for the teacher and the facilitator to identify the classroom or instructional conditions in which the student is most likely to experience reading difficulties. Finally, following this meeting the facilitator meets with the student to initially assess his/her performance on the critical reading skill of concern.

Different approaches can be taken to pinpointing the skill that will be addressed. As a general rule, only one skill should be targeted initially for intervention, and the skill selected should serve as an important building block for additional skill development. In many instances this skill is likely to be one in which the student falls below current grade level or placement level. For example, it may be found that a student in second grade struggles to decode unknown words. His teacher may report that the student still has not mastered short-vowel sounds, based upon his performance in class. In this instance, mastery of short-vowel sounds would be needed for the student to progress. This skill would be considered a building block for future reading success. This skill was also expected to have been mastered earlier in the curriculum (i.e., it is not typically addressed during second-grade classroom instruction). We often recommend that the skill be selected from the school's reading curriculum or from the state's learning standards. Other sources could be used as well (see Table 3.1 in this book). Regardless of the source used, it is important that the skill you select is specific enough that it can be assessed. The following is an example of specific learning objectives from our state's (Virginia's) Standards of Learning for first grade.

1.6   The student will apply phonetic principles to read and spell.

a) Use beginning and ending consonants to decode and spell single-syllable words.

b) Use two-letter consonant blends to decode and spell single-syllable words.

c) Use beginning consonant digraphs to decode and spell single-syllable words.

d) Use short vowel sounds to decode and spell single-syllable words.

e) Blend beginning, middle, and ending sounds to recognize and read words.

f) Use word patterns to decode unfamiliar words.

g) Read and spell simple two-syllable compound words.

h) Read and spell commonly used sight words.

Note how each of these objectives represents *related yet distinct* skills. Assuming a student is struggling to use decoding skills to read unknown words, the teacher and facilitator might decide that one (but not all) of these skills should serve as the critical starting point to begin individualized interventions. Initial focus on a single skill does not mean that only one skill will be focused upon throughout the entire time a student receives intensive support; instead, skills targeted for intervention should be changed as a student demonstrates improvement. The student should always be working toward an end goal that allows the gap between the student and his/her peers to be narrowed.

After pinpointing the skill that needs to be addressed through intervention, the PST facilitator and the referring teacher should discuss the instructional conditions in which the student struggles with this skill. For example, Jeremey is a first-grade student who is reportedly struggling to retain letter sounds. During the interview with Jeremey's teacher, the facilitator asks if Jeremey has ever demonstrated that he knows letter-sounds. After reflecting on the question, his teacher, Mrs. O'Cain, reports that he does seem to know many of the letter-sounds in isolation (e.g., when shown a letter and asked to say the sound it makes), but when asked to match letter-sounds to pictures or identify sounds at the beginning of a word, he is typically incorrect. Moreover, she notes that Jeremey seems to perform worse when required to work in small groups with his peers. As many teachers have observed in the past, some students are often inconsistent in their ability to display their reading skills. Teachers have often noted that on some days certain students are successful and other days they are not. Although such inconsistent responding may appear random, it usually has more to do with the varying types of instructional activities or tasks students are being asked to perform. This discussion between facilitator and teacher also focuses on the extent to which this skill has been emphasized in the curriculum. For students struggling to learn how to read, the frequency with which they need to practice their skills or the extent to which they need skills taught in a very direct manner may not be well matched to the adopted curriculum.

It is also important to determine whether a student might actually have the skills needed to be successful but often fails to exhibit them due to a lack of motivation. Determining whether a student cannot apply a skill or chooses not to apply it is not always easy. In such cases, additional data collection will be needed. Further understanding regarding whether a student can perform a skill and under what conditions will prove useful to the team as the members attempt to appreciate a student's learning needs and design appropriate interventions.

In addition to interviewing the teacher, a member of the team should be prepared to directly assess the student's reading skills prior to the initial PST meeting. As a general rule, this assessment should minimally include an assessment of the student's accuracy in performing the target skill. Results of this assessment will help to verify the problem and its severity. In the event that the student has not mastered this skill, we recommend assessing prerequisite skills in an effort to determine which skill(s) the student has indeed mastered.

Although a number of reading assessment tools exists, we generally recommend *criterion-referenced* assessments. These assessments sample numerous critical skills from the curriculum and help to evaluate whether the student has reached a specified "criterion" level of performance. Importantly, the assessment should include the specific skill that is of primary concern to the teacher. It may be the case that the teacher has a broad concern regarding some aspect of reading without knowing which specific skill to pinpoint for assessment. In selecting or constructing these kinds of assessments, it is important to understand the developmental reading process that unfolds as individuals become more successful readers. Findings from the National Reading Panel (2001) suggest that specific, critical skills must be developed if students are to become successful readers, including the development of phonemic awareness, phonics skills, oral reading fluency, comprehension, and vocabulary development. As noted earlier, we recommend using Table 3.1 to assist with this process of identifying key skills that might be part of this initial assessment.

The final objective of Step 1 is for the PST facilitator and the teacher to generate a problem statement that will be shared with the entire PST. Problem statements are designed to ensure that all members of the team are focused on the defined concern and will assist with intervention efforts. To communicate clearly and to increase the likelihood of consistency in problem-solving efforts, we recommend that a common format be used in stating the problem. This statement should include a quantified definition of the problem based upon the results of the initial assessment. For example, the following problem statement might be formulated for a student struggling with decoding skills: *When asked to read single-syllable, short-vowel words, Marcus correctly reads 50% of the words presented to him.* Alternatively, if the use of decoding skills is inconsistent, a problem statement might reflect the conditions in which the student struggles. For example: *When asked to read single-syllable, short-vowel words within a small-group instructional setting, Michael is highly inaccurate.*

To summarize, during the first step of problem solving, the primary goal of the PST is to identify a problematic reading skill that will become the focus of the individualized intervention. The target skill should be viewed as critical to the development of more proficient reading. In addition, by the end of the problem identification phase, the PST should have a clearer understanding of the types of instructional activities in which the student struggles and whether related concerns exist (e.g., low motivation or behavior concerns).

Step 2: PST Hypotheses Development Meeting

Once a target skill has been identified for improvement, the PST must determine how best to help the student. This help includes the development of an individualized intervention intended to improve the student's targeted reading skill. Problem solving in Tier 3 intervention processes is individualized because it assumes that each student struggles for a different reason. The goal of the second step of the problem-solving process is to uncover that reason. Consequently, the PST will focus its discussions on exploring reasons that might explain the struggling reader's difficulty with the target reading skill. At the outset, it is important to remember that the problem-solving approach does not attempt to determine whether a student has a disability or an underlying disorder. Neither is it the team's goal to identify all possible factors that might explain why the student is struggling. The reason for this is that many explanatory factors simply cannot be changed (e.g., IQ, socioeconomic status, parental marital difficulties). Instead, the team focuses on attempting to identify and address only those barriers that are considered modifiable/changeable in the school setting.

Interventions are most beneficial when they help students directly build reading skills or address barriers to optimal learning that can actually be changed. As a general rule, barriers that can be changed include student behavior that may interfere with learning (e.g., off-task behavior), problematic aspects of the classroom environment related to student learning (e.g., absence of appropriate reading materials), inadequate instruction (e.g., no direct teaching of critical phonics skills), and poor curriculum (e.g., lack of planned activities allowing students to continue practicing newly acquired skills). Barriers that cannot be changed, such as difficulties in the home environment, are not considered as part of this discussion. Finally, underlying cognitive abilities that are correlated with reading success (e.g., verbal working memory) are not considered, because interventions intended to address those abilities are not commonly implemented by teachers, and evidence is limited as to whether they actually result in improvement of reading skills.

The PST coordinator should lead a discussion in which ideas are generated regarding why the student is struggling. All team members should have the opportunity to express their perceptions of and impressions about the student's difficulties. That said, the team's approach to formulating these ideas should be based upon information collected in Step 1 as well as information provided by the grade-level team regarding the student's response to the Tier 2 intervention. The process should unfold in a way that hypotheses about, or generates ideas for, each of the following areas: (1) instruction/curriculum, (2) learner, and (3) classroom environment. Each of these areas and how they are understood within the problem-solving process are discussed next.

Instruction/Curriculum

Hypotheses/ideas in this area largely focus on the match between current skill development and the type of instruction being provided. Assuming your Tier 1 and Tier 2 practices incorporate differentiated instruction that is based upon valid assessment data, then it is quite possible that you have already accomplished this "match." However, at Tier 3 it is important to consider how instruction might have an impact on the individual learning needs of a particular student. As students learn new skills, they generally go through a process in which accurate use of the skill develops first, followed by fluent use of the skill, and finally by use of the skill in new ways or in new situations. For example, individuals learning to drive a car first focus on all the steps they must get right: starting the ignition, releasing the emergency break, checking their mirrors, etc. Simply remembering to do all of these things comes first. Eventually, new drivers begin to go through each of these steps in an efficient and seamless manner without even thinking—that is, their efforts become fluent. Finally, they can comfortably transfer their driving skills to new situations (e.g., driving a friend's car, driving their own car on the highway, driving at night). Although driving a car and reading are hardly the same, the point is that each of these skills develops in a progressive manner, and just as instruction for the emerging driver must be tailored to the stage of development, the same is true about reading instruction for the developing reader. Imagine asking a new driver, just learning to drive, to handle an 18-wheel truck? The result could be disastrous. The bottom line is, we want to ensure that the instruction that is provided matches a student's current skill level. In ensuring that this is the case, the PS team might consider a number of questions:

1. Is the student's current instructional level accurately identified?
2. Does current instruction match the student's instructional reading level?
3. Have critical reading skills been taught in a direct, explicit, and systematic manner?
4. Have the reading skills that the student must still acquire been clearly identified?
5. Are instructional goals well articulated, measurable, and closely monitored?
6. Is the student mastering important reading skills before being expected to learn more difficult skills?
7. Do the materials used to instruct the student appropriately emphasize the skills that the student needs to learn?
8. Does the student receive repeated opportunities to master new skills with immediate feedback?
9. When provided with opportunities to practice an important reading skill, is the student actually paying attention and actively working on the skill?
10. Does the student experience high rates of success when working independently?
11. Does the student have many opportunities to practice newly acquired skills independently?

This list of questions should not be considered exhaustive. After all, instruction is complex, and given the circumstances regarding the difficulties a student might be experiencing, additional questions may need to be considered. Of particular importance is determining whether the student is receiving the appropriate type and amount of instruction, given his/her current level of skill development.

Learner

The PST may also generate ideas regarding those difficulties that are related to learner-based characteristics. The learner characteristics of primary interest to the PST include sensory difficulties (e.g., vision and hearing), motivational level, and whether the learner has acquired the necessary academic support skills (e.g., does he/she know how to follow directions, work with other children?). We recommend that documentation indicating that the student has passed recently administered hearing and vision screenings be made available for the initial meeting. These issues must be followed up with students who have failed these screenings. Because vision and hearing difficulties can impede or prevent the student's reading progress, it is impossible to plan effectively until they are remedied.

As mentioned earlier, a student may have mastered a particular skill but fail to demonstrate or perform that skill when asked. A student experiencing this type of difficulty has been described as having a *performance deficit* and may appear unmotivated and disengaged (Duhon et al., 2004; Gresham, 1981). Such students may perform erratically or inconsistently and may also demonstrate behavior difficulties that interfere with their learning (Daly, Witt, Martens, & Dool, 1997). In order to increase the chances of successful academic performance, the PST may need to develop an intervention that addresses the factors influencing the behavioral concern. One approach taken by PSTs is to engage in a process known as functional behavioral assessment (FBA) (Gresham, Watson, & Skinner, 2001). The purpose of FBA is to identify situations in which the problem behavior is likely to occur and to identify the factors that maintain the problem behavior. Once these situations are identified, efforts can be made to change them so that problem behavior decreases and students are better able to focus on performing academically. Trained members of the PST are responsible for conducting the FBA. It is important to understand that team members conducting FBAs will need specialized training. Fortunately some school psychologists and special educators have received this training.

In addition to being motivated to learn and not engaging in behaviors that interfere with learning, most young students gradually develop a set of behaviors/ skills that allows them to become academically successful. These skills have been referred to as *academic enablers* and include social skills, study skills, and engagement (DiPerna, 2006, p. 7). Indeed, research has suggested that students experiencing academic difficulties are likely to demonstrate lower levels of these behaviors compared to peers not experiencing difficulties (Elliott, DiPerna, Mroch, & Lang, 2004). *Engagement* represents the extent to which a student actively participates in instructional activities involving reading. Importantly, *active participation* means that the student actually responds to instructional prompts and is doing the academic work that has been assigned. Engagement may be a particularly important academic enabler in the primary grades (K–2) (DiPerna, Volpe, & Elliott, 2002), and level of engagement is directly influenced by instruction provided in the classroom (Greenwood, 1996). It appears that the amount of time allocated for direct instruction of both academic skills and academic enablers has an impact on engagement and learning outcomes (Greenwood, 1996). Moreover, prosocial behavior and academic achievement are related (Malecki & Elliott, 2002). It appears that students who know how to ask for help, when to ask for help, and how to engage in positive and friendly interactions with peers and teachers may perform better in the classroom. Importantly, social skills are learned, and many programs exist that can teach these skills at school. Finally, study skills are those behaviors that allow a student to work independently on instructional activities with the goal of acquiring or improving existing academic skills. As applied to reading, some of those behaviors might include self-monitoring to ensure comprehension, organizing oneself to accomplish tasks in a timely manner, and recognizing when instruction or an assigned activity is confusing.

Classroom

Finally, it is important to understand that the classroom environment, or ecology, can also have an impact on student learning. The classroom environment is influenced by more than just the instruction that is delivered; it also includes classroom management and the social–emotional climate of the room. It is important to note that teachers who differentiate their instruction, who provide sufficient opportunities for practice and high levels of feedback, and who set goals also seem to have well-managed classrooms (Gettinger & Kohler, 2006). In well-managed classrooms students clearly know and understand classroom rules and routines, as well as the consequences for rule violations. Moreover, teachers of well-managed classrooms spend time explicitly teaching expectations and use positive and proactive strategies to prevent behavior problems (Simonsen, Fairbanks, Briesch, Myers, & Sugai, 2008). These teachers use physical proximity to prompt desired behavior from their students (Shores, Gunter, & Jack, 1993) and prevent problems from occurring by reminding students of expectations (Colvin, Sugai, Good, & Lee, 1997). It would seem that teachers who are successful in managing classroom behavior and instruction can manage multiple tasks at once and are aware of what is happening in their rooms. What seems particularly important to understand is that well-managed classrooms increase the likelihood that students will be meaningfully engaged in academic work. And as just noted, research indicates that active engagement has a direct impact on student outcomes (Greenwood, 1996). When attempting to improve reading outcomes, engagement in small-group reading instruction as well as independent reading practice with appropriately leveled reading materials seem important (Taylor, Pearson, Clark, & Walpole, 2000).

To summarize, the second step of the problem-solving process requires the team to explore various hypotheses/reasons that might be contributing to the referred student's difficulties. It is also important to understand that the team will often need to collect additional assessment data to confirm the hypotheses generated. The types of assessment procedures that are used to evaluate hypotheses include (1) review of records, student work products, or instructional materials; (2) additional interviews with teachers, parents, and/or the student; (3) classroom observations; and (4) possibly additional direct assessment of the student. To implement this step it is particularly important that the PST include members who have training in the direct assessment of student skills as well as in the assessment of instructional environments. We recommend that the PST document the hypotheses generated and the steps that will be taken to confirm those hypotheses. What follows is an example that highlights the second step of the problem-solving process.

Jenny, a second grader, is struggling with fluency. Her teacher's problem statement is: *When asked to read second-grade reading passages, Jenny reads 48 WCPM, whereas the average fluency rate for second-grade students during the middle of the year is 72 WCPM* (Hasbrouck & Tindal, 2006). As we can see from this problem statement, Jenny is well below expected levels of reading fluency performance. During their problem-solving meeting, team members generated a number of hypotheses that might help to explain Jenny's fluency difficulty. First, the team considered the instruction that Jenny had been receiving. Information regarding her Tier 2 intervention was examined. The focus was on decoding and building Jenny's sight vocabulary. Jenny had made adequate progress in these areas but the GOM (oral reading rate) indicated that her improved decoding skills and sight vocabulary were having minimal impact on reading fluency. Her teacher confirmed that in the classroom Jenny typically read very slowly. When asked about the opportunities that Jenny had to read in the classroom, her teacher reported that the class typically read a story together and then worked in smaller groups to engage in word study activities. Jenny's teacher also reported that the students were able to select books and then read independently.

Upon examination of the initial fluency data that were collected by the PST facilitator, it was revealed that Jenny read the second-grade passages with 97% accuracy, suggesting that her ability to decode second-grade material was adequate. Thus, the team hypothesized that Jenny might not be receiving enough opportunity to practice reading at her instructional or independent level in order to develop her fluency skills. The team decided to conduct an observation of Jenny during independent reading time since this was the primary time when she had opportunities to practice developing reading fluency. Three key findings were revealed during this observation: (1) Jenny spent about 5 minutes finding a book she wanted to read; (2) the book that she chose was actually at her frustrational level; and (3) once she did begin reading the book, she frequently veered off-task and was engaged with the book for only 65% of the time she was supposed to be reading. As a result of this follow-up observation, the team felt comfortable confirming the hypothesis that Jenny did not have enough opportunity to practice her developing reading skills. This information was important to developing a Tier 3 reading intervention.

Step 3: PST Intervention Planning Meeting

When previous attempts to improve a student's reading skills fail, everyone, including the student, is likely to experience frustration. Development of individualized interventions provides the PST with an additional opportunity to assist a student in need. Keep in mind, research tells us that even empirically supported interventions may not be 100% successful with every student. However, the problem-solving process attempts to increase the chances of a successful intervention because an intervention is selected or developed that is intended to address the reason behind students' difficulties. When considering the development of individualized interventions, the team should develop an intervention plan that will serve as a blueprint for implementation. Thus, Tier 3 intervention plans should include information that addresses the *how, what, when,* and *who* of implementation.

Developing the Intervention Plan

An *intervention plan* is a set of instructions that provides teachers or other support personnel with all the information they need to implement an intervention. In other words, it is a blueprint for instruction with specific students. Thus, the plan should indicate which professionals are responsible for implementing and evaluating the intervention, how frequently the intervention will be implemented, when it will be scheduled, and the way it is to be implemented.

Once the PST discusses and agrees upon an intervention, a written plan should be completed to document the team's decision. More importantly, the plan should be specific enough that the individual responsible for implementing it is able to use it as an implementation guide. Importantly, the intervention plan should provide step-by-step directions regarding how the intervention should be implemented. Figure 7.3 provides the step-by-step portion of an intervention plan for increasing reading fluency with connected text. This plan is based upon a meta-analysis of

---

Step 1: Read the selected passage to the student.

Step 2: Ask the student to read the passage.

Step 3: Provide the student with feedback, including the following:
- Number of errors made
- Words read correctly
- Graph performance

Step 4: Engage in correction procedures.
- Review the first error by saying the word to the student and having the student reread the word correctly.
- Next, have the student read the word in the sentence from the text.
- Repeat this process for each error made.

Step 5: Reread the entire passage a second time.
- Provide feedback (Step 3 above).
- If the same word(s) is read incorrectly again, then additional correction is provided.
- Correction = sound out the word for the student. Have the student repeat the sounding-out process, then read the whole word, and read within a sentence.

Step 6: Reread a third and fourth time with feedback and error correction (if necessary).

FIGURE 7.3. Reading fluency intervention.

research studies examining repeated reading procedures (Therrien, 2004). As can be seen in the figure, very specific directions are provided for the repeated reading intervention. These directions are straightforward and can be easily followed.

One of the greatest challenges to PSTs is generating intervention ideas. We believe that this challenge can be overcome when schools spend time developing an *intervention library* that contacts interventions categorized to address different types of needs. For example, intervention ideas might be organized to address either skill-based or performance-based problems. In addition, interventions could be organized to address different types of instruction-based difficulties, such as acquisition, fluency, and generalization/transfer issues. However, the first step for the team is to actually populate their libraries with intervention ideas that have an empirical basis. Many resources are available that provide helpful, detailed intervention plans for the individual student level. A list of some of these resources is provided in Figure 7.4.

In addition to having a library of empirically supported interventions, the actual intervention should meet additional criteria. First, the intervention should target the critical reading skill identified by the team. Remember that at Tier 3,

---

Reading-Specific Titles

- Bean, R., & Swan Dagen, A. (Eds.). (2012). *Best practices of literacy leaders: Keys to school improvement.* New York: Guilford Press.
- O'Connor, R., & Vadasy, P. (Eds.). (2011). *Handbook of reading interventions.* New York: Guilford Press.
- Walpole, S., & McKenna. M. (2012). *The literacy coach's handbook* (2nd ed.). New York: Guilford Press.

Broader RTI Titles

- Brown-Chidsey, R., Bronaugh, L., & McGraw, K. (2009). *RTI in the classroom: Guidelines and recipes for success.* New York: Guilford Press.
- Burns, M., Riley-Tillman, C., & VanDerHeyden, A. (2012). *RTI applications: Vol. 1. Academic and behavioral interventions.* New York: Guilford Press.
- Howard, M. (2009). *RTI from all sides.* Portsmouth, NH: Heinemann.
- Howard, M. (2010). *Moving forward with RTI: Reading and writing activities for every instructional setting and tier: Small-group instruction, independent application, partner work, whole-group engagement, and small-group collaboration.* Portsmouth, NH: Heinemann.
- Mellard, D. F., & Johnson, E. S. (Eds.). (2007). *RTI: A practitioner's guide to implementing response to intervention.* Thousand Oaks, CA: Corwin.
- Owocki, G. (2010). *The RTI daily planning book, K–6: Tools and strategies for collecting and assessing reading data and targeted follow-up instruction.* Portsmouth, NH: Heinemann.
- Rathvon, N. (2008). *Effective school interventions* (2nd ed.): *Evidence-based strategies for improving student outcomes.* New York: Guilford Press.
- Sailor, W. (2009). *Making RTI work: How smart schools are reforming education through schoolwide response-to-intervention.* San Francisco: Jossey-Bass.
- Southall, M. (2011). *Differentiating reading instruction for success with RTI.* New York: Scholastic.
- Whitten, E., Esteves, K., & Woodrow, A. (2009). *RTI success.* Minneapolis: Free Spirit.
- Wright, J. (2007). *RTI toolkit: A practical guide for schools.* Port Chester, NY: Dude.

FIGURE 7.4. Selected publications with intervention resources.

the intervention is focused upon a single skill. Thus, the team should select an intervention that has been shown to be effective in addressing the primary skill of importance. Other skills might be expected to improve from the intervention as well, but the team should focus mostly upon the primary skill of concern. Second, the intervention should be matched to the stage of skill development that was identified in the assessment (Daly, Lentz, & Boyer, 1996). In other words, the intervention should consider whether a student primarily needs to improve accuracy, fluency, or generalization of the reading skill. A student who is just acquiring a skill and remains largely inaccurate may need instructional interventions that provide a clear and sufficient explanation of how to engage in the skill. These students will likely require instruction to be adapted so that very small units of information are initially provided and that instructional and practice items are limited to a few examples. Interventions aimed at improving accuracy will likely include the teacher's modeling of how to use the skill, opportunities for the student to practice the skill, immediate feedback for incorrect responses, and repeated opportunities in which the student correctly uses the skill. An example of an individual-level accuracy-based intervention for improving letter-sound recognition is "incremental rehearsal" (Volpe, Burns, DuBois, & Zaslofsky, 2011). In this intervention students are directly taught unknown letter-sounds over a period of several intervention sessions and then practice recalling those sounds while also recalling the sounds of letters that they have already mastered. In addition to repeated exposure and practice with the unknown sounds, the key to this intervention appears to be the tightly controlled ratio in which students are exposed to an unknown sound followed by exposure to several known sounds.

Once a student has mastered a skill, he/she will need opportunities to practice that skill in order to become proficient in its use. Fluency interventions can be geared toward students who are highly accurate but generally slow in their oral reading rate. In their review of the literature, Daly, Lentz, and Boyer (1996) found that interventions requiring students to practice reading repeatedly and the use of reinforcement for meeting goals were effective in increasing oral reading fluency.

As discussed earlier, it is also possible that some students will demonstrate inconsistencies in their performance and simply may not be engaged or motivated, despite having adequately developed reading skills. In the event that the skill is present but not consistently performed, the intervention would focus upon increasing the likelihood that the student exhibits the skill. These students will likely require interventions that encourage greater involvement and participation. A specific example of this type of intervention is the "Mystery Motivator" (Rhode, Jenson, & Reavis, 1992). In this intervention, the student is required to meet some predetermined goal, such as a specific amount of work completed or a specific degree of accuracy in the work, to earn a privilege. For example, a student might be given independent work to complete while the teacher works with other students. In the event that the goal is met, the student then has an "opportunity" to earn a valued privilege, such as free time or possibly a valued object such as a small toy. What seems important about this intervention is that the student does not know when the "opportunity" for earning the privilege is present; thus he/she is likely to work hard all of the time. After meeting this goal, the student and the teacher use an invisible ink highlighter on the motivator chart to reveal whether the privilege is available on that particular day. This intervention has proved effective in addressing a variety of academic and behavioral problems (Kraemer, Davies, Arndt, & Hunley, 2012; Madaus, Kehle, Madaus, & Bray, 2003; Moore, Waguespack, Wickstrom, Witt, & Gaydon, 1994).

Additional important factors that the team should consider when selecting an intervention have to do with the match or "contextual fit" between the classroom and the demands of the intervention. Pragmatic considerations such as the resources needed to implement the intervention, the time required for it, and whether the intervention is complex are important factors that have been linked to whether the intervention will be seen as acceptable or consistently implemented (Elliott, Witt, Galvin, & Peterson, 1984; Witt, Martens, & Elliott, 1984). We cannot overly stress the importance of this point because an intervention that is not implemented is of no help to a struggling student.

Implementation of interventions also raises the issue of intervention support. Teachers should not be alone in implementing interventions. We take an "all-hands-on-deck" approach in that the entire team as well as other qualified individuals may be responsible for supporting or directly implementing the intervention.

Implementing the Intervention Plan

Once the intervention has been selected, the team will need to consider when the intervention will be implemented, how frequently, and where. As a general rule we believe that individual interventions should be implemented when children are well rested and can be focused. Student level of engagement is an important factor. Shorter intervention sessions will be more effective than longer sessions if the student's level of interest progressively wanes. Most individualized interventions that target specific skill development can be accomplished in 20–30 minutes, and it is best if these interventions occur every day. Because they are individualized and require the student's focus, it is important that a quiet space be selected for the intervention. We realize that space is a precious commodity in elementary schools; however, it is crucial that Tier 3 interventions take place in a quiet space with few distractions. Further, if the classroom teacher is responsible for implementing the intervention, then steps should be taken to ensure that adequate supervision can be provided to the rest of his/her classroom.

Interventions aimed at *performance difficulties* should occur during specific instructional times during the day. For example, students who are not progressing because they are highly distracted and more interested in gaining the attention of their peers would need an intervention to be implemented during those times when these distractions are the greatest. Keep in mind that putting these interventions in place all day long can render them less effective, as it may become too burdensome on the teacher to keep them up for the duration of the day.

One of the most commonly asked questions about Tier 3 interventions has to do with the length of time that interventions will need to be implemented. Our answer to this question is part philosophical and part empirical. From a philosophical perspective we believe that interventions should be implemented until they are successful. Thus, if an intervention fails we must try another one, and if that one fails—we try again. The ultimate goal of RTI and the problem-solving process is to find solutions, not endorse failure. Tier 3 interventions represent the last option to providing early intervention supports to students, and teams should consequently make efforts to keep working until students begin to experience success.

Finally, we have also been asked whether the selected intervention should be implemented exactly as indicated or whether deviations from the plan are permissible based upon an individual student's needs. In general, we like to encourage teams to stick to the specific parameters of a plan as much as possible so as to ensure that the plan is effective. Although some deviations to implementation are to be expected and may be indicated depending on the needs of the student, too much "drift" from how the intervention is supposed to be implemented may compromise positive effects.

Step 4: PST Intervention Follow-Up Meeting

As with the Tier 2 interventions showcased in this book, interventions implemented within Tier 3 must also be monitored to determine their effectiveness. The procedures outlined for progress monitoring in earlier chapters are applicable at Tier 3. That is, both MM and GOM should occur. Importantly, just because a student is receiving Tier 3 support does not necessarily mean progress monitoring measures will change. For example, Nicole began receiving Tier 2 intervention to assist her in learning letter-sounds. Although she received Tier 2 instruction for many weeks, however, she never was able to master all of the letters. Once Tier 3 interventions were started, the team continued to assess Nicole's mastery of the letters in order to see if the more intense intervention worked better. Moreover, the team monitored Nicole's fluency with letter-sounds during both Tier 2 and Tier 3 interventions. Assessment of student progress and review of progress monitoring data should occur frequently during Tier 3—that is, at least once per week. Similar to Tier 2, assessment data should examine the student's progress relative to defined goals. This usually means evaluating progress at particular points in time (i.e., comparing the student's current score to a benchmark score), which is referred to as *level* data, and by examining progress across time to compare growth in the student's scores to preset target levels of growth, which is known as *slope* data. The various methods for interpreting these data go beyond the scope of this book. We recommend that the PST have individuals trained in the various ways of interpreting progress monitoring data in order to make the best possible decisions about individual students.

Intervention Fidelity

Finally, in addition to measuring student growth through progress monitoring, information should be collected that helps the PST determine if the intervention is being implemented the way that it was intended to be implemented. This step is important because the intervention process assumes that students may improve when they are provided with instruction or intervention that research has previously shown to be effective. If our instructional efforts deviate too greatly from these proven practices, then we may not be providing students with the best possible instruction. Moreover, if a student does not show improvement in his skills, we cannot be sure if the lack of improvement is due to ineffective instruction or to some other cause (e.g., a disability).

In the end, the decisions made by the PST are based upon an assumption that the intervention or instruction is being implemented with high levels of integrity. When your medical condition is treated with medication, your physician assumes that you are following the regimen of treatment as prescribed. If your condition does not improve after several days, then it is likely that your doctor will want to confirm that the medication was taken as prescribed. Given that important decisions are being made about a struggling student's education, it is imperative that data be collected on whether interventions are being implemented as intended. We assume that everyone wants to help students and has the best intentions, but we also know that it can be difficult to sustain implementation of an intervention over several weeks because many barriers can get in the way. The PST does not collect these data to judge those implementing interventions; instead, these data are collected to determine whether the student is responding to instruction or not.

Various methods have been proposed for collecting intervention integrity data. One approach, discussed in previous chapters, is use of an intervention log. In this approach the interventionist completes a form documenting that the intervention was implemented, what was done on that particular day, and notes about student attendance. This approach is generally non-time-consuming and is a good way to document work that has been completed. A second approach is to have a member of the PST occasionally observe during an intervention session. Using this approach, the observer can use a checklist to determine whether important steps have been included in the instruction. Fidelity checklist items have been provided in previous chapters for Tier 2 intervention instruction. Similar checklists might be constructed by the PST for Tier 3 intervention as well. The primary advantage of this approach is that it provides a more objective source of information regarding implementation of the intervention. Moreover, the observer can provide valuable feedback that may be useful in improving future implementation of the intervention.

Conclusion

Some students will not respond positively to Tier 2 intervention instruction, and it is important to have a system in place to address the needs of these students. This level of intervention, referred to as *Tier 3* intervention, is strengthened when it utilizes a problem-solving approach to design individual interventions. The problem-solving approach focuses on student resilience and skills, rather than on deficits. The problem-solving approach can be organized and efficient when enacted by a problem-solving team (PST), which implements four phases of problem solving. The PST works to appropriately identify the problem and analyze it, then determines appropriate intervention(s), and finally evaluates the intervention using various forms of data.

References

Adams, M. (1990). *Beginning to read: Thinking and learning about print.* Cambridge, MA: MIT Press.

Afflerbach, P. (1998). Reading assessment and learning to read. In Osborn & F. Lehr (Eds.), *Literacy for all: Issues in teaching and learning* (pp. 239–263). New York: Guilford Press.

Albrecht, S. F., Skiba, R. J., Losen, D. J., Chung, C.-G., & Middelberg, L. (2012). Federal policy on disproportionality in special education: Is it moving us forward?. *Journal of Disability Policy Studies, 23,* 14–25.

Bear, D. R., Templeton, S., Invernizzi, M. R., & Johnston, F. R. (2012). *Words their way: Word study for phonics, vocabulary, and spelling instruction* (5th ed.). Upper Saddle River, NJ: Pearson.

Bergan, J. (1977). *Behavioral consultation.* Columbus, OH: Merrill.

Bentum, K., & Aaron, P. G. (2003). Does reading instruction in learning disability resource rooms really work?: A longitudinal study. *Reading Psychology, 24,* 361–382.

Betts, E. A. (1946). *Foundations of reading instruction.* Oxford, UK: American Book Co.

Blachman, B. A., Ball, E. W., Black, R., & Tangel, D. M. (2000). *Road to the code: A phonological awareness program for young children.* Baltimore: Brookes.

Bond, G. R., & Dykstra, R. (1967). The cooperative research program in first-grade reading instruction. *Reading Research Quarterly, 32*(4), 348–427.

Bransford, J. D., & Stein, B. S. (1984). *The IDEAL problem solver.* New York: Freeman.

Brophy, J., & Everston, C. (1976). *Learning from teaching: A developmental perspective.* Boston: Allyn & Bacon.

Chall, J. S. (1967). *Learning to read: The great debate.* New York: McGraw-Hill.

Chall, J. S. (1983). *Stages of reading development.* New York: McGraw-Hill.

Christ, T. J. (2006). Short-term estimates of growth using curriculum-based measurement of oral reading fluency: Estimating standard error of the slope to construct confidence intervals. *School Psychology Review, 35,* 128–133.

Clay, M. (1993). *An observation survey of early literacy achievement.* Portsmouth, NH: Heinemann.

Colvin, G., Sugai, G., Good, R. A., III, & Lee, Y. Y. (1997). Using active supervision and pre-correction to improve transition behaviors in an elementary school. *School Psychology Quarterly, 12*(4), 344–363.

Cook, C. R., Burns, M. K., Browning-Wright, D., & Gresham, F. M. (2011). *A guide to refining and retooling school psychological practice in the era of RtI.* Palm Beach, FL: LRP Publications.

Common Core State Standards Initiative. (2010). *Common Core State Standards for the English language arts and literacy in history/social science, and technical subjects.* Washington, DC: CCSSO & National Governor's Association.

Cunningham, P., & Hall, D. (2008). *Making words first grade: 100 hands-on lessons for phonemic awareness, phonics and spelling.* New York: Allyn & Bacon, Pearson.

Daly, E. J., Witt, J. C., Martens, B. K., & Dool, E. J. (1997). A model for conducting a functional analysis of academic performance problems. *School Psychology Review, 26,* 554–574.

Daly, J. E., Lentz, F., & Boyer, J. (1996). The instructional hierarchy: A conceptual model for understanding the effective components of reading interventions. *School Psychology Quarterly, 11,* 369–386.

Deno, S. L. (2003). Developments in curriculum-based measurement. *The Journal of Special Education, 37*(3), 184–193.

DiPerna, J. C. (2006). Academic enablers and student achievement: Implications for assessment and intervention services in the schools. *Psychology in the Schools, 43,* 7–17.

DiPerna, J. C., Volpe, R. J., & Elliott, S. N. (2002). A model of academic enablers and elementary reading/language arts achievement. *School Psychology Review, 31,* 298–312.

Dolch, E. W. (1936). A basic sight vocabulary. *Elementary School Journal, 36*(6), 456–460.

Downing, J. (1969). How children think about reading. *The Reading Teacher, 23,* 217–230.

Duhon, G. J., Mesmer, E. M., Gregerson, L., & Witt, J. L. (2009). Effects of public feedback during RTI team meetings on teacher implementation integrity and student academic performance. *Journal of School Psychology, 47*(1).

Duhon, G. J., Noell, G. H., Witt, J. G., Freeland, J. T., Dufrene, B. A., & Gilbertson, D. A. (2004). Identifying academic skill and performance deficits: The experimental analysis of brief assessments of academic skills. *School Psychology Review, 33,* 429–443.

Ehri, L. (2005). Learning to read words: Theory, findings, and issues. *Scientific Studies of Reading, 9,* 167–188.

Ehri, L. C., & Wilce, L. S. (1980). The influence of orthography on reader's conceptualization of the phonemic structure of words. *Applied Psycholinguistics, 1*(4), 371–385.

Elliott, S. N., DiPerna, J. C., Mroch, A., & Lang, S. C. (2004). Prevalence and patterns of academic enabling behaviors: An analysis of teachers' and students' ratings for a national sample of students. *School Psychology Review, 33*(2), 297–304.

Elliott, S. N., Witt, J. C., Galvin, G., & Peterson, R. (1984). Acceptability of positive and reductive interventions: Factors that influence teachers' decisions. *Journal of School Psychology, 22,* 353–360.

Evans, M. A., Bell, M., Shaw, D., Moretti, S., & Page, J. (2006). Letter names, letter sounds, and phonological awareness: An examination of kindergarten children across letters and of letters across children. *Reading and Writing, 19,* 959–989.

Forness, S. R. (2001). Special education and related services: What have we learned from meta-analysis? *Exceptionality, 9*(4), 185–197.

Fry, E. (1980). The new instant word list. *The Reading Teacher, 34*(3), 284–289.

Fuchs, D., Mock, D., Morgan, P. L., & Young, C. L. (2003). Responsiveness-to-intervention: Definitions, evidence, and implications for the learning disabilities construct. *Learning Disabilities Research and Practice, 18*(3), 157–171.

Fuchs, L. S., & Deno, S. L. (1991). Paradigmatic distinctions between instructionally relevant measurement models. *Exceptional Children, 57*(6), 488–499.

Gettinger, M., & Kohler, K. M. (2006). Process–outcome approaches to classroom management and effective teaching. In C. M. Evertson & C. S. Weinstein (Eds.) *Handbook of classroom management* (pp. 73–95). Mahwah, NJ: Erlbaum.

Greenwood, C. R. (1996). Research on the practices and behavior of effective teachers at Juniper Gardens Children's Project: Implications for the education of diverse learners. In D. Speece & B. K. Keogh (Eds.), *Research on classroom ecologies: Implications for inclusion of children with learning disabilities* (pp. 39–67). Hillsdale, NJ: Erlbaum.

Grisham, F. M., Watson, T. S., & Skinner, C. H. (2001). Functional behavioral assessment: Principles, procedures, and future directions. *School Psychology Review, 30,* 156–172.

Hall, S. L. (2006). *I've been DIBEL'd, now what?: Designing interventions with DIBEL data.* Longmont, CO: Sopris West.

Halladay, J. (2012). Revisiting key assumptions of the reading level framework. *The Reading Teacher, 66*(1), 53–62.

Hasbrouck, J., & Tindal, G. A. (2006). Oral reading fluency norms: A valuable assessment tool for reading teachers. *The Reading Teacher, 59,* 636–644.

Horn, W., & Tynan, D. (2001). Time to make special education "special" again. In C. E. Finn, A. J. Rotherham, & C. R. Hokanson (Eds.), *Rethinking special education for a new century* (pp. 259–287). Washington, DC: Thomas B. Fordham Foundation and the Progressive Policy Institute. Retrieved from *www.ppionline.org/documents/SpecialEd_ch12.pdf.*

Hunt, L. C. (1970). The effect of self-selection, interest, and motivation upon independent, and frustrational levels. *The Reading Teacher, 50,* 278–282.

Invernizzi, M. R., Bear, D. R., & Templeton, S. (2011). *Jo's words their way: Word study for phonics, vocabulary, and spelling instruction* (5th ed.). Boston: Allyn & Beacon.

Invernizzi, M. , Meier, J. D., Swank, L., & Juel, C. (1997). *Phonological awareness literacy screening for kindergarten (PALS-K).* Charlottesville, VA: University Printing Services.

Kim, Y. S., Petscher, Y., Foorman, B. R., & Zhou, C. (2010). The contributions of phonological awareness and letter-name knowledge to letter-sound acquisition: A cross-classified multilevel approach. *Journal of Educational Psychology, 102,* 313–326.

Kounin, J. S. (1970). *Discipline and group management in classrooms.* New York: Holt, Rinehart & Winston.

Kraemer, E., Davies, S., Arndt, K. J., & Hunley, S. (2012). A comparison of the mystery motivator and the get 'em on task interventions for off-task behaviors. *Psychology in the Schools, 49*(2), 163–175.

Kuhn, M. R., & Stahl, S. A. (2003). Fluency: A review of developmental and remedial practices. *Journal of Educational Psychology, 95*(1), 3–21.

LaBerge, D., & Samuels, J. (1974). Towards a theory of automatic information processing in reading. *Cognitive Psychology, 6,* 293–323.

Ladner, M., & Hammons, C. (2001). Special but unequal: Race and special education. In C. E. Finn, A. J., Rotherham, & C. R. Hokanson (Eds.), *Rethinking special education for a new century* (pp. 259–287). Washington, DC: Thomas B. Fordham Foundation and the Progressive Policy Institute. Retrieved from *www.ppionline.org/documents/SpecialEd_ch12.pdf.*

Lemons, C. J., & Fuchs, D. (2010). Phonological awareness of children with Down syndrome: Its role in learning to read and the effectiveness of related interventions. *Research in Developmental Disabilities, 31*(2), 316–330.

Lindamood, C. H., & Lindamood, P. C. (1998). *The Lindamood phoneme sequencing program for reading, spelling, and speech.* Austin, TX: Pro-Ed.

Madaus, M. M. R., Kehle, T. J., Madaus, J., & Bray, M. A. (2003). Mystery motivator as an intervention to promote homework completion and accuracy. *School Psychology International, 24*(4), 369.

Malecki, C. K., & Elliott, S. N. (2002). Children's social behaviors as predictors of academic achievement: A longitudinal analysis. *School Psychology Quarterly, 17,* 1–23.

Marcell, B. (2011). Putting fluency on a fitness plan: Building fluency's meaning-making muscles. *The Reading Teacher, 65,* 242–249.

McCarthy, P. A. (2008). Using sound boxes systematically to develop phonemic awareness. *The Reading Teacher, 62*(4), 346–349.

Moore, L. A., Waguespack, A. M., Wickstrom, K. F., Witt, J. C., & Gaydon, G. R. (1994). Mystery motivator: An effective and time efficient intervention. *School Psychology Review, 23,* 106–117.

Murphy, J. (2004). *Leadership for literacy: Research-based practice, PreK–3.* Thousand Oaks, CA: Sage.

Murray, B. (2012). *Murray's reading genie.* Retrieved from *www.auburn.edu/academic/education/reading_genie.*

Nation, K., & Hulme, C. (1997). Phonemic segmentation, not onset–rime segmentation predicts early reading and spelling skills. *Reading Research Quarterly, 32,* 154–167.

National Early Literacy Panel. (2008). *Developing early literacy: Report of the National Early Literacy Panel.* Washington, DC: National Institute for Literacy.

National Institute of Child Health and Human Development. (2001). *Report of the National Reading Panel. Teaching children to read: An evidence-based assessment of the scientific research literature on reading and its implications for reading instruction* (NIH Publication No. 00-4769). Washington, DC: U.S. Government Printing Office.

National Reading Panel. (2001). *Teaching children to read.* Jessup, MD: National Institute for Literacy.

Opitz, M. F., & Rasinski, T. V. (2008). *Good-bye round robin, updated edition: 25 effective oral reading strategies.* Portsmouth, NH: Heinemann.

Paige, D. D. (2011). That sounded good!: Using whole-class choral reading to improve fluency. *The Reading Teacher, 64,* 435–438.

Piasta, S. B., Petscher, Y., & Justice, L. M. (2012). How many letters should preschoolers in public programs know?: The diagnostic efficiency of various preschool letter-naming benchmarks for predicting first-grade literacy achievement. *Journal of Educational Psychology, 104*(4), 945–958.

Powell, W. R. (1970). Reappraising the criteria for interpreting informal inventories. In D. L. De Boer (Ed.), *Reading diagnosis and evaluation* (pp. 100–109). Newark, DE: International Reading Association.

Rasinski, T. V. (2000). Commentary: Speed does matter in reading. *The Reading Teacher, 54*(2), 146–151.

Rasinski, T. V. (2004). Creating fluent readers. *Educational Leadership, 61*(6), 46–51.

Rasinski, T. V. (2012). Why reading fluency should be hot! *The Reading Teacher, 65*(8), 516–522.

Rasinski, T. V., & Padak, N. (2000). *Effective reading strategies: Teaching children who find reading difficult* (2nd ed.). Upper Saddle River, NJ: Merrill.

Rasinski, T. V., Yildirim, K., & Nageldinger, J. (2011). Building fluency through the phrased text lesson. *The Reading Teacher, 65*(4), 252–255.

Rhode, G., Jenson, W. R., & Reavis, H. K. (1992). *The tough kid book: Practical classroom management strategies.* Longmont, CO: Sopris West.

Riedel, B. W. (2007). The relationship between DIBELS, reading comprehension, and vocabulary in urban first-grade students. *Reading Research Quarterly, 42,* 546–567.

Rosenfield, S. A., & Gravois, T. A. (1996). *Instructional Consultation Teams: Collaborating for change.* New York: Guilford Press.

Share, D. L. (2008). Orthographic learning, phonology and the self-teaching hypothesis. In R. Kail (Ed.), *Advances in child development and behavior, 36,* 31–82.

Simonsen, B., Fairbanks, S., Briesch, A., Myers, D., & Sugair, G. (2008). Evidence-based practices in classroom management: Considerations for research to practice. *Education and Treatment of Children, 31*(3), 351–380.

Snow, C. E., Burns, M. S., & Griffin, P. (1998). *Preventing reading difficulties in young children.* Washington, DC: National Academies Press.

Spear-Swerling, L., & Sternberg, R. J. (1996). *OFF-track: When poor readers become "learning disabled."* Boulder, CO: Westview Press.

Stahl, S. A. (1998). Teaching children with reading problems to decode: Phonics and "not-phonics" instruction. *Reading and Writing Quarterly, 14*(2), 165.

Stahl, S. A., Kuhn, M. R., & Pickle, J. M. (1999). An educational model of assessment and targeted instruction for children with reading problems. In D. H. Evenson & P. B. Mosenthal (Eds.), *Advances in reading language research: Reconsidering the role of the reading clinic in a new age of literacy* (pp. 249–272). Stamford, CT: JAI Press.

Taylor, B. M., Pearson, P. D., Clark, K., & Walpole, S. (2000). Effective schools and accomplished teachers: Lessons about primary grade reading instruction in low-income schools. *Elementary School Journal, 101*(2), 121–166.

Therrien, W. J. (2004). Fluency and comprehension gains as a result of repeated reading: A meta-analysis. *Remedial and Special Education, 25*(4), 252–261.

Treiman, R., Tincoff, R., Rodriquez, K., Mauzaki, A., & Francis, D. (1998). The foundations of literacy and learning the sounds of letters. *Child Development, 69*, 1524–1540.

United States Congress 101st. (2004). *Individuals with disabilities education improvement act: Sec. 614.b.6.B.* Retrieved from *www2.ed.gov/policy/speced/guid/idea/idea2004.html*.

Vellutino, F. R., & Scanlon, D. M. (1987). Phonological coding, phonological awareness and reading ability: Evidence from a longitudinal and experimental study. *Merrill–Palmer Quarterly, 33*, 321–363.

Vellutino, F. R., Scanlon, D. M., & Lyon, G. R. (2000). Differentiating between difficult-to-remediate and readily remediated poor readers: More evidence against the IQ–achievement discrepancy definition of reading disability. *Journal of Learning Disabilities, 33*(3), 223–238.

Vellutino, F. R., Scanlon, D. M., Small, S., & Fanuele, D. P. (2006). Response to intervention as a vehicle for distinguishing between children with and without disabilities: Evidence for the role of kindergarten and first-grade interventions. *Journal of Learning Disabilities, 39*(2), 157–169.

Volpe, R. J., Burns, M. K., DuBois, M., & Zaslofsky, A. F. (2011). Computer-assisted tutoring: Teaching letter sounds to kindergarten students using incremental rehearsal. *Psychology in the Schools, 48*(4), 332–342.

Vygotsky, L. (1986). *Thought and language.* Cambridge, MA: MIT Press.

Walpole, S., & McKenna, M. (2012). *The literacy coach's handbook: A guide to research-based practice (solving problems in the teaching of literacy)* (2nd ed.). New York: Guilford Press.

Witt, J. C., Martens, B. K., & Elliot, S. N. (1984). Factors affecting teachers' judgments of the acceptability of behavioral interventions: Time involvement, behavior problem severity, and type of intervention. *Behavior Therapy, 15*, 204–209.

Worthy, J., & Broaddus, K. (2002). Fluency beyond the primary grades: From group performance to silent, independent reading. *The Reading Teacher, 55*(4), 334–343.

Yopp, H. K. (1995). A test for assessing phonemic awareness in young children. *The Reading Teacher, 49*(1), 20–29.

Ysseldyke, J. E., Algozzine, B., Richey, L., & Graden, J. (1982). Declaring students eligible for learning disability services: Why bother with data? *Learning Disability Quarterly, 5*(1), 37–44.

Index

An *f* following a page number indicates a figure; a *t* following a page number indicates a table.